BITTERSWEET MEMORIES:
A History of the Peoria State Hospital

To: KEN & ANNE

I CAN'T BEGIN TO EXPRESS MY GRATITUDE FOR THE WAY YOU ACCEPTED LISA & GABI INTO YOUR FAMILY.

BEST WISHES!

Gary T. Lisa

BITTERSWEET MEMORIES:
A History of the Peoria State Hospital

by
Gary L. Lisman

with memories collected by
Arlene Parr

Namsil Publications
Bartonville, Illinois 61607

Contact the author at
(309) 697-5870.
Lisman, Gary L. Bittersweet Memories: A History of the Peoria State Hospital
by Gary L. Lisman
p. cm. Includes index and bibliographical references.

1. Peoria State Hospital--History 2. Psychiatric Hospitals--Illinois--History I.   Title.
Note for Librarians: A cataloguing record for this book is available from Library and Archives Canada at www.collectionscanada.ca/amicus/index-e.html

Cover Design by Gary Lisman
Front: Bowen Building after Peoria State Hospital closed, picture by Lisa Helms.
Back: Leg irons on a patient in an unknown county almshouse, picture from Milner Library.
ISBN 1-4120-3336-5

Printed in Victoria, BC, Canada. Printed on paper with minimum 30% recycled fibre.
Trafford's print shop runs on "green energy" from solar, wind and other environmentally-friendly
power sources.

TRAFFORD
PUBLISHING
Offices in Canada, USA, Ireland and UK
This book was published on-demand in cooperation with Trafford Publishing. On-demand publishing is a unique process and service of making a book available for retail sale to the public taking advantage of on-demand manufacturing and Internet marketing. On-demand publishing includes promotions, retail sales, manufacturing, order fulfilment, accounting and collecting royalties on behalf of the author.

Book sales for N ca and international:
Trafford Publishing, 6E–2333 Government St.,
Victoria, BC v8t 4p4 CANADA
phone 250 383 6864 (toll-free 1 888 232 4444)
fax 250 383 6804; email to orders@trafford.com
Book sales in Europe:
Trafford Publishing (uk) Ltd., Enterprise House, Wistaston Road Business Centre,
Wistaston Road, Crewe, Cheshire cw2 7rp United Kingdom
phone 01270 251 396 (local rate 0845 230 9601)
facsimile 01270 254 983; orders.uk@trafford.com
Order online at:
trafford.com/04-1163

10 9 8 7 6 5

About the Author

Gary was born on May 20, 1949 in Memphis, Tennessee but grew up in Peoria, Illinois. Upon graduation from Manual High School in 1967, he accepted a job at Keystone Steel and Wire Company. Except for a tour of duty with the Navy, he would work there for the next sixteen years as a millwright in the steel mill.

In 1983, he accepted a position at Commonwealth Edison, an electrical generating company, at Powerton in Pekin, Illinois. It was at this time that he decided to return to school. It would take twelve years to earn a bachelor's degree from Illinois State University in 1995.

After graduation, he was accepted into the masters program at Illinois State University. As part of his course work, he enrolled in a seminar class which stressed the importance of local history. It was while researching and writing a paper for this class that he discovered the Peoria State Hospital and its rich history.

Gary is now retired, which afforded him the time required to write this book. He and his wife, whom he met in Junior High School, were married in 1968. They have one daughter and four grandchildren. They reside within walking distance of the Peoria State Hospital Grounds.

About the Contributor

Arlene was raised on a farm near the southeastern Illinois city of Olney, but has been in the Peoria area since 1965. She worked at Zeller Mental Health Center for 30 years, primarily in Staff Development and Training. She also served as the professional librarian the last nine years while attending Illinois Central College's library program. She became interested in the history of mental health while overseeing the museum of artifacts that had been preserved from the Peoria State Hospital. From this interest she and others formed a committee in 2000, the year she retired, with the goal to preserve the history of mental health in central Illinois. The Mental Health Historic Preservation Society of Central Illinois became the official name, and Arlene was instrumental in getting 501(c)(3) nonprofit status for the society.

She took over as the director of the society from Dr. James S. Ward when he retired and moved to Arizona in 2001. Arlene spent much of her time researching, collecting memories, and spearheading several fund-raisers. The society was then able to fund the printing of the book, *Asylum Light,* published in 2004. Dr. James S. Ward was the primary author of *Asylum Light,* with many other contributors. Arlene compiled these contributions, along with the memories collected, into the book.

Because of this experience, Gary Lisman, a member of the society, who was researching for a book of his own on Peoria State Hospital, asked Arlene to contribute memories and other expertise to his book. The result of their shared efforts is *Bittersweet Memories.*

She and her husband live in East Peoria and are the parents of a married son and a daughter.

This book is dedicated to those thousands of men and women who, at one time or another, called Peoria State Hospital, no matter how briefly, "home."

Acknowledgments

This project, on the surface, appears to be the collaboration of two individuals: myself, Gary Lisman, and my very good friend, Arlene Parr. It would, however, be a mistake to assume that this was the case. There would be no book had it not been for the help and support of our respective spouses, Cathy Lisman and Dan Parr.

I cannot begin to relate how much my wife, Cathy, contributed not only to the writing of this book, but to me personally. I am sure that there were many times that she would have rather been gardening, or spending time with our grandchildren. Instead, she helped by keeping me focused on the project at hand, and would spend countless hours reading my numerous rough drafts. She also listened patiently to my incessant ramblings about the Peoria State Hospital for hours on end. Without her efforts and understanding, it is quite likely that this book would still be a pile of incoherent drafts and notes.

For all of your hard work and understanding, Cathy, the only thing I can say is -- thank you and I love you.

Although my wife was my main source of support, help, and inspiration, there were many others who helped in making this book possible. Among these individuals are my parents, Walter and Verna Lisman, and my daughter, Lisa, and her husband, Jeff Helms. There are countless librarians throughout the state who aided me in obtaining the materials I needed. I am especially grateful to Julie Niemeier and Jason Zimmerman, the research librarians at Alpha Park Library. I also received a great deal of encouragement and support from the members of the Mental Health Historic Preservation Society of Central Illinois, especially Dr. James S. Ward. Lastly, I must acknowledge my good friend and partner on this project, Arlene Parr. To all of you I say thank you.

Gary L. Lisman

Acknowledgments

I am privileged to be a part of this tremendous project -- to preserve the history of Peoria State Hospital.

Gary and I have put in many hours to bring to the reader this fascinating story in history and memories. I especially would like to thank all the people who have so graciously given me their memories. I echo Gary's acknowledgments. His wife, Cathy, has been a real asset. I am eternally grateful to Helen Arney and her Saturday Writer's Group to which I belong, for all their help in proofing. Helen was tremendous as she devoted extra hours of her time to finish the proofing.

I also would like to thank Steve Clore of the Zeller family for sharing pictures and contact information on other Zeller members; Marian Steffen of the Zeller family for sharing letters; Louise Suits for her genealogical help, and Jeff Helms for his computer expertise. Gloria LaHood and Marilyn Leyland of the Peoria Historical Society have been an inspiration to me with their help and encouragement. Another name must be mentioned -- Judith Hollenberg, now retired -- who did much research and preserved history for the Department of Mental Health while working in Springfield. She was such an inspiration to me when I was working at Zeller Mental Health Center in Peoria.

My husband, Dan, has supported me in many ways, and has sacrificed some fun times while I was "married" to this project. Thank you, dear one. I would like to acknowledge my sisters, Velma VonAlmen and Bernadine Dasch; our son, Eric, and his wife, Bing Parr; our daughter, Casandra and her precious baby girl, Jennis; my goddaughter, Beverly Daniels and her precious baby boy, Gaige; and my four brothers, Junior, Eugene, Howard, and Lee Scherer, and all the rest of my great big family. Also friends Kay Reardon, Mary Karmenzind, Rosemary Trowbridge, Janelle Crump, and Linda Molyneux for their encouragement. I feel my wonderful parents have sent love and encouragement from heaven. Also, a special thank you to my little friend, Jessica Lappin, for her help with my picture.

And thank you, Gary Lisman, for having confidence in me by including me in this great adventure!

A "haunting" note: "Monuments and Memories," Chapter IX, was especially hard to lay out, as when a revision was made and text was moved to another page it literally disappeared. Some of it was later found hiding behind pictures or on the master page. Could the cemetery spirits have been playing games? I will never know!

Arlene Parr

Contents

Foreword

In 1895 the citizens of west-central Illinois decided it was time to relieve families, jails, almshouses and society at large of the "lunatics." Such a sentiment had existed starting with Dorothea Dix's impassioned plea to the Illinois General Assembly in 1847. She provided graphic descriptions of the unimaginable suffering of the mentally ill without care. The Illinois Asylum for the Incurable Insane at Bartonville became the seventh asylum in Illinois. Peoria State Hospital (so renamed in 1909) was important because it collected these poor creatures in one area under the care of professionals who were trying to understand and help them. It relieved families of their care. It was a far better setting than jails, almshouses, etc. It focused attention and interest on this group of heretofore rejected members of the population. It stirred vocations in the care of the mentally ill. It was an important era in the care of the mentally ill and social attitudes toward them.

We should recount the heroic efforts of those who anguished in the care of these unfortunates. The coping and conquest of mental maladies by individual patients should be told. Their inspirational odysseys would benefit every reader. The story needs telling.

We should care about the mentally ill because it is now known that it spares no class, age, gender, and race. We benefit by reliving treatment styles of the past. Clues to effective management have led to discoveries in research and care. Medical breakthroughs of the modern era began with the antipsychotic drugs formulated in the early 1950s. This was closely followed by the synthesis of antidepressants. Several generations of these drugs have evolved. This had effectively made the treatment style of 1902 anachronistic. Never will we return to the massive institutions of one hundred years ago.

Peoria State Hospital existed from 1902 until the end of 1973. Its impact on the neighboring community was immense. It helped dispel ideas of a demon driven disease to a universally prevalent one capable of "infecting" anyone. Humane treatment was now encapsulated by a scientific coating. Prejudice and avoidance were largely overcome. Peoria State was a hospital, an instrument of social change and an institution where brave people resided, both as staff and patients.

James S. Ward, M.D.
Author of *Asylum Light: Stories from the Dr. George A. Zeller Era and Beyond,*
Copyright 2004, and in the practice of psychiatry for some 35 years, including the superintendency of Zeller Zone Center, and regional zone administrator.

Introduction

A few miles from the city of Peoria, Illinois, at the bottom of a beautiful bluff overlooking the Illinois River, are the remains of an old set of stairs. For more than a half-century after the turn of the twentieth century these stairs led from a train station, located at the bottom of the steep hill, to the grounds of the Peoria State Hospital. This stairway, partially covered with weeds and debris like the hospital itself, is today a forgotten reminder of the once stately facility which was located there.

It is impossible to know just how many patients, nurses, doctors, workers, and visitors used these stairs over the years to gain access to the hospital grounds. These stairs, depending upon what one reads or to whom one talks, were a stairway to heaven, to hell, or to somewhere in between. Only one thing is sure: everyone who climbed these stairs was profoundly affected by what he or she found there.

It was in 1902 that the first trainload of patients arrived at the brand new facility. By 1973, the year that the hospital closed, it had become a relic of the past, a sad reminder of the unfulfilled dreams of many of the people who had founded it more than seventy years earlier.

The plagued history of the Peoria State Hospital is easy to recount; the less obvious are the many reasons for its demise. One has to be cognizant that the face of mental health care is always changing. Although the Peoria State Hospital was considered state of the art in the early 20th century, new procedures, treatments and pharmaceutical discoveries had, according to many experts, rendered the Peoria State Hospital an unnecessary facility. The advent of new drugs used to treat the numerous mental health problems was perhaps the biggest factor in closing a long-term care facility such as the Peoria State Hospital. These new drugs, when properly administered, allowed many patients to be reinstated into society more quickly. Lengthy, if not permanent, care in a facility such as the Peoria State Hospital now was replaced by a wave of drug therapy.

At the same time, newer facilities, like the Zeller Zone Center, located on University Street in Peoria, began in 1967 to offer better treatment for those in need of mental health care. These two events, along with the political atmosphere in Illinois, would ultimately lead to the closing of this once-proud institution.

Before 1907, people throughout the Peoria area took great pride in having what was then called the "Illinois Asylum for the Incurable Insane at Bartonville" located in their midst. Their feelings did not change when the facility was subsequently renamed "Illinois General Hospital for the Insane," or finally, the "Peoria State Hospital" in 1909.

Early in its history and, indeed, throughout most of its years of operation, the hospital and its adjacent grounds was almost park-like in its appearance. This is a far different scene from the one that would be found after its closing in 1973. There are very few original buildings remaining and those that are still in existence have, for the most part, fallen into a state of disrepair. Most who visit this site today are still drawn to the Bowen Building's beauty, but always with a certain measure of trepidation. This building, perhaps single-handedly, stands as a monument to the Peoria State Hospital. By viewing this one building it is still possible to sense the grandeur that once was the Peoria State Hospital, but not without also feeling the decay and decline that has overtaken the facility today. This decay can be readily seen in the two following photographs.

The first photograph, which was taken around 1902, stands in stark contrast to the second photograph, taken one hundred years later in 2002.

Alpha Park Library

Bowen Building: Circa 1902

Lisa Helms

Bowen Building: Circa 2002

"Marvelous Progress Made at Bartonville Insane Asylum," that appeared in the Peoria Star on Sunday, February 10, 1907, stressed that view clearly as it sought to praise not only the work being done but the physical layout of the hospital itself. At this time, the Peoria State Hospital was considered to be a modern, state of the art, progressive facility. It was, perhaps, one of the finest examples of social reform regarding the care and treatment of the mentally ill to be found anywhere in the United States. The Peoria State Hospital, the paper's reporter noted, sought to ease the plight of those poor unfortunates who had been kept in county almshouses, jails, private homes, and, in some cases, penned up like wild animals before it was founded.

According to the <u>Star</u>:

> *In front of the Administration building of the Illinois Asylum for the Incurable Insane at Bartonville there stood a stone pedestal, on the top of which there is a sundial. On the four sides of the base of this pedestal have been chiseled the words, "Non-restraint, Non-imprisonment, Non-resistance, and Eight Hour Day."*
>
> *The words quoted above are supposed to express in brief the policy of the administration in dealing with the mentally unfortunate confided (sic) to its care by the state of Illinois. The casual observer will see no deeper significance.*
>
> *These four terms mark an epoch in the treatment of the insane an era of progress, a stage of progress believed to be impossible for centuries. Considered separate and apart from each other they still mean a great deal. Grouped together they mean more. Yet there is a deeper significance than in the mere words, for behind them is the broad idea of giving to each of the poor, deranged minds that which the Constitution grants to all men - a chance of betterment.*[1]

The same article continued:

> *Out at the Bartonville Asylum as it is commonly called, they are reverting to the old simple life, the life which gets as near to nature as possible and which clings to her through all its days. They are giving the insane man and woman a chance halting not at the step which marks improvement of physical conditions but pushing on to a point where the mental atmosphere is purified and the diseased mind grapple with problems as free and unhampered as the mind of a child.* [2]

Nothing remains the same, and even by mid-century the hospital had become an ever-sad illusion of good intentions gone awry. Rick Baker took a far darker view of the Peoria State Hospital in his book <u>Mary, Me in Search of a Lost Lifetime</u>:

> *...by 1973, when the governor of Illinois finally ordered the place closed, it was an overpopulated, understaffed, antiquated, murderous pile of infection. State investigators found that by 1973, the state hospital which had once been looked upon as something to strive for, was a nightmare where people sat with large, open sores, eating their own feces a place where naked lunatics leaned casually against hallway walls and masturbated on whoever happened to be passing by; a place where unlicensed doctors diagnosed massive brain hemorrhages as "slight abrasions" and treated them with iodine; a place where therapy was abandoned in favor of something called "life support" (which meant something like this to state employees at the institution; We can't help these crazy assholes. About all we can do is try to keep them from killing us); a place where crying, naked men and women were years before lined like stockyard cattle to await electroshock treatment, and when the electricity knocked them unconscious, attendants would disconnect the wires and toss the people into a huge tub of cold water to revive them. Peoria State Hospital stood on the hills near the river like some once great mastodon being devoured by parasites. Finally, the governor, in his mercy, ordered a bullet be put through its head....* [3]

One must wonder what happened at this facility over the years to cause such a discrepancy in the accounts of the patients and the care they received at the Peoria State Hospital. Surely, not all of the patients lived the pristine existence as described by the <u>Peoria Star</u> in 1907. Conversely, however, one must also believe that not all of the patients suffered from the intolerable and incompetent care as described by Rick Baker sixty-six years later.

This book seeks to understand what happened at the hospital during its fascinating history and to do so to as accurately as possible. In the end, the individual reader will be allowed to draw his or her own conclusions regarding the Peoria State Hospital and the thousands of men and women who, at one time or another, called it, no matter how briefly, "home."

Chapter I

The Birth of the Peoria State Hospital

Many historians, when researching a topic, ask when something happened as opposed to why something happened. We know from the existing records that the cornerstones for the Peoria State Hospital were placed on June 6, 1896, on a parcel of land near Bartonville, Illinois, about five miles south of Peoria, Illinois.[1] As vital to our understanding of the past as such facts are, it is surely of more interest and, perhaps, importance to ask why then, 1896, and why Bartonville, Illinois?

The first question, "why then," is fairly easy to answer. By the end of the nineteenth century a series of profound social changes and thinking were taking place throughout the country regarding the care of the mentally ill.

Prior to this, there were no state institutions for the care and treatment of the mentally ill in Illinois - or in most of the country for that matter. The mentally ill were housed or, perhaps a better word would be incarcerated, in local community almshouses or jails.

Mental illness was being looked at quite differently at this time. Governor John P. Altgeld spoke of the revolutionary changes which were occurring concerning the treatment, care and thinking of the mentally ill. It was his dedication speech in Peoria, Illinois, on June 6, 1896, for a new mental health asylum which was to be built there that Governor Altgeld emphasized how horrible the past had been:

> *There was a time when the unfortunates of the world were left to die by the wayside. At times they were taken out and destroyed. They were considered a burden and a drawback. The insane at that time were supposed to be afflicted and possessed of the devil or an evil person. The idea that the insane were suffering from a different kind of disease was never thought of. They were chained to the floor or penned up: they were treated worse than animals.* [2]

There were a growing number of physicians in the late eighteenth and early nineteenth centuries starting to specialize in the treatment of the mentally ill. It was now believed that insanity was a disease of the brain and that, in many cases, it could be cured.[3] One of the concepts that these physicians brought to bear was the construction of institutions built strictly for the care of the mentally ill. According to Thomas Kirkbride *". . .the view that the mentally disturbed patient could best be treated away from home in an institutional setting was becoming increasingly accepted."* [4] This trend was associated with the steady increase in the construction of insane asylums or, as they were otherwise termed, state hospitals for the mentally ill.

Thomas Kirkbride, an innovator of the design and construction of facilities designed especially for the mentally ill, would write in his book, <u>On the Construction, Organization and General Arrangements of Hospitals for the Insane</u>, in 1880:

> *". . .proper custody and treatment of the insane are now recognized as among the duties which every State owes to its citizens; and as a consequence, structures for the special accommodation of those laboring under mental disease, provided at the general expense, ample in*

number, and under the supervision of the public authorities, will probably, before any long period, be found in every one of the United States." [5]

The state of Illinois, like the rest of the country in the latter part of the nineteenth century, would also embark upon an endeavor to provide a safe haven for its mentally ill citizens.

Dorothea Dix, an early advocate for the humane treatment of the mentally ill, addressed the Illinois Senate and House of Representatives in January of 1847. She described in great detail the plight of the mentally ill not only in Illinois but in the United States as well. She stated that, *"Scenes of misery have met my view, which no language, however vividly combined can adequately describe. . ."* [6]

Immediate action was needed to ease the plight of those afflicted. Mental illness, Dix said, *". . .is not confined to rank, age, sex, or condition. All are liable to its attacks; and all are directly concerned to secure means for its cure. This can be done only by the establishment of a hospital adapted expressly to this end."* [7]

As a result of her efforts and many other like-minded individuals, the legislature would pass the "Act of Incorporation, an act to establish the Illinois State Hospital for the Insane," on March 1, 1847.[8] This act led to the first public mental health facility in the state located in Morgan County near the city of Jacksonville, Illinois. The facility would be known as the Illinois State Hospital for the Insane. The name of this facility would later be changed to the Jacksonville State Hospital.[9] It was the forerunner of all future such institutions built in Illinois.

Society had been profoundly affected by the Industrial Revolution. Education was more accessible to the masses, cities were growing. Agriculture, once the main stay of the American economy, was now being supplanted by the specialization of labor in the modern industrial plants. According to David Gallahar, as a result of this new urbanization emerging from the Industrial Revolution:

> *An urban-industrial society had emerged in which form, public institutions performed more and more of the function previously discharged by the church, family and local community. These traditional institutions could no longer adequately deal with the problems of an increasingly complex society. Thus, new and specialized structures of state government began to carry out various functions deemed vital to the welfare of the American people.* [10]

Illinois would make a step towards accepting responsibility for the care of the mentally ill in 1847. It was at this time the state created committees known as the Local Board of Charities. These local boards were responsible for visiting and inspecting the various institutions throughout the state that fell under their jurisdiction. The state of Illinois, however, would not officially accept full responsibility for the mentally ill until 1907. It was then that a law was passed which required all mentally ill persons be transferred to various state hospitals.

These trustees were appointed by the governor and answered only to the governor. By 1869, the state had created the Board of State Commissioners of Public Charities. This commission would operate for approximately forty years and effectively take over the duties of the Local Board of Charities.

Although not as complex as why now, it is definitely worth exploring the question as to why the Bartonville location was chosen for the hospital. Peoria, like the rest of the country, was in dire need of a public mental health facility. The social economic revolution which was taking place resulted in several local municipalities expressing a wish to have a state facility for the mentally ill erected in their communities.

The economic benefit to one's community was a major reason for obtaining a state facility. There would be an immediate influx of jobs and money due strictly to the construction of such a large facility. It was reported that the new facility would be a big benefit, not only to Peoria and Bartonville, but the county as well. <u>The Peoria Daily Transcript</u> claimed that:

> *It will be a benefit to all classes of trade, for the 5,000 inmates must be fed and clothed, and the thousands of visitors who will be attracted here annually must spend money. It is the greatest thing ever offered Peoria, better than two or three manufacturing enterprises, for the people know it will be here forever, and that it will run every day the year around.*
>
> *It will be a big thing for the farmer, for it will afford a wonderful home market for produce of all kinds, butter, eggs and poultry. These 5,000 people must be fed, and the food will have to be purchased. It can be got more advantageously in Peoria than anywhere else, and thus the benefit will be here.* [11]

The immediate effect that such a facility would have upon a community cannot be minimized, but there was another reason for securing a mental health facility. As previously stated, there was a sense of altruism taking place at this time regarding society's responsibility for the humane care and treatment of the mentally ill. This new altruistic phenomena was a major factor for the Peoria area.

What was needed was a catalyst to start the wheels of government; that catalyst proved to be the Peoria Women's Club. The members clearly believed in the club's motto taken from <u>Oedipus Tyrannus</u>: "To help another from what one has, or is, is the most noble deed." For more than a decade the members worked diligently until their wish for a state hospital came to fruition. One could rightfully claim that without the ambitious members of the Peoria Women's Club the Peoria State Hospital would, in all probability, have not been erected.

Dr. George A. Zeller, who would become the longtime head of the Peoria State Hospital, considered the Peoria Women's Club to be the single most significant group when it came to the acquisition of a state facility for the mentally ill for the area. He wrote, *"The birth of the women's club movement in the decade of 1880-1890 brought new pressure to bear on the subject. In Peoria, in particular, the question was energetically pushed by Mrs. Clara P. Bourland, Mrs. Anna Petherbridge, and Mrs. S. O. Loughridge."* [12]

The <u>Fifth Biennial Report of the Trustees, Superintendent and Treasurer of the Illinois Asylum for the Incurable Insane at Peoria</u> contained the following:

> *As local federations of charities multiplied and as county supervision of the almshouses became more strict the necessity of State care for incurables became more and more apparent, and finally culminated in the formation of an organization of Peoria women, headed by that able, energetic and public spirited woman, Clara Parsons Bourland, then as now, president of the Peoria Women's Club.*

These women agitated the question through the local and State press, before meetings of men and women in many localities, they besieged the conventions of both parties and secured endorsements of their views, and finally sent a lobby to Springfield to present the matter to the Legislature, where, in the session of 1895, they finally succeeded in securing an appropriation of $65,000 for the erection of a main building so constructed as to permit of extensive additions. [13]

Who were these women and the organization that they represented? The Peoria Women's Club was founded on January 20, 1886, the outgrowth of a previous club known as the Peoria Art's Society. [14] **The Peoria Star** reported:

The "Peoria Women's Club" was similar to earlier women's organization the earliest of which was formed in 1868, much to the consternation of the men at this time. It was widely accepted that women who organized and joined these clubs often would and should meet with prejudice and dismay. The "Peoria Women's Club" was no different and the members of this first club joined, "braving prejudice, ridicule and opposition voiced by men in general and even by a few women." [15]

Apparently, Clara Parsons Bourland, the founder and president of the Peoria Women's Club for twenty-five years, knew that society, in general, was opposed to women voicing their opinions in the public forum. *"Until then they had no intellectual existence separate from that determined by the kinds of husbands, fathers and brothers they had."* [16] To assuage such fears, she enlisted a few other like-minded individuals and formed a society for the study of art which, according to the **Peoria Star**, *". . .seemed ladylike enough. And the suspicious breathed easily."* [17] Although the society continued to grow, their efforts were still restricted to the so-called arts and *"gave no grounds for masculine fears."* [18]

This group of genteel women, however, was about to change in a profound way. Around 1882 Clara Parsons Bourland took a trip to Europe. What she saw and experienced there led to a major role change for the Peoria Women's Club. Upon, *". . .returning home, she set about organizing a real club that should not only bring this heritage to Peoria women, but should also use its influence for the betterment of the community."* [19] Their initial goals were: *". . .mutual sympathy and counsel and united effort towards the higher civilization of humanity. They set up four main departments: art and literature, home education, philanthropy and reform, and music."* [20]

It was from this point that the Peoria Women's Club would begin to lobby tirelessly in their efforts to have a hospital built in the Peoria area. The Peoria Women's Club, like Dorothea Dix, would diligently pursue their beliefs and desires regarding the care of the mentally ill.

David Gallahar could have been writing about the Peoria Women's Club instead of Dorothea Dix when he wrote:

While other Victorian women, if they stepped outside the domestic circle at all, circulated petitions and formed benevolent associations to influence a masculine system from which they were excluded, Dix invaded the system itself, grasped the levers of government, and exercised substantial power. [21]

It was the hope of the Peoria Women's Club that the state would assume the responsibility for the care of those unfortunates who were now housed in jails, almshouses, and, in some cases, pens not fit for animals, let alone human beings. Their hope was that the candidates and party representatives in attendance at the various conventions would support them in their efforts in securing humane care for the mentally ill.

According to Dr. Zeller, it was at the request of these ladies he introduced a resolution at the Republican County convention of 1892. He urged upon the legislative nominees in attendance the necessity of providing the state care for the insane inmates of the almshouses. A similar resolution was adopted in the conventions of the other political parties that year also. (See Appendix I: Copy of the resolution.)

Regardless of the motives of either party or the politicians involved, it was not until the middle of Governor Altgeld's term in office that the movement would gain enough momentum to have a law passed. Apparently, Governor Altgeld had, as Zeller claimed, "*. . .a tender regard for the interest of the insane.*"[22] It was during this period that the state not only established an institution in the Peoria area, but also set up the Illinois Western Hospital for the Insane at East Moline as well. It was a momentous occasion as, Zeller later wrote, "*Few states have organized two state hospitals at a single session.*"[23]

One reason for the rapid and relatively easy passage of this act to fund new mental health facilities throughout the state was that, "*many members of the Legislature were or had been members of County Boards of Supervisors and, as such were aware of the deplorable conditions under which the insane were kept in the almshouses.*"[24] Therefore, when the bill: "An Act to Provide for the Location, Erection, Organization and Management of an Asylum for the Incurable Insane" was presented in the 1895 session, it speedily became law on June 21, 1895.[25] This sense of government altruism may have been exacerbated due to the economic situation faced by many at this time. "*It was a time of intense financial distress and it may be that the inability of the average citizen to extend private aid made the public officials all the more heedful of the needs of the unfortunates.*"[26]

As stated earlier, it was at the urging of the Peoria Women's Club that George A. Zeller would introduce a resolution at the Republican state convention of 1892, requesting those in attendance and those who were to be nominated as to the dire need of the mentally ill. [27]

Interestingly, the adoption of such a resolution by the Republican Party may not have been strictly for altruistic reasons. Political ambitions were, perhaps, involved also since neither party wanted to appear ambivalent regarding the issue of the need for the care of the mentally ill. Dr. Zeller alludes to this when he wrote, "*. . .a similar resolution was adopted in the conventions of the other parties that year.*"[28]

It would take more than popular public support and the intense lobbying of the Peoria Women's Club, however, to insure that a facility for the care of the mentally ill would be built in the Peoria area. Several other cities were interested in obtaining a mental health facility for their respective communities. Governor Altgeld commissioned a committee consisting of John Finley of Peoria, Henry Alexander of Joliet, and John McAndrews of Chicago to select a building site.[29]

One of the major obstacles that had to be overcome before construction could begin was the securing of a suitable site for the facility. Governor Altgeld had stipulated that the city obtaining such a facility would have to donate the land where the facility would be built. The land was eventually obtained from a Mr. Joseph B. Barton, who donated a portion of his homestead for this project. [30] According to Dr. Zeller, *"When Governor Altgeld stipulated that the city obtaining the institution would donate the site, the public spirit of the city speedily rose to the occasion and a half section of land, situated in the village of Bartonville, was tended to the state free of charge.*[31]

Once the land was secured it still had to meet certain criteria before the final approval for construction would be given. The basis for the criteria, mandated by the governor, can be found in Thomas Kirkbride's book, **On the Construction and General Arrangements of Hospitals for the Insane.** It was at a meeting of "The Association of Medical Superintendents of American Institutions for the Insane," held at Philadelphia in May of 1851, that several proposals were adopted regarding the construction of hospitals for the insane. Two of the proposals proved to be crucial for the community which would receive approval for a state facility in their area.

First: "Every hospital for the insane should be in the country, not within less than two miles of a large town, and easily accessible at all seasons."[32]

The Bartonville location was actually more than two miles away from Peoria: however, due to rapid growth, the location would soon meet such a requirement. The location was especially desirable because of its easy accessibility. There were two reasons for this. First, there was a road which ran near the site. Secondly, there was a passenger train that traveled south out of Peoria. This train made daily stops at the foot of the grounds at a depot that was located there.

Second: "No hospital for the insane, however limited its capacity, should have less than fifty acres of land, devoted to gardens and pleasure-grounds for its patients. At least one hundred acres should be possessed by every State hospital, or other institution for two hundred patients, to which number these propositions apply unless otherwise mentioned.[33]

The site, as originally donated, was made up of two parcels. The first was one hundred fifty-eight acres on the bluff. The second parcel contained one hundred and sixty acres, which was located below the first parcel.[34] There were also several acres of land directly adjoining this site that was unimproved. This land was appropriated in 1912, which gave the hospital five hundred seventy acres of land, of which one hundred eighty-three constituted the main facility. The remaining two hundred and fifty-two acres were detached farms which served not only as a source of meat and produce, but as a place of rehabilitation for many of the patients.[35]

With the land appropriated and the governor's approval it would seem that the Peoria Women's Club had apparently accomplished their goal. They had secured a state hospital for the insane to be located near Peoria, Illinois. Their hope would not become a reality, however, until February 10, 1902, when the first patients arrived. Why it took nearly six years to open the hospital is the heart of Chapter II.

The Peoria State Hospital would, until its final closing in 1973, stand as a testimonial to the tenacity of the Peoria Women's Club.

Eighty-five years after the formation of the Peoria Women's Club, in 1971, the **Peoria Observer** would celebrate the anniversary of the Peoria Women's Club and its accomplishments. The **Observer** listed many of the club's achievements and concluded ". . .ranking among the club's greatest accomplishments during its early years was lobbying for humane treatment of the mentally ill, which eventually resulted in the construction of the Peoria State Hospital at Bartonville." [36]

Chapter II
The Walls Came Tumbling Down

"It was an architectural death-trap. . . ." <u>Charleston Plaindealer</u>

June 6, 1896, was an auspicious day for Peoria, Illinois, and the surrounding area. This was to be the day that the cornerstones for the Peoria State Hospital were to be laid. The <u>**Peoria Daily Transcript**</u> carried the following artist's depiction of what the facility would look like upon its completion.

The event *". . .marked an epoch in the history of Peoria, for it is the first state institution ever accorded to this city."*[1] These stones represented the fruition of many months of effort by the citizens of Peoria, Illinois, to have a mental facility built in their area.

Foremost, among these citizens, were the members of the Peoria Women's Club. It is readily apparent that these women were very influential in the securing of the new facility. Their president, Clara Bourland, not only addressed the crowd assembled there that day, she would travel there in a buggy with another prominent member of the club, Mrs. Anna Petherbridge. Their carriage was second in line located behind Mayor Allen, Judge Worthington and Walter Baker. This prominent position in the parade surely attests to their importance.

Mother Nature apparently sensed the importance of this day, for it rained nearly every day during the week but this day *". . .dawned bright and pleasant."* [2]

Peoria and the surrounding area were being decorated in a fashion that one would expect to see for the Fourth of July. Work on the decorations had taken place for several days in an effort to:

> *. . .clothe the city in her holiday attire. Flags, bunting and the decorations extended from the lowly cottage of the humble toiler to the stately mansion of the millionaire, from the shop to the public buildings and mammoth business blocks, all attesting to the pride and loyalty of the occupants. Some of the decorations were elaborate. The city hall was decorated from the tip of the flagpole to the ground. Bunting was draped across the entire front in graceful folds and fathered in the center at a portrait of Governor Altgeld. The large flags floated from the courthouse, the government building and other public buildings, while the large dry goods houses spread yards upon yards of bunting across their fronts. There was very general decoration, both of business houses and residences.* [3]

Bartonville, like Peoria, was also decorated from end to end. The <u>Peoria Daily Transcript</u> reported that, *"The stores and cottages of the villagers were elaborately decorated, and Bartonville people did themselves proud in every way."* [4]

Governor Altgeld arrived by private car from Galesburg where he had delivered an address at the commencement exercise of Lombard University. His wife had come from Springfield by private car also. She would be at his side during a ceremony which was to take place later that afternoon in the village of Bartonville, located just south of Peoria. The National Hotel, where the Governor and his wife would stay, was filled to capacity with *". . .distinguished men from different parts of the state, prominent politicians and professional men, and not a few ladies called to pay their respects to the visiting ladies and the distinguished visitors."* [5]

It was estimated that by noon the city was filled with three thousand citizens from all over the state.[6] Some arrived by boat, but most came by rail. It was reported that, *"All the trains brought in large delegations and especially those from the south, east and west, which offered reduced rates."* [7]

People started to assemble all along the parade route two hours ahead of the time slated for a parade that would go from the National Hotel in Peoria to a site near Bartonville, Illinois. A crowd estimated at five thousand had gathered at Bartonville to witness the laying of the cornerstones for a new state mental health facility which was to be located there. [8]

Clara Bourland **Peoria Women's Club**

Once the parade arrived at the site the fanfare would continue well into the afternoon. Governor Altgeld was last to speak to the large contingent of dignitaries and interested citizens. Strangely, however, his remarks did not refer to the Peoria Women's Club and their role in securing the facility for Peoria. The governor's speech in its entirety can be seen in Appendix II.

The stones were constructed from Quincy, Massachusetts, granite and came from one of the oldest quarries in the United States. One of the stones weighed two thousand two hundred pounds and was engraved on one side with the following: *"Erected A.D. 1896, John P. Altgeld, Governor, Commissioners, John Finley, Peoria, President. Henry Alexander, Joliet, Secretary. James Andrews, Chicago, Treasuruer. Lonsdale Green, Chicago, Architect. E. J. Malloy, Chicago, Contractor. John Warner, Peoria, Superintendent."* [9]

The stones also included a time capsule which held several items. For a list of these items see Appendix III. It is not known what happened to these original stones; they may have been destroyed or perhaps reused in the eventual rebuilding of the facility.

It was upon these stones that the hopes of many were to be laid. As massive and impressive as they were they could not support the facility which was being erected. Just a year later the walls of this magnificent building would come tumbling down.

What had happened? Who was to blame? These questions were never adequately addressed by the press or the government. What can be surmised is a story that includes mismanagement, lies, and corruption.

As auspicious as the groundbreaking ceremony had been, the ensuing inspection of the facility by Governor John Tanner, on December, 22, 1897, just months after the groundbreaking would result in an infamous decision. Governor Tanner had decided to have the nearly completed facility razed and start over. The building was deemed unsuitable for two reasons. First, it appeared to be in danger of collapse. Secondly, it did not, according to the governor, *". . .comply with the conditions required in these modern times for buildings for the insane."* [10]

The original building was designed on what is commonly referred to as the *"Kirkbride Plan."*

This plan has been described *". . .as gothic, and would have been more at home in the Rhine River Valley or perhaps on the moors of Scotland."* [11] This is not a description which leads one to picture a place which would tend to assuage one's fears. This is especially true of the inmates, as they were referred to at this time, who were to be treated there.

There are few pictures to be found of the original building. One did, however, appear years later in the <u>Limestone Independent News</u> claiming, *"It Looks Like a Castle but It Isn't."* Most people who are familiar with the Peoria State Hospital are still unaware that this building ever existed.

The decision to raze the structure would ultimately delay the opening of the Peoria State Hospital for the Incurable Insane until February 10, 1902.

The cost of this decision was estimated to be fifty thousand dollars. [12] The <u>Peoria Herald</u> reported that the decision to tear down the building would result in a *". . .loss of about forty per cent, but that is but a drop in the bucket when compared with a million and half dollars, which will probably be spent on the buildings before they are completed."* [13]

The Second Biennial Report of the Trustees and Treasurer of the Illinois Asylum for the Incurable Insane at Peoria gives one some insight as to what went so horribly wrong.

Governor John Tanner appointed a new board on March 17, 1897, to replace the former board which had overseen the construction that was taking place. The reason for the removal of this board is not immediately clear; however, one must be cognizant that the members of these boards were appointed by the governor. Therefore, it is entirely possible that the original board was replaced for political reasons and not due to any wrongdoing on their part regarding the construction of the asylum. The new board did seek to distance themselves from the controversy surrounding their predecessors and the problems associated with the construction that was underway. In a rather scathing statement they claimed that the previous board had:

> *. . .failed to so far as we are informed, to keep any record of their proceedings; and it is for that reason impossible for us to state when or how they organized the board, or what steps were taken to secure a suitable site, or what were the reasons and considerations which induced the adoption of the actual site selected, or what steps were taken to secure proper architectural plans, or what bids were received for the construction of the asylum in accordance with the plans adopted. All that is known upon the subject, except from hearsay and common rumor, is contained in the following list of expenditures made by the former board.* [14]

The problem was further exacerbated when it was discovered that the book containing the expenditures had eight pages missing.[15] It is astonishing that this discovery of incomplete and missing records did not lead to an in-depth investigation at this time.

Shortly after the new board was assembled, they made a visit to the asylum being built in Bartonville. The first impression of the members of the board, upon arriving at the site, was very positive. They reported:

> *. . .the Asylum was placed by the former board upon the edge of the bluff, about two hundred feet above the level of the river, in a very conspicuous position, being visible from the other side of the river for several miles in either direction, and the prospect from the top of the bluff is one of the most beautiful, probably, to be found in the State of Illinois. The building was large and showy, without being extravagant in ornamentation. . . .* [16]

Once they entered the building, their opinion regarding the facility was dramatically different. Regarding the interior, they reported, in part, that:

> *. . .an examination of the interior, however, showed that it was poorly adapted to the purpose for which it was meant to be used. The wing which had been constructed was in effect a barrack, and presented a barn like appearance of cold discomfort. The house was an oblong box cheaply built of brick nor furred, but plastered directly on the wall, and in places the plastering, which appeared to be a single white coat, was not more than a sixteenth of an inch in thickness. The system of heating and ventilation was entirely inadequate. In each of the large rooms partitioned off for the use of patients there was a single flue, which, if used for the introduction of hot air, offered no exit for ventilation, and if for ventilation, there was no possibility of introducing fresh air. As planned, the wing would furnish not one of the facilities or conveniences required in a public charitable institution, except that a place was provided for water closets and a bath tub. A worse plan for an institution for the care of the insane was never devised.* [17]

The new board decided that the asylum should be completed but only if changes could be made in the wings not yet completed. Also, there would have to be substantial repairs made to the partially completed portion of the structure.

They employed the private architectural firm of Messrs. Reeves and Baillie to make the needed design changes. These changes included the construction of two additional wings to be known as ward number two and ward number three and an administration building which would take the place of ward number four.

Once the new plans were accepted, the general assembly appropriated $53,000 for the project's completion. Bids for the project were opened on August 26, 1897. There were four bids submitted but they all exceeded the amount appropriated by the General Assembly. See chart below:

Bidders	Administration Building	Wings	Total
M. F. Powers, Chicago	$17.983.00	$71,347.00	$89,320.00
V. Jobst	16,100.00	74,500.00	90,600.00
John McDonald	18,782.00	74,500.00	95,282.00
Peoria Steam Marble	20,564.00	89,290.00	109,854.00

The board was forced to make certain omissions from the original plans and make changes in their building specifications. Even with these changes, the lowest bid, which was submitted by M. F. Powers of Chicago, was for $84,430. The board was left with no other option and accepted the bid by M. F. Powers, which was $31,430 over the appropriated amount.

This contract was never signed due to further problems discovered by the board. Before the contract could be signed, Mr. Powers, accompanied by Reed, the local trustee, went to view the institution and grounds one last time. What they found there was quite disturbing. Something had gone terribly wrong; the building was still under construction, but it was in danger of collapse.

It was at that time that several cracks were found in the walls on the inside and some on the exterior of the building. These cracks were not considered to be a problem initially. Mr. Powers, in fact, remarked that cracks occur in nearly all buildings. His initial confidence in the structure failed, however, when he entered the large day room in the extremity of the wing. It was there that a rather large crack caught his eye, which he said, "must be due to a settlement." [18] This discovery led to further investigations of the site to see if the building had been placed over an abandoned mine.

It was a well-known fact that much of this area had once been mined for coal, but the dispute was whether or not the building stood directly over entries and rooms of the abandoned coal mines located in the area. The first board had always contended that it did not. This discrepancy led to an inquiry to determine the exact location of the entries and rooms of the abandoned coal mines. It was thought that perhaps one or more of the mines under the building had collapsed, resulting in what is referred to as a "squeeze."

In order to ascertain the exact locations of the mines, the board utilized the services of John S. Stevens, an attorney for the trustees. Stevens was able to obtain an incomplete map of the area from Joseph Sholl, the former owner of the coal rights under the land in question. The map was originally begun ten years prior to the construction of the asylum. It showed, in ink, mines one, two, and three. At a later date, the entries to mines four and five were penciled in.[19] It is not evident if the prior board had seen this map and, if they had, it is not known if the entries to mines four and five were penciled in at that time.

Stevens would take sworn affidavits from the former owners of the mine and some of the miners who had worked the area in question. This testimony, when compared with a survey of the surface made by Jacob Harman, civil engineer, concluded that the building did, in fact, stand almost directly over the abandoned coal mines. Even with this information, there was a difference of opinion regarding the severity of the problem. According to the board, it was *". . .claimed by some of those familiar with the facts in the case, that the 'squeeze' having taken place, there can have been no further settlement after the erection of the building, while by others this is denied."* [20]

Armed with this information, the board sought the services of a consulting engineer and architect. They submitted their findings to the board on October 4, 1897.

> *In accordance with your request, we have visited the site of your asylum at Peoria, and have made a careful examination of its topography and have noted as far as possible the character of the underlying soil and rock. We have also made an examination of the building now standing there on and of its plans, and of the plans prepared by Mr. Lonsdale Green, architect, for a completed asylum building, of which the buildings now standing are intended to be a part. Further, we have examined carefully the plat of actual and approximate locations of the mining operations which have been carried on under said site, and by searching examination of miners who had been employed upon said mining works, we have endeavored to verify the lines laid down on said plat and to obtain full information as to the extent to which coal and other material had been taken out from under said premises, as also with regard to the "squeeze or collapse which had some years ago occurred. . . .* [21]

By December of 1897, the problems associated with the buildings at the facility were becoming a political quagmire. The members of the board were coming under public scrutiny as the problems of the facility came to light. There were rumors that all or part of the board would be asked to resign or be replaced as a result of the problems at the site. Henry Alexander, the president of the board of trustees for the asylum, sought to silence these rumors and assuage the public fears when he stated:

> *. . .there is absolutely no truth in the rumors that I have decided to resign. I have heard these stories several times but I have not thought of resigning. The members of the board are on good terms and are working in harmony. There is no friction and nothing that would cause me to step down. We are also working in perfect harmony with the state board of charities and have had no trouble of any kind. That board is doing its duty thoroughly just as we expected it to and it cannot be blamed for that. So far as I know no differences have arisen between the local and state boards. The question of the asylum site and building is in their hands and we will await their decision. The present trouble is to be regretted but no one is to blame but the citizens of Peoria themselves.* [22]

A special meeting of the board was to take place in Peoria on December 1, 1897. The purpose of this meeting was to further investigate the problems at the site and adopt plans to remedy the situation there. Henry Alexander made the following statement after their meeting that night: *"As far as the present buildings are concerned they are solid and I entertain no fears as to their safety. I am convinced that additional buildings will be erected on the present site."* [23]

Obviously, there was something amiss concerning the construction of the new hospital buildings. Less than two weeks after the special meeting of the board, it was reported that Governor Tanner would personally make a trip to Peoria to inspect the site.

Prior to this announced visit by the governor, it had been reported that the general public was not satisfied with the report by experts who had inspected the sites and ruled that the buildings were in no danger of collapse. Others, however, sought to complete the project. Among these were Dr. Frederick Wines, secretary of the state board of charities, the members of the board of trustees of the asylum and, according to The <u>**Peoria Herald**</u>, *". . .quite a number of prominent personages of the city have taken a deep interest in the matter and have endeavored to prevent the removal of the buildings."* [24]

Governor Tanner's visit to the site led him to make the decision not only to stop any further construction at the site, but to have the building which was nearly completed torn down. According to the governor,

> . . .there may be some occasion to doubt that they would settle more than they have, they are totally unfitted for the purpose for which they were erected, that they are faulty in construction, and they do not comply with the conditions required in these modern times for buildings for the insane. [25]

The reason for the building's failure was not immediately ascertained. It was concluded that even though the building was indeed built atop abandoned coal mines, it was highly unlikely that this resulted in the collapse of the buildings being erected at this site. In fact, as the hospital grew in later years, other buildings were erected on this site without developing similar problems.

Perhaps the biggest factor in the building's failure can be attributed to poor construction. Had the governor not decided to have the building removed and replaced, the result could have been catastrophic. The builder had apparently attempted to profit through the use of substandard material.

Before proceeding with the destruction of the building one final inspection of the site was made. What they found during this last inspection proved the situation at the site to be even worse than originally thought. The Second Biennial Report reported that the final inspection was carried out by R. D. Lawrence of Springfield, one of the State Commissioners of Public Charities, who is a practical contractor and builder; by F. W. Menke of Quincy, president of this board, who is also a practical contractor and builder; aided by Messrs. Reeves and Baillie, architects; and Jacob A. Harman, civil engineer, of the city of Peoria. Jack Meyers wrote in his unpublished history of mental health care in Illinois that the political repercussions were so great that these men were brought to the area under great secrecy to determine the cause and remedy for the situation.[26] Once the inspection was completed, according to Joe Mehr, their recommendation was simple and direct. *"Knock it Down!"* Obviously, the building was even worse than expected, and like Jericho the walls would come tumbling down.

> . . .cracks in the building, of which there were several hundred, were observed and measured from time to time, and it became apparent that they were increasing in length and width and number, until finally two of them opened to such an extent that daylight could be seen through them from the inside of the building. The building was pronounced to be unsafe, by the common consent of all these gentlemen, and its loss inevitable. [27]

The cause of the building's demise became readily apparent to those involved as the building was being demolished and their worst fears were being realized. Once the foundation was reached, it was decided that faulty construction and not the "squeeze" of the mine, was the reason for the building's failure. The foundation was described as being of *"such flimsy construction, that it was unequal to the sustaining of the walls erected upon it."* [28]

The board further reported:

> *. . .When the foundations were reached, they were found to be of such shoddy material and construction that very little of the stone in them was available for future use. A portion of the foundation has been left for the inspection of members of the General Assembly. In places the outside stone on the inside of the wall was thin stone, standing on edge, and packed with spawls and small rubble stone filled in with sand and mortar, as though they had been thrown in with a shovel. Our first opinion was that the cracks in the wall which rendered the demolition of the building necessary were occasioned by its having been erected over the entrances and rooms of an abandoned coal mine, but the character of the foundation upon examination proved to be such as to render it certain that the building would not have stood under any circumstances nor in any location. Our decision to take the building down is, therefore, more than justified; and, if this statement should be questioned, all that is necessary is for the doubter to visit the location and look at the foundation for himself.*[29]

The consequences of the building's demise took several directions. The total cost to the state and the taxpayers was never officially reported, but it had to be substantial. For example, the intitial loss was estimated to be at least fifty thousand dollars. It was hoped that much of the material could be salvaged and reused. By salvaging some of the materials, such as brick and stone, door frames, windows and window frames, flooring, structual iron, etc., the state would save approximately fifteen thousand dollars.[30]

Then there was the delay in the opening of the facility. It would be six years after the intial groundbreaking ceremony before the facility would be ready to accept patients.

The political fallout was rather substantial as well. The original board had to be replaced by the governor.[31] One of these members would eventually face twenty counts of malfeasance in office.[32]

Even though the losses involved were great, the six-year delay was, in retrospect, well worth the wait. The concept used in the original construction, the "Kirkbride Plan," was not now considered to be the best design for the treatment of the mentally ill. The "Kirkbride Plan" for the construction of mental health facilities had been replaced by what was referred to as the "Cottage Plan."

These cottages bore little resemblance to the harsh and foreboding look of the original hospital. Now when the first one hundred patients arrived, in February of 1902, they found waiting for them a modern park-like facility based on the "Cottage Plan." This new facility was certainly more comforting to the eye than the stark prison setting as originally designed. One can surmise that the outward appearance of the facility did a great deal to alleviate the fears of the patients that would arrive there for years to come.

Chapter III

Day One: Arrival of the First Patients

The long wait for the opening of the Illinois Asylum for the Incurable Insane was finally, officially, over with the arrival of the first group of inmates on February 10, 1902. Surely, the opening of the most modern facility of its kind in the state would be an auspicious event. This was not to be the case. The arrival of the first patients met with little or no fanfare, which was in stark contrast to the gala festivities that had taken place there six years earlier. There were no large crowds of onlookers; the governor was not there with his entourage of local and state dignitaries; there were no bands or banners to announce the arrival of the patients.

Even the weather was quite different. August 6, 1896, can only be described as picture perfect, whereas the weather on February 10, 1902, was far from perfect. In fact, it was a typical cold, drab winter day, not a day conducive for a celebration. It could be argued that the weather was the reason that many of those who had been present for the groundbreaking ceremony chose to shy away from the grounds on this very important day. The weather would certainly have impacted the attendance, but the scandals that were associated with the hospital was more than likely the main cause of the indifference shown toward the actual opening. Fortunately, the dismal weather and poor turnout was not an omen of things to come.

The <u>Peoria Herald Transcript</u> reported that, *"there were quite a few people on hand to see them."*[1] At first this gives the impression that the patients were met by a large crowd of onlookers, however, this was not entirely the case. In reality, if not for the small gathering of doctors, nurses, and the curiosity seekers, the importance of the patients arrival may have been overlooked.

Sadly, some of those on hand to greet this first group of patients had come to observe their arrival much like they would go to a carnival side show. To their chagrin, however, the first patients were the less severely afflicted ones transferred from the Jacksonville asylum. There were:

> *. . .neatly dressed and some of them looked very much like prosperous business men and students. One young man resembled a young preacher very much. Another looked as though he might have lost his mind while delving into the mysteries of some deep subject. These are the more cleanly patients and the more filthy ones will not be removed for some weeks.*
>
> *As far as excitement or anything unusual was concerned all the visitors were disappointed. The cars were pulled into the asylum grounds and the patients alighted the same as ordinary people at Union Station. The attendants opened the door of one car and they filed out and stood by the car. Then the other car was opened and these patients filed out. When the last man had stepped from the car one of the attendants said "Come on boys and walked towards one of the cottages. The patients followed peacefully and spent their time leisurely looking over their new home. The only word spoken by any of them was by a man about fifty years old who seemed to be dealing for a faro game. Another old man wanted to stand on one side and watch the other patients march by.*[2]

The first patients, and subsequent arrivals, came to the asylum by rail where they were met at a train station located just below the asylum grounds. The patients would be transported by rail for many years to come, but the lack of excitement generated by them caused the public to eventually lose interest in their arrivals.

Terminal Station at the foot of the asylum grounds. Circa 1904   **Alpha Park Library**

What these first patients saw was a new and modern facility designed by Dr. Frederick H. Wines. His plan was a derivative of the Cottage Plan. *"The Cottage hospitals were a complex of many buildings separate from each other and housing sixty to one hundred and fifty persons, rather than one or two large structures housing one to two thousand or more persons, which was the standard approach to mental hospital construction from about 1850 to 1900."* [3]

There were only seven cottages available for use at this time. Three of them were to be occupied by the male patients and two by the female patients. The other two cottages had to be used for quarters for the male and female attendants until the construction of more buildings was completed. All of the cottages looked similar to the one below.

Alpha Park Library

Due to the lack of cottage space, it was necessary to house some of the women patients temporarily in the employees' building. According to Dr. Carriel, the interim superintendent at the Illinois Asylum for the Incurable Insane, "*. . .it was thought best to use the building originally intended, and known as the employees' building, for female patients. To do this it was necessary to screen the windows, and make some changes in the interior. These proved quite satisfactory, and the building as it stands today is well adapted for the purpose for which it is used.*" [4] The Bowen Building, or employees' building as it is referred to in the papers of the time and the Biennial Reports, can be seen in the following picture:

It had taken six years and an expenditure of millions of dollars for the Asylum for the Incurable Insane to reach a point where the facility could finally accept patients. There was still a great deal of controversy as to who was responsible for the many problems that had led to numerous and costly delays in the opening of the Peoria State Hospital. Suffice to say, there was enough blame to go around.

Col. Mack Tanner, secretary of the State Board of Charities and the only state official in attendance that day, tried to put an end to the controversy surrounding the facility by saying, "*. . .there were blunders made it is true but the present board of commissioners have succeeded in bringing about very satisfactory results from the chaotic state in which they found the affairs of the asylum when they assumed control.*"

The new trustees would report that:

> *In assuming charge of the affairs of this institution, we did not fully realize the actual condition of affairs which we soon found to exist. While the board which immediately preceded us did much to unravel the complications which had been increasing for the past six years, yet we found many unfinished contracts, unsettled and unadjusted claims of subcontractors, arising from the failure of the general contractors of the main buildings, as also several contracts which had been supposed to be completed had been accepted and settlements made, which were incomplete and unsatisfactory, and which required additional contracts and expense to complete, ready for the opening of the institution.* [5]

Although all of the problems associated with the facility had not been completely resolved, patients started arriving. Dr. H. B. Carriel, the acting superintendent, stated in his report to the Board of Trustees of the Illinois Asylum for the Incurable Insane:

The, institution was opened for the reception of patients February 10, 1902. On this date one hundred male patients were admitted from the Illinois Central Hospital at Jacksonville. February 13, forty seven males and 52 females were admitted from the eastern hospital at Kankakee. February 15, fifty nine males and fifty one females were admitted from the Illinois Northern hospital at Elgin, and fifty males from the Illinois Southern hospital at Anna. April 4, twenty males and thirty females were admitted from the Western hospital at Watertown, fifteen female patients from the Central hospital at Jacksonville, sixty five female patients from the Cook County hospital at Dunning. April 5, eight male patients from the Central hospital. May 7, one male patient from the Winnebago county almshouse, and June 25, one female patient from the Winnebago county almshouse, making a total of six hundred thirty eight patients received. [6]

Over the next few months several more patients would arrive at the asylum and, with each arrival, the amount of attention paid to them would decrease dramatically. By April of 1902, there were six hundred and thirty-four patients at the facility and only one local paper saw fit to report the arrival of one hundred and twenty patients from throughout the state on April 4, 1902. The arrival of the first patients and subsequent arrivals did not generate a great deal of public interest regarding the facility, but it did mark the beginning of bold and innovative treatment for the mentally ill housed there. A new era of treatment was about to begin and the Peoria State Hospital would be at the forefront of mental health care, not only in Illinois, but throughout the country for many years to come.

Chapter IV
Dr. Zeller's Appointment

Dr. Zeller would not officially assume his role as superintendent of the Illinois Asylum for the Incurable Insane, now known as the Peoria State Hospital, until November 1, 1902, nearly eight months after the first patients had arrived. He had been appointed to this position in 1896, following the election of Governor Tanner, in what can only be described as an act of political patronage. Conventional wisdom would dictate that appointments made in this manner are, more often than not, disastrous. Fortunately for everyone associated with the Peoria State Hospital this did not hold true with this appointment. James Dalzell, regional administrator and superintendent of Zeller Mental Health Center, stated that, in fact, Dr. Zeller, *". . .was a man who was really wedded not only professionally but emotionally to this part of the country. A man who was obviously the perfect superintendent to start Peoria State Hospital."*

One might ask, why was this nondescript doctor from central Illinois singled out for this position? In reality Dr. Zeller was a prominent physician and Republican supporter in central Illinois. He had been elected three times as chairman of both the city and county Republican Central Committee, and in 1895 and 1899 had the dual role of being chairman of both the city and county central committees simultaneously. According to Dr. Zeller's autobiography:

> *In 1896, my prominence in the councils of the party brought me forward as a candidate for the state treasurer. I made a creditable showing in the convention, but a Chicago man was slated. I was told that if I would wait until 1898 I would be named without opposition. By that time, I realized that I had no business aspiring to an office of such grave responsibility.* [1]

Due to his loss, Dr. Zeller may have abandoned his desire to seek public office for himself. He did, however, continue in his position as chairman of the county central committee. Dr. Zeller's efforts, as chairman, would not go unnoticed. By his own admission it was due to his active participation in getting John Tanner elected governor in 1896 that he was offered the superintendency of the Illinois Asylum for the Incurable Insane. According to Dr. Zeller his appointment, unlike an elected office, *". . .here was something in my own line and I was glad to accept."* [2]

On February 15, 1898, the battleship USS Maine was shattered by an explosion which caused the ship to sink and the death of two-thirds of her crew. This incident marked the beginning of the Spanish-American War. As a result, *"Patriotic feelings ran high and the pressure for precedence of call was tremendous."* [3] With this in mind, Dr. Zeller, who was superintendent in name only with no wages forthcoming at this time and, believing that the opening of the facility was a long way off, volunteered to serve with the Army in the Philippines.

While he was away serving in the Philippines, Richard Yates was elected to replace Governor Tanner. Again, Dr. Zeller's past political activities proved to be an asset. Because he had campaigned with Governor Yates in previous elections, he was well known to Yates and he was reappointed as superintendent at Peoria State Hospital.

Why was Dr. Zeller's absence significant to the history of the Peoria State Hospital and Dr. Zeller? Simply put, as a result of his absence Dr. Zeller would not have any influence on the construction and the administration of the Peoria State Hospital for nearly four years. It was during his absence that the Peoria State Hospital would be rebuilt and readied for the eventual influx of patients. If Dr. Zeller had been available to direct the construction, perhaps he would have halted entirely, or minimized, the installation of the heavy iron gratings and bars that adorned many of the cottage windows. He may have also reduced the number of seclusion rooms with heavy doors and restraint apparatus that were being readied for the influx of patients.

Upon his return home Dr. Zeller commented that, *"I found everything moving along as if I had merely been away overnight."* [4] Things had actually changed a great deal, especially the Peoria State Hospital. Gone was the ponderous castle-like structure that, at best, can only be described as a foreboding hulk. In its place was a system of cottages and buildings that would surely put the most troubled patient at ease. The newly rebuilt Peoria State Hospital was certainly modern, and aesthetically pleasing to the eye. All was not as it appeared on the surface though; therefore, Dr. Zeller's programs and innovations for the treatment of the mentally ill would be temporarily delayed.

Dr. Zeller, in uniform, while serving in the Philippines.

Zeller Family

Dr. Zeller Takes Charge

While Dr. Zeller was away serving his country in the Philippines during the construction phase of the hospital, the board of trustees decided it would be in the best interest of the State to have an experienced superintendent on the grounds to assist them in the completion and furnishing of the institution. On July 1, 1901, they elected Dr. F. C. Winslow, formerly of the Illinois State Hospital for the Insane at Jacksonville, to be superintendent. The board said that they, *". . .found him an able and efficient officer, rendering us valuable advice and assistance in many ways until he passed away, having died suddenly in Chicago, October 10 of the same year."* [5]

In December, 1901, the board, at their regular meeting, would appoint Dr. H. B. Carriel as acting superintendent, pending the arrival of Dr. Zeller. Dr. Carriel held this position until Dr. Zeller relieved him on November 2, 1902. For Dr. Zeller, this marked the beginning of a thirty-six year love affair with the institution that would be known as the Peoria State Hospital.

Dr. Carriel eagerly awaited the day when Dr. Zeller would officially relieve him of duty. Dr. Zeller wrote that, *"out at the asylum the physician who was temporarily in charge pending my arrival was anxious to be relieved so he could return to his institution at Moline."* [6] Dr. Carriel was indeed anxious for Dr. Zeller to assume control of the institution, but he was not going back to Moline. He was going to assume control of the Central Hospital at Jacksonville. The same board that had named him interim superintendent had selected him on July 1, 1902, to be the full-time superintendent at Jacksonville.[7]

Dr. Zeller, being acclimated to the official formalities of the military, was quite surprised at how simple the transfer of responsibilities was accomplished. According to Dr. Zeller, *"The assumption of office was so simple that it surprised me. There was no invoicing, no checking in and out, no accounting for property as I had been accustomed to in my various changes of assignment in the army. It seemed a loose way of surrendering and taking over a million dollars worth of property, much of it expendable."* [8]

The ease of this transfer would pale once Dr. Zeller realized what lay ahead of him as the superintendent. He was a resolute man with a deep sense of what was needed; however, he was also cognizant that the responsibility for the future of the Peoria State Hospital was in his hands. With this in mind, he immediately set to work putting his vision for the hospital into effect, knowing full well that if his vision failed it would have been not only ruinous to his reputation, but would have, more than likely, resulted in his removal from state service.

Chapter V

New Facility - Old Ideas

"The gravest danger to this service is precedent -- the tendency to leave a thing so because it has always been so. It was this disposition that kept the insane in shackles and dungeons a thousand years longer than human intelligence warranted."   Dr. George A. Zeller

Dr. Zeller's initial impression of the hospital for which he was assuming responsibility was less than favorable. He even expressed his dislike of the hospital's name, the Illinois Asylum for the Incurable Insane. According to him, *"The ponderous name of the institution conveyed neither cheer nor hope."* [1]

Dr. Zeller would cope with the stigma that he associated with the hospital's name for the next several years. He was so bothered by the name that he would on many occasions proclaim that, *". . .it must not be presumed, from the name of this institution, that he who enters here leaves hope behind."* It was on July 1, 1910 that Dr. Zeller happily wrote in the Eighth Biennial Report:

> *Gentlemen--I have the honor to submit the eighth biennial report of this institution, covering the two years ending June 30, 1910. In doing so, it might be well at the outset to explain that the repeated changes in the name of this institution illustrate in themselves the change in the public attitude toward that considerable element of society so unfortunate as to be afflicted with mental aberration, and for whose special care the State maintains eight large public institutions.*
>
> *Fifteen years ago the great concern of the charitably disposed was to have the incurably insane removed from the almshouses, and out of this movement this institution sprang. It fulfilled its mission admirably and the name, Illinois Asylum for the Incurable Insane, seemed quite appropriate. Instinctively, however, the mind shrank from a condition, from which the very name indicates that hope had vanished, and the Legislature of 1907 very considerately changed the name to the Illinois General Hospital for the Insane. This name we retained only two years. The sting was still there. The word "insane" grated harshly on the ear and offended the eye. Finally, in 1909 when the general reclassification of names was presented to the Legislature our present name, The Peoria State Hospital, was legally adopted.*
>
> *I cannot recite in this brief report the change in sentiment that came over the public as each change in name occurred. Those who sent their friends here under the original title did so out of desperation, realizing the patient was indeed incurable and that the name, however repulsive, was grimly proclaiming a fact. Later, under the name of General Hospital for the Insane they brought their friends here because the insanity was amply demonstrated and required hospital care.* [2]

So, from 1909 until 1973 when the hospital closed, it would be known as the Peoria State Hospital. A name that was synonymous with some of the best mental health care available not only in Illinois but the United States as well.

The name was not the only thing that Dr. Zeller was displeased with when he assumed control. He felt that the *"intent of the institution had, from his perspective, been subverted. The reason for the creation of the Asylum for the Incurable Insane was to rescue those chronically mentally ill people who were languishing in almshouses in counties across the state."* [3] When he took over, he soon discovered of the 690 patients present, none of them had come from the poorhouse, as the county homes were designated at that time. The state had played an enormous game of musical chairs with the patients from other hospitals. *"In not a single instance had the institution risen to the situation it was specifically charged to remedy."* [4] Actually, the hospital had little choice regarding the first patients. To be in compliance with the law, the first five hundred inmates were to be taken from the established hospitals for the insane, and only then could the hospital start receiving patients from the almshouses. Dr. Zeller was of the idea that those already receiving care in a state hospital should not usurp the needs of those individuals languishing in the almshouses.

> . . .it is not until the almshouses are reached that the people begin to realize what a blessing this institution is to the State.
>
> It is at such time that the closets give up their skeletons and society for a brief moment again becomes conscious of the existence of individuals long supposed to be dead. [5]

It was in 1839 that the Illinois legislature authorized County Commissioner's Courts, and these courts could establish tax-supported almshouses or poorhouses once the voters from the county approved their establishment. Also included in this act was a provision as to whom would be placed in these facilities. According to this law, *"all persons unable to provide for themselves because of bodily infirmity, idiocy, or other unavoidable cause were to be sent to the care of the almshouse. Once the almshouses were created, they often were used to confine people with mental illnesses; usually those who were in the terms of the day, furiously mad."* [6]

Perhaps many had already forgotten the deplorable conditions that had preceded the advent of the state hospital system. It is evident that Dr. Zeller, to his credit, could not and would not forget. He was constantly reminded of the horrors that many of his patients had suffered at the various almshouses. This was due to his close association with a very special patient, Rhoda Derry.

Of the thousands of patients that would eventually call the Peoria State Hospital home, Rhoda Derry's story is perhaps one of the saddest. Her care and condition were so shocking that her story has been retold many times. She was perhaps the most striking object lesson conceivable regarding the difference between the almshouse care of the mentally ill, and the treatment the mentally ill received at an asylum. This does not mean that the care received at the almshouses was innately bad, only that many of these facilities were not designed for this type of care. For example, Dorothea Dix reported the following conversation with the "master" of the poorhouse at Galena: *". . .there madam,"* said the keeper with emotion, *"there is the only place I have for keeping the furiously insane, when they are sent to the poorhouse - a place not fit for a dog - a place where they become daily worse, and where their cries, vociferations, and blasphemies, with other offenses, drive all the peace and quiet from the place. The sick have no respite, and the family at large not rest."* [7]

It is only fitting that Rhoda's story be told at this time. It has been said that, *". . .appropriation committees from legislatures who were unwilling to provide funds for the institution gazed upon her, heard the story of her miserable existence in a poor farm, shuddered, relented and voted money so that the unfortunate insane might be taken from the county almshouses and cared for in the state asylums."* [8]

In an effort to do her justice, two accounts will be given in their entirety. The first one tells us why she would become a ward of the state, and the other one chronicles her care as a patient at the Peoria State Hospital. The first story came from the February 10, 1907, <u>**Peoria Star**</u> article, "Marvelous Progress Made at Bartonville Insane Hospital." The second story is taken from Dr. Zeller's autobiography.

Some of the Inmates:

> Some queer characters may be found among the 1900 patients. One of the most noted cases was that of Rhoda Derry. Rhoda died last fall at the advanced age of 67 years. She had a history which is probably without a parallel in the world. As a striking example of the evils of almshouse treatment of insane she did more for suffering humanity than almost any woman in the country.

Rhoda Derry was born in Adams County, Illinois. She was the daughter of a wealthy farmer and was a strikingly handsome girl. While yet in her teens she was wooed by a son of a neighboring farmer. The young man's family, however, were opposed to the match. In order to prevent the young couple from marrying, the boy's mother visited the girl and threatened to bewitch her if she did not release her son from the engagement. The mother so wrought upon the girl's fears that she became insane and strange to say exhibited all the signs of one possessed of an evil spirit.

Shortly after the threat, Rhoda came home one night, jumped on the bed and stood on her head spinning around like a top. She declared that the "Old Scratch" was after her. For a time she was taken care of by her relatives, but was finally sent to the Adams county poor house. There she remained for forty years.

For inhumanity nothing has ever been heard to equal the treatment afforded this poor girl in the Adams County poor house. For years she lived in a basket of straw cared for solely by other feeble minded patients. During this time her limbs became drawn up until her knees almost touched her chin. There they remained day after day and week after week until the muscles became atrophied. It was impossible for her to move either her legs or her hips.

After a while the basket of straw was dispensed with and a square box set on legs, was submitted. This box had holes in it so that the excretions would drop into a pan beneath. Mice and other vermin crawled into the box, made their nests and reared their families at the very side of the poor creature

Under such treatment her malady became more pronounced. With her long fingernails she scratched her eyes out. With her fists she beat her face until all her front teeth had been knocked out. She lost, to a degree, the power of speech and became a hideous object. Placed on the floor she hopped along on her hands, so doubled up that she looked more like a toad than a human being.

From these surroundings, in 1904, Rhoda was brought to the Bartonville asylum. She was taken to the hospital for women, bathed regularly and lived for the first time in forty years, in a bed, between clean white sheets. [9]

The "Box Bed," Rhoda's home for forty years. Alpha Park Library

Twentieth Century Witchcraft

In a former report, mention was made of the remarkable case of Rhoda Derry. She died in October, 1906, and the following letter was sent to Honorable C.B. McCorry, judge of the Adams County Court. Its publication is deemed appropriate at this time as it deals with a unique case and with a condition, God grant, that will not recur in Illinois:

I have the honor to report that Rhoda Derry, of your county died in Hospital A, in this institution, on October 19th. The passing of this most unfortunate woman calls for more than a formal notice, as she was alone in her class and it is not likely that her duplicate could be found in the United States or in the world. Her mental affliction dating back half a century makes her a connecting link between the time when the revival of interest in the insane began, and the present. Blind, deformed, demented and helpless, she lay for forty-three years in the Adams County almshouse, her eyeballs having been plucked out by her own hand in some of the outbursts of insane fury which her keepers were unable to control. More than once she was the subject of a special report at the hands of the State Board of Charities, and it seems almost beyond belief that the public conscience could so long tolerate a condition against which every humane instinct rebels. Leading up to the cause of her final transfer to this institution, I hope I may be pardoned for quoting the letter of your State's attorney:

In going over our insane paper we have one woman about sixty-six years old, who has been in our county house forty-three years, became insane at about twenty-two or twenty-three years of age. She has never taken medicine and seems to be in good health. She is drawn up so her knees touch her breast, is rather stout, weighs about one-hundred-fifty pounds, is blind and cannot attend to the wants of nature. Up to three or four years ago, she tore off her clothes and unless tied would be naked. She is kept in a box in which straw must be changed several times a day. She has occasional violent spells and beats herself and whatever else comes in her way. In that way she beat out her own eyes. She eats with her hands only and swallows everything she can get hold of. As a rule, now they keep a slip or gown on her. Our authorities have no way of keeping her hidden from the public or taking scientific care of her. Her identity is practically unknown. Neighbors ascribe her malady to witchcraft.

The autumn of 1904 found us with eight new cottages with a capacity of 100 each and a general letter sent out to the county judges brought to above reply and immediate authority for transfer of twenty women inmates from your almshouse was granted. We practically doubled our population in the three full months and among the 700 inmates received there were necessarily many deplorable cases but none to compare with "Rhody." I remember the night of her arrival. There had been a washout and the special car containing the Quincy contingent was many hours late, and did not reach here until one o'clock in the morning. We had been receiving patients all day and took our conveyances to the railroad crossing to meet these latest arrivals. Mr. Hoarn and a number of supervisors accompanied the party and assisted in carrying, or leading a very motley group of inmates from the car. When all were seated, two of the party handed up a common clothes basket and we started up the hill. Presuming the basket contained the clothing of the party, we were not prepared to see the bundle move about and begin to jabber, and interest was at once centered upon the strange guest. That interest has never abated in the two years Rhody has been with us. She immediately became the object of solicitude on the part of the nurses and she has never been a moment out of their sight night or day. She was placed in a comfortable and clean bed and it was changed as often as spoiled and no nurse every complained because of the demands made upon her time for caring for Rhody. Her unfortunate plight had been given wide publicity by reporters who were noting the new arrivals and few visitors went away without asking to see the "woman who was brought here in a clothes basket." As our hospital facilities developed, Rhody was given even better attention and her appreciation of special delicacies was only equal to her delight at being given a chew of tobacco. We never allowed her to become the object of curiosity, but when real students of social problems came along, we took them to the bedside of Rhody and her case alone called down more blessings upon the State than all the eighteen hundred others we are caring for. No one ever blamed the almshouse authorities for her former care and all seemed to feel that they gave her the best they could afford and I often told them that fact that she was not without considerate care, but somehow visitors went away with the feeling that this one case alone justified the erection of this institution and no person ever saw her without becoming a firm convert to the belief in state care of the insane.

When the weather grew pleasant the nurses would place Rhody on a mattress on the porches. She was too deformed to even sit in an invalid chair and at one time when she was transferred from one cottage to another, the clothes basket was again brought into requisition as the most available litter. Time, which had spared her to become an object lesson to the State and arouse its latent sense of justice to the unfortunates, was slowly accomplishing its mission and her emaciation, always notable, became more pronounced until only a bundle of bones tightly covered with skin remained, and when the final summons came, it found her surrounded by her faithful nurses, without even a bedsore upon her deformed body. Tell me such a life was lived in vain! Where are all the relatives of this once prominent family? All have preceded her to the grave. They, no doubt, lived useful lives but none made such an impression upon the public thought of the day as this unfortunate woman. She reached the allotted three score years and ten and is buried in grave number 217, asylum cemetery.

The nurses who cared for her in life were at the side of the grave when the last honors were paid her and, when they returned to their duties, instead of feeling relieved that a great burden was lifted from their hands, all were crying.

The impression of a humane service, dutifully rendered has shed its halo about them and the institution is better for having cared for her, the State is better for the knowledge that justice was finally done this long neglected woman. [10]

Rhoda's grave marker #217. **Gary Lisman**

Chapter VI

A Revolution in Mental Health Care

"The world hates change, yet it is the only thing that has brought progress." Charles F. Kettering

Long since removed from the front of the Bowen Building, there was once a stone pedestal, on top of which there was a sundial. Etched on the four sides of this pedestal were the words: Non-imprisonment, Non-restraint, Non-resistance, and the Eight Hour Day. These words briefly expressed the policy of the Peoria State Hospital regarding its care of the mentally ill housed there.

At the time, and even perhaps today, most would fail to see any great significance in these simple phrases, but upon further reflection it is obvious they in many ways marked a new era in mental health care. Considered separate and apart from each other, they still mean a great deal. Grouped together they mean more. Yet, there is a deeper significance than in the mere words, for behind them is the broad idea of giving to each of the poor, deranged minds that which the Constitution grants to all men - a chance of betterment.

Non-imprisonment

The man behind these prophetic words was Dr. George A. Zeller, a man without any experience in the care and treatment of the insane. This was a man whose impact on mental health care would prove to be incalculable.

After finishing his tour of duty with the United States Army in the Philippines, Dr. Zeller assumed his position as superintendent. He was disappointed to find that, in his absence, the state had installed heavy iron gratings and bars on the windows and doors, and that there were rooms designed as seclusion rooms that had heavy doors with peepholes which allowed the staff to monitor those so restrained. It was not unusual, in many mental health hospitals of the day, for a patient to not only be placed in such a room, but to be also physically restrained by the use of various mechanical apparatus.

This was completely unacceptable to Dr. Zeller and he immediately started to implement drastic change, starting with the removal of the bars and grates from the windows and doors from as many of the cottages as possible. This was not only a humanitarian act, but it was a way to add to the bucolic atmosphere that the hospital sought to achieve. Early on, he decided that the Peoria State Hospital would, in fact, be a state home with *". . .particular emphasis on the word home."*[1] After all, he was under the opinion that the role of the hospital was *". . .to restore individuality and remove from the surroundings of the inmate of imprisonment."*[2]

It must be noted that this was a learning process for all those involved. Initially, the bars were removed from the general dining rooms only. Once the success of this had been determined, it was decided to remove them from the windows and doors of a select few of the patient cottages. Then, *"encouraged by the many expressions of approval on the part of visiting friends and relatives of inmates, and by the absence of any attempt at escape, we cautiously continued the innovation."*[3] This pattern would continue until all but one cottage for each sex had been so treated. It was thought that perhaps the, *"limit of liberation had been reached."*[4] After further deliberations with those in charge of these wards it was determined, by the staff and Dr. Zeller, that they would dispense with the bars and guards in these cottages as well. So by October of 1905, the last vestige of imprisonment was gone and placed in storage in the belief that never again it would, *"be applied for the imprisonment of the unoffending."*[5]

Gradually, the gratings and bars were removed and by November 1, 1905, exactly three years after he had taken control of the hospital, he had 2,000 patients living there without a bar on any window or a locked room.

This is nothing short of amazing, when in fact, many of the patients were, in truth, a danger not only to themselves but, in many cases, to the public as well. Dr. Zeller reported in 1904 that:

> . . .*this institution contains the most violent, destructive and habitually untidy inmates of any in the State and, collectively cannot likely be duplicated anywhere in the United States. They are the picked cases from more than 7,000 insane.*
>
> *I have visited and carefully inspected every hospital for the care of the insane in Illinois, as well as numerous almshouses, and I fail to find anywhere a ward which, in violence or distracting, equals the 58 women in Cottage No. 4, group "B."*
>
> *We have with us many homicides, two of whom are life-time convicts.*
>
> *We have a woman who choked two women to death, and a man who inflicted a fatal bite upon another and subsequently killed two women with a fire poker.* [6]

He had many of the offensive bars and screens put into storage and a picture was prominently displayed in the Sixth Biennial Report. This picture served as a constant reminder that there was no place or need for such apparatus, not only at the Peoria State Hospital but at any institution that was responsible for the care of the mentally ill.

The bars did eventually serve a purpose, but not as they were originally intended. They were used once again as cages, not for the patients, but for a zoo. One could, possibly, make the argument that this was not just a zoo designed for the pleasure of the patients and staff but as a metaphor showing that humans should not be caged like the animals caged here. Or as Dr. Zeller wrote:

> . . .*the antics of the deer and playfulness of the bears drew the attention of the hundreds of visitors who not only were interested in what might be considered an incipient zoo, but commented most favorably that equipment that had been used in imprisoning humans was now harboring wild animals.* [7]

Six thousand dollars worth of gratings that Dr. Zeller had removed from the doors and windows of the asylum's buildings, and later used to construct a zoo on the grounds.

By 1910 this zoo was the home of thirteen deer, and twelve of these animals had been born and raised there. There was also to be found there a number of red foxes and coyotes in separate pens. Perhaps the strangest sight of all was a young black bear, which had been donated to Dr. Zeller and the hospital by the state of Washington. Eventually, the bear became so tame that he was permitted, while under the supervision of two patients who had trained him, to visit all parts of the hospital. His frequent visits to the cottages were reportedly met with the intense delight of the patients housed there. [8]

When Dr. Zeller left the institution in 1913 to become the state alienist, his replacement, Ralph Hinton, apparently had little interest in the zoo. He allowed the zoo to fall into a state of disrepair and it eventually became nonexistent.

Gary Lisman

The top two pictures show all that remains of the zoo's foundation. The bottom two pictures show a portion of the zoo's wall embedded with a portion of the screen that had been used for the cages.

It is not known what happened to the bears that were housed there, but many of the animals were simply allowed to escape. The herd deer had grown to fifteen and, according to Dr. Zeller, *". . .are still seen to this day in the woods along the Sangamon and Mackinaw rivers nearby."* A pathetic incident occurred ten years later. Eight of the deer came out of the woods, approached an old habitat, gave a look around and scampered down the hill at the approach of a group of patients.[9]

The following is a story that was written about the zoo by Haskel Armstrong for the **Peoria Herald Transcript** in June of 1913.

Bars Made For Insane Now Form Zoo Cages

One of the queerest freaks of fate to be displayed to the human race is to be found in the grounds of the Peoria State Hospital for the Insane at Bartonville. Here in the only institution for insane in the world where bolts, locks and bars are not used nor known by the inmates, insane or declared so by commissions and therefore worthy of imprisonment or restraint, are building a zoo for the caging of wild animals, and every grate, bar, chain and lock in the construction of the cages and pens, has at some time in the past served to cage human beings. Such is the mockery of fate. The main corral, around an acreage of sufficient size to farm and in which are all the cages and the pens, is made from the iron-barred grates which were taken from the doors of the same hospital when Dr. George A. Zeller, the present superintendent, took charge several years ago. There are scores of these "strong doors" made into one endless fence about the zoo.

"Crazy Crib" Holds Rabbits:

Within the corral are the cages, and these too were all made from the grates and barred doors of the cottages. Here and there on the doors of the enclosure for the beasts are chains and locks, which in the past served to bind "violent" patients, and in one corner, as if in mockery of the thing itself, is a "crazy-crib," once made to hold a maniac, and now holding rabbits.

The work of building this zoo is supervised by Dr. Eugene Cohn, assistant superintendent of the institution, but the spading of the earth, the setting of the posts and the fastenings of the joints in the many cages, together with the care of the animals is being done by the patients of the "crazy-house."

Zoo Nearly Complete:

Work on the zoo at the Peoria State Hospital has been carried forward to such an extent that the place begins to show signs of completion. The inner cages and yards for the larger animals have been completed, and only the work of arranging for the smaller pets remains. Concrete dens and caves made to resemble the natural rock homes of the wild beasts, have been built for the bears, wolves, foxes, and similar animals. "Natural" watering places have been put in for all, and "digging pits" prepared. These last extend to all classes of animals which have a tendency in the wild state to dig or burrow into the earth. They were prepared by sinking concrete basins to a depth of four to six feet about areas varying from ten to forty feet square, and filling these basins with earth. About the top are the wire net cages and the whole makes possible burrowing for the animals without the danger of them digging out of captivity.

In the main corral for the deer a natural deep ravine and a densely wooded acre or two, furnish a "natural" home and the aid of the concrete artist in preparing watering places and "springs" has given them what they can and do enjoy. There are at present twelve deer in the corral and one which runs at large over the grounds all of the same herd. Six fawns are expected a little later in the summer, and these will all be kept in the herd.

Bears Have Bath Rooms:

An interesting feature of the zoo is the bear den, in which two black bears scarcely out of the "cub" stage, roll and frolic like two pups. In the bear cage just at the base of a "hill" built in a realistic way of rock and cement is a bath tub. This bath tub was one discarded from the hospital, and though porcelain, has been so damaged as to be worthless. One of the brighter "bugs*" of the asylum fixed up the tub in a setting of stones and concrete to resemble a mountain pool, turned water into it, and now has both the bears trained to take "a bath" at his command. The bears enjoy it so much that the "bug" has been given permission to fix up the other cages in the same way, and all animals are now to have real "bathrooms" in their apartments.

Rabbits form a large part of the zoo in numbers, there being several hundred now at large in their new digging pits. Every species of rabbit and hare is to be found in the lot, from the blooded Belgian hare to the lowly cottontail, and cross-breeds. The rabbit cages and yards extend over a large part of the main corral and are moved about from day to day to give their inmates fresh grass on the stands.

In the fox department of the zoo, but three members are to be found, but a family of seventeen is soon to be added to the lot, and all given into the new dens and yards.

Have 200 Squirrels:

A consignment of nearly two hundred squirrels is to be received in small lots during the next month, and all the furry animals are to be turned into a specially built cage of wire netting to include several of the large trees in the corral and deer park. Close to two hundred squirrels were loosed in the grounds of the hospital two years ago, but all have been killed by trespassing hunters and coal miners. Because of this the newcomers will be caged but in such a way as to be almost free.

Raccoons to the number of twenty, will be received at the zoo within the next few days, and will be added to the collection of animals already there.

All these animals to be received are to be sent in from southern points in Illinois and lower Mississippi river states, and most of them are gifts to the zoo by outsiders or members of the staff of the hospital.

While birds do not at present form a part of this collection of inhabitants of the wild, it is planned to, in the near future prepare "roosts" where pheasants, doves, eagles, owls and other birds common to captivity, can be kept for the pleasure and enjoyment of inmates and visitors on the hospital grounds.

Non-restraint

Another of Dr. Zeller's programs involved the reduction and the eventual banning of all forms of mechanical restraints. By June of 1904 he wrote that mechanical restraint had been reduced to a minimum and at the Peoria State Hospital it was only employed periodically to the violent inmates on

---

*Bug was a derogatory term applied to the patients.

the male side. This was quite an achievement, but he would not be satisfied until the use of mechanical restraints was no longer accepted as the norm.

Dr. Zeller's observations as to how restraints were used only served to strengthen his belief that nothing good was accomplished through the use of restraint apparatus. There were others opposed to the way the mentally ill were being restrained but it must be remembered that it was Dr. Zeller who actually made a concerted effort to rid the state hospitals of these offending apparatus. Thirty-two years prior to Dr. Zeller's assuming control of the Peoria State Hospital, Dr. Andrew McFarland would state, in a report to the State Board of Charities in 1870 that:

> . . .in a large institution perhaps only one-fourth of the patients would require this method of treatment.
> . . .for those who do not need it (restraint), the bolts and bars found in all our asylums are not only of no advantage, they are positively injurious. They irritate many patients and retard their recovery.

Dr. Zeller echoed these sentiments in a paper that he presented at the conference of the Governor, the State Board of Charities, and the Institutional Superintendents, held in Springfield, Illinois, on October 19, 1906. In this paper he adamantly proclaimed:

> I am not called upon to recite my own experience in dealing with this subject, yet why should I take such a decided stand against mechanical restraint if I were not able to point in a successful year in which not one vestige of it has been employed? Its utter uselessness has been demonstrated in a hundred cases who wore restraint so long that it seemed a befitting garment. Our working details are filled with men and women who are daily expending upon some useful occupation the energy that once was spent in madly chafing at the restrictions that were limiting the movements of the body. Note the dog that bounds at you when you enter the yard and frisks about you as you walk up the path, and then note the tethered dog tearing at his chain and threatening to tear you to pieces. It is the same with human beings, sane or otherwise. Insanity, like bodily disease, is but a disordered function. The function still remains, no matter how far the disease has progressed. Impaired though it may be, the insane mind is still capable of receiving some impressions. The horse, with supposedly no mind at all, never fails to find his own stall in the largest stable, and the dog will recognize his master among 10,000 men. The child is not more tractable than the average insane person. One might as well bar from school an unruly child, because it entails a burden upon the teacher to successfully direct it, as to fly to mechanical restraint because its abolition increased the work of those who care for the insane. As well let the victim of infectious disease die, because his care would entail danger of contagion to the nurse. As well leave a battle unfought, because to meet the enemy might expose the soldier to bullets! Men who serve have no right to take their convenience into consideration beyond that of the good of their charges; and if mere numbers are needed, the State has never limited its force, and all of us in the public service have unlimited resources at our command. Therefore, how can we excuse ourselves, if in a failure to avail ourselves of them we inflict physical and mental torture and resort to the devices of the dark ages in meeting conditions which experience has shown can be solved without the employment of such means. [10]

Eventually, it was decided that the use of mechanical restraint was more for the convenience of the attendant, rather than the good of the patient. Dr. Zeller, in his continuing effort to ban restraints, made the following observation:

. . .that the amount of restraint increased in proportion to the previous experience of the attendant. I found that when I cited this or that case that might be handled without restraint, I not frequently had a response echo from a recruit who seemed willing to give the patient a chance; but ever suggest such a thing to the hospital tramp* and you were invariably confronted with a hundred reasons why it could not be done.[11]

By October of 1905 he had banned all use of such restraint altogether. *Only a ". . .few experienced attendants mourned its disappearance, but even they gave in to the new order of things."* [12] In fact, at that time, the hospital employed more than 100 attendants who had never seen the restraints in use, and their only knowledge of them was the collection that was contained in the hospital museum of discarded institutional antiquities. They would not know how to apply them even if they were made available.

---

*Asylum tramp was a term used to describe those employees who had previous asylum experience. Mack Leiter, his maintenance man since the early days of the opening of Peoria State Hospital claimed that, "it soon became known among people seeking employment that those with asylum experience need not apply. Should, nevertheless, an "asylum tramp" become employed by withholding his past, the eagle eye of the superintendent soon discovered this oversight, and the tramp was discharged."

"HUMANE" APPARATUS

"One of the most potent causes of preservation of mechanical constraint has been the ingenuity of the dealer and manufacturer, who has artfully adopted the name "Humane Restraint Apparatus" and by that means has caused many who were using it to lapse into a position of false security, when in fact, the most humane apparatus is inhumane. I have in my museum what any of you would shrink from as the most repulsive of restraining devices: the Utica crib; and yet, hanging upon the wall are apparently harmless appliances a hundred times more cruel. The Utica crib is nothing more than a bed with strong and high wood sides and ends and a swinging door over the top. In it the patient has perfect bodily freedom, limited only by the dimensions of the enclosure.

Let any one witness the writhings and contortions of a patient in a restraint sheet tied hand and foot in bed, or study the interference of respiration while wearing the straight jacket or camisole with arms crossed the breast and the hands tied across the back by means of the blind sleeve, and see if he would not prefer even the monstrosity known as the Utica crib."

Dr. George A. Zeller

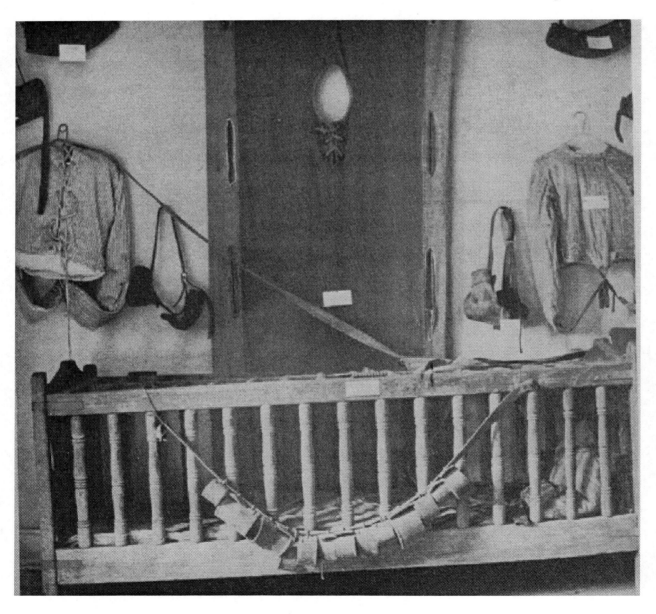

DISCARDED APPARATUS
CONSISTING OF SHACKLES,
HANDCUFFS, MANACLES,
AND BALL AND CHAIN.

ILLINOIS LAW CONDITIONS ALLOWING RESTRAINT

No patient shall be placed in restraint or seclusion in any hospital or asylum for the insane in the state except, by the order of the phyician in charge all such orders shall be entered upon a record kept for that purpose, which shall show the reason for the order in each case and which shall be subject to inspection by the state Commissioners of Public Charities and each record shall at all times be open to public inspection.

SAFEGUARD AGAINST SOMETHING OBJECTIONABLE

The law itself would appear as a safeguard against to cover application of something in itself objectionable and herein lies the absurdity of the law. It the application of mechanical restraint is construed so serious a matter as to call for legislation specifying under what conditions it may be practiced, then why tolerate it all and above all why give it legal sanction?

Search the Statues of Illinois and you may fail to find anywhere a clause legalizing the infliction of bodily injury except in the case of hangman alone and then only after a verdict has been rendered by a jury of his peers and the pardoning power of the Chief Executive has been sought in vain. When men executed upon the order of an assistant physician there will be some excuse for the restraint law of Illinois."

This exhibit of discarded restraining apparatus remained on display as a constant reminder of what had once been considered the norm in mental health care.

In the early 1950s, the National Mental Health Association sought to collect these cruel relics of the past. It was their desire to have them melted down and cast into a "Mental Health Bell." On April 13, 1953, at the McShane Bell Foundry in Baltimore, Maryland, these inhumane restraints were cast into a three hundred pound bell. It is not known if any of the restraints accumulated at the Peoria State Hospital were included in this symbol of hope. The bell has become the symbol of the National Mental Health Association. They proudly claim that this *"huge bell serves as a powerful reminder that the invisible chains of misunderstanding and discrimination continue to bind people with mental illnesses and rings out hope for improving mental health and achieving victory over mental illness."*

"Cast from shackles which bound them, this bell shall ring out hope for the mentally ill and victory over mental illness."

(Inscription on the National Mental Health Bell)

Non-resistance

The use of narcotics to subdue patients may seem less obtrusive than the use of the mechanical restraints. They were, however, in a word an insidious practice. It is hard to imagine what the patient was going through as they were not only suffering from some form of mental illness which may have caused them delusions, but now they were being given narcotics which would, in some cases, exacerbate their delusions.

While the patient was suffering the effects of narcotics it was virtually impossible to communicate with them. This would make it extremely difficult, if not virtually impossible, for their caretakers to discover and treat the source of their illness. If patients are kept constantly sedated they, in many instances, tended to be slow to respond to therapy. Even worse, many of the skills taught to them while they were drugged would not be retained once the effects of the drugs wore off and the patients returned to a drug-free state.

There was another problem directly associated with the use of these narcotics to control patients, "withdrawal." In the event that patients did recover sufficiently from their mental illness that their daily dose of mind-controlling drugs could be stopped, there was a distinct danger of drug dependency. Now, the patient faced a life of drug addiction or the rigors of withdrawal.

One can only imagine the bedlam that must have existed once the hospital ceased using drugs as a means to control the unruly patients. This is one case, however, where one can rightly claim that the end justified the means. Once off the drugs, according to Dr. Zeller, *"It is a source of the utmost satisfaction to see and converse with patients to whom narcotics and hypnotics once seemed indispensable who are now comparatively rational beings two years after the administration of the last dose."* [13]

Eight-Hour Day

The implementation of an eight-hour work day was both innovative and controversial. Dr. Zeller felt, rightfully so, that those employees who were forced to work longer hours were, in many cases, too exhausted to properly care for their charges. Up until this time it was not unusual for employees to work thirteen to fourteen hours a day.

Most of the opposition to this new idea was budgetary, as there was a concern that this reduction in hours would require the employment of even more attendants and, therefore, materially increase the payroll. He knew that if the implementation of an eight-hour day significantly affected the hospital budget, the idea of a shortened work day would not be accepted.

He set about to assess the schedules and manning requirements for the various cottages. He wanted to ascertain if it would be possible to properly supervise the cottages with fewer attendants on duty at any one time. If this could be accomplished he could implement an eight-hour schedule for the attendants without significantly increasing the payroll.

What he found was that every ward had more attendants than were required. A ward that normally had four attendants scheduled there could, at least four times a week, get by with only three attendants when one of them had the afternoon off. Also, since every employee working these longer hours was entitled to every other evening off, then the ward was often under the supervision of just two attendants. It was surmised that the minimum number of attendants actually needed was two. If this were the case, then under the old schedule it would require that every attendant worked thirteen hours every day and fifteen hours every other day, and once a week, when, *"keeping what is known as 'late,' the attendant would be on duty for nineteen hours with one afternoon off per week."* [14]

His solution to the problem was solved when he had the hospital do a systematic recleassification of all the patients. Once this was accomplished, Dr. Zeller was, in some cases, able to reduce the amount of attendants needed in some of the cottages. The excess attendants were now available not only to supplement the needs of those cottages that contained the more violent, untidy and destructive patients, but to schedule more time off for all of the attendants. To his surprise, this was accomplished without increasing the work force. In fact, he claimed that they were actually able to reduce the number of employees.

This seemingly simple reclassification and reassigning of some attendants not only proved acceptable in regards to the treatment meted out to the patients, but it also proved to Dr. Zeller and his superiors' satisfaction that the decreased work day did not significantly affect the payroll. The chart included, taken from the Sixth Biennial Report, shows the results of Dr. Zeller's reorganization.

**TABLES SHOWING THE NUMBER OF EMPLOYEES REQUIRED UNDER THE EIGHT HOUR DAY
AS COMPARED WITH THE FOURTEEN HOUR DAY**

COTTAGE	Number of Attendants Old Regime 14 and 10 hours daily		EIGHT HOUR SCHEDULE		
	Day	Night	6:00 a.m. to 2:00 p.m.	2:00 p.m. to 10:00 p.m	10:00p.m. to 6:00 a.m.
No. 1 "A" 62 feeble old ladies	3	1	2	2	1
No.2 "A" Womens' Infirmary-62 infirm and untidy women	4	1	2	2	1
No.3 "A" 62 very untidy women	4	2	3	3	2
No.4 "A" Women's epileptic colony-62 epileptic women	5	2	2	2	1
No.5 "A" Employees' hospital, operating room and forty 4 working patients.	4	1	2	2	1
Women's' Hospital Tent colony fr 16 consumptives annexed --81 sick women	9	3	3	3	2
No1 "B" Mens' epileptic colony -- 61 epileptic men	4	2	2	2	1
No.2 "B" Mens' 62 extremely untidy men	5	2	2	2	2
No.3 "B" Mens' infirmary -- 62 infirm men	3	1	2	2	1
No.4 "B" Home for aged men -- 62 old men	2	1	2	2	1
Mens' Hospital Tent colony for 10 consumptives annexed 77 sick men.	9	2	3	3	2
Domestic Ward 64 working women	3	1	1	1	1
Supply Ward 150 working men	4	1	2	2	1
Dormitory Ward 47 selected women (mild)	2	1	1	1	1
No.1 "C" 125 semi-disturbed men	5	1	3	3	1
No. 2 "C" 125 partly employed m en	8	1	2	2	1
No.3 "C" 125 old men	4	1	2	2	1
No.4 "C" 125 extremely violent men	9	3	5	4	3
No.5 "C" 125 extremely violent women	9	3	5	4	3
No.6 "C" 125 quiet women	4	1	2	2	1
No.7 "C" 125 old ladies	4	1	2	2	1
No.8 "C" 125 partly employed women	4	1	2	2	1
TOTAL	108	33	52	50	30
GRAND TOTAL		141		132	

Once the news of Dr. Zeller's innovations started to emerge a great deal of attention was focused on him and the hospital; however, not all of it was favorable. Even Dr. Zeller would have periods when he thought that, perhaps, they had gone too far. Fortunately, he had the support of Dr. George W. Michell.* Dr. Michell was one of Dr. Zeller's most loyal supporters and, according to Dr. Zeller, *"he was even bolder than I when I began to hesitate about enforcing this or that policy, he stood firm against all discouragement and we invariably won our point."* [15]

It is noteworthy that Dr. Zeller was, at this time, not considered an expert or trained specialist in the care and treatment of the mentally ill. It would be easy, therefore, for us to assume that his lack of training and experience would be a detriment but, in actuality, it allowed Dr. Zeller to assume control unburdened with any preconceived ideas. He was, therefore, free to institute many of his innovations without prejudice. As a result, he found himself to be constantly at odds with the so called "experts." Over time he developed a genuine mistrust of the "experts" because they continued to hold to conventional precedent and outworn traditions and, as a group, objected to the *". . .abolition of archaic methods and the substitution of modern, humane and scientific standards."* [16] He wrote in his autobiography that:

> *A reputable textbook published late in the eighteenth century declared that "after all, severe and repeated flogging is the best treatment for the insane." Not that I mean to convey the idea that flogging was permitted in our American institutions at the opening of the twentieth century, but I do say that abominations nearly as cruel as that were tolerated as late as 1915. Not only tolerated but approved. And why approved? Because the authorities relied upon "experienced" help for their information as to how the insane must be handled. It was the old story of precedent, the stagnation of clinging to tradition, of closing the mind to the new "agitators" who were clamoring for the abolition of archaic methods and the substitution of modern humane and scientific standards. We preceded cautiously along these lines as anyone must who is departing from established and recognized customs.* [17]

It is hard to imagine what the "experts" reaction was to Dr. Zeller's innovations. Suffice to say, there would be a fair amount of trepidation among his peers. They could not fathom how he could manage a facility with 1,800 patients without any mechanical or medicinal restraint, no cells, no cell rooms, or other places of seclusion or confinement. Even harder for them to accept was the fact that there was not a bar, grating, or screen on any of the doors or windows. In fact, many of the wards and cottages were unlocked night and day. Apparently, some of Dr. Zeller's detractors were so alarmed as to the conditions that now existed at the Peoria State Hospital that they voiced their concerns to his superiors in Springfield. According to Dr. Zeller, they had reported *". . .that a reign of terror existed in our neighborhood and that our paroled patients were committing all sorts of depredations."* [18]

As a result, unbeknownst to Dr. Zeller and the rest of his staff, an investigator was sent to the area by the State Board. After spending three days of visiting numerous homes and interviewing many of the people from the area, the investigator found that there was no basis for the complaints. In fact, quite the opposite was found. He had come expecting to find an *"excited and hostile community;"* what he found was a community that was in support of Dr. Zeller and his new open-door policies. Due to this investigation, the board encouraged Dr. Zeller to not only continue what he had been doing but to expand it to the rest of the hospital.

Rhoda Derry's story and the erection of a zoo out of the discarded gratings and screens are two dramatic examples of how the face of mental health care was changing, not only in Illinois, but in the entire country. The catalyst for this change in thinking is directly associated with Dr. George Anthony Zeller's progressive thinking.

* Dr. Michell served as Dr. Zeller's aide for a short period. He eventually left Peoria State, and opened two private hospitals for the care of the mentally ill in the Peoria area.

It can be argued that many of the innovations attributed to Dr. Zeller had been in effect elsewhere. One of the earliest proponents of humane care for the mentally ill was Philippe Pinel. Pinel, a French physician, was one of the key figures in the quest for humane treatment for the mentally ill. He argued that they should be treated as sick individuals instead of as "wild animals." In 1794, after facing a great deal of resistance from authorities, he was eventually given permission to remove the chains of the patients under his charge at Bicetre Hospital in Paris. His actions gave credence to the idea that through purposeful activity and being comforted, the "insane" could be restored to reason. Dr. Zeller was aware of Dr. Pinel's efforts, and was greatly influenced by his methods and ideas.

So it can be argued that Dr. Zeller was not the first to institute humane treatment for the mentally ill. It cannot, however, be denied that it was this country doctor from Spring Bay that championed these changes in the State of Illinois and eventually the rest of the country as well.

Chapter VII
The Nursing School

". . .that mighty army of self-sacrificing women who in all ages forsook pleasure and comfort and even gave up life itself in order to minister to the suffering." Dr. George A. Zeller

It takes a very special person to be a nurse, and it takes an exceptional person to be a nurse in a mental health facility. Dr. Zeller was well aware that, in order for his plans for the Peoria State Hospital to come to fruition he would need a dedicated staff, and at the heart of this staff was the nurse. (See Appendix IV, <u>What Is The Meaning Of Psychiatric Nursing</u>)

"Dr. Zeller," said Dr. James Ward, *"from his first days at the 'asylum' recognized the importance of a nursing care staff trained to a new concept of care for the mentally ill."* [1] With this in mind, Dr. Zeller's "Training School for Nurses" was opened in 1906. The program was designed so that, upon completion of a three-year program, the graduating nurse would be certified by the state. He wanted a program that would, in his words, *". . .give to our diploma the value and dignity worthy of such a document."* [2]

To get an idea as to how difficult the course was, when the training started in 1906 there were one hundred and five participants; by the end of the first year, which was compulsory, the number of participants had dwindled drastically. Two years later when the graduation was held on June 18, 1909, just twelve* of the original hundred and five participants had completed the course.[3]

In order for the program to succeed everyone involved needed to make personal sacrifices. The medical staff was now not only responsible for patient care; they were now responsible for training the future nurses. Due to the implementation of the eight-hour day, it was necessary to hold classes three times per day; therefore, it was necessary for the medical staff to rearrange their already full schedules.

Dr. Zeller, always mindful of budgetary constraints, insisted that the trainees receive instruction on their off time. *"This sacrifice,"* Zeller said, *"was one of the conditions assumed by those who entered the service."* [4] Having the future nurses, most of which served as attendants, take classes while they were off duty alleviated the need for replacement personnel. It also assured that only the most dedicated would apply for admission to the school.

The first class started in 1906 under the tutelage of Mary Bird Talcott, chief nurse of the asylum. This class completed the program in 1909 and, in June 18 of that same year, the school would hold its first commencement. The ceremony was the first of many which would take place at the Peoria State Hospital.

---

* (It appears that the Peoria Evening Journal may have miscounted or misprinted the number of graduating nurses. The picture of this first class shows thirteen graduates surrounding Mary Bird Talcott, the chief nurse of the asylum.)

Left to Right: Eva Roberts, Viola M. Gordon, Iva M. Culp, Gertrude P. Manzer, Effie Wills, Lillian Herrine, Mary Bird Talcott, Orpha L. Koger, Grace Williams, Carrie D. Harty, Eulah May Jackson, Anna J. Joiner, Ella M. Williams, and Harriett L. Parish

On this particular evening the guest speaker was Dr. J.A. Petitt of Ottawa, the past president of the Illinois State Medical Society and "Nursing the Mind" was to be the subject of his speech. The Reverend B.G. Carpenter, pastor of the Universalist Church gave the invocation. Dr. Zeller presented the diplomas, while music would be furnished by an orchestra composed of inmates of the asylum.[5]

The evening's program was to end with a banquet and a dance. It was to be held in the large general dining hall used by the attendants at the facility. It was expected that there would be at least sixty couples participating in this affair.

The nurses' school was, obviously, a source of great pride for Dr. Zeller but, as happy as he was with the school, he took even greater pleasure in the success and achievements of the graduating nurses. He reported in his Ninth Biennial Report that, *". . .those of our nurses who took the Civil Service Examination later passed with high marks, one of them standing number one in a field covering the entire state, many of the contestants being graduates of large General Hospitals. Four of our graduates have been promoted to the position of Supervising Nurse."* [6] They also made history as they were the first institutional graduates ever to attain the position of chief nurse in an Illinois institution.

The "Training School for Nurses" continued to evolve and, by 1914, the state had opted for a two-year program instead of the original three-year program for the trainees. The following is a summary of the new two-year course of study for the junior and senior years:[7]

JUNIOR YEAR.

Practical Nursing.	Dietetics.	Nervous and Mental Diseases.
Urinalysis.	Anatomy and Physiology.	General Medicines.
Bandaging.	Toxicology.	Materia Medica.
Bacteriology.	Physiology.	
Chemistry.		

SENIOR YEAR.

General Medicine.	Infectious Diseases.	Gynecology.
Pediatrics.	Practical Nursling.	Dermatology.
Hydrotherapy.	Genito-Urinary Diseases.	Eye, Ear, Nose, and Throat.
General Surgery.		
Obstetrics.		

Note: This Junior Senior Year Notation doesn't seem right but this is how it is in the Biennial Reports!

The school continued to follow this format for the next two years. The only change made to the program during this period was the addition of more hours of study to some of the subjects. There was, however, a major change at the Peoria State Hospital. Dr. Zeller was no longer the superintendent.

Dr. Zeller was appointed superintendent of the Peoria State Hospital in 1896. His appointment, by his own admission, was a result of his political activities. In the 1912 election the power and influence of the Republican Party diminished greatly, not only on the national level, but on the state and local levels as well. As a result, Dr. Zeller would be replaced as superintendent. He was well aware of his precarious position and wrote quite candidly about it in his autobiography.

> *My activities in behalf of the Republican Party were too well known to afford me any protection against any aspirant belonging to the successful party and although the newly elected governor, Edward F. Dunne, had visited our institution on several occasions and was outspoken in his advocacy of its manner of conduct. I knew that sooner or later such pressure would be brought to bear upon him that it would be very embarrassing for him to retain me. His party had been out of power sixteen years and his followers had a legitimate claim for recognition. This I did not gainsay, nor did I make the slightest effort to offset any of the arguments advanced by the various candidates for my position; in fact, I took out one of them through the premises and showed him in detail the workings of the institution. He was the most eligible and worthy of all the candidates, and be it said to his credit, he withdrew his name from further consideration after a thorough survey of the field.*
>
> *With the sole exception of the superintendent, the entire institutional force was under the protection of the civil service law* and had little to fear on account of the radical change of the state government from one party to that of its opponent. The superintendency was purposely excluded in order to give the governor a free hand in the selection of executives whose views harmonized with those of his party. Against this, no argument could avail and I resigned myself to the certainty that my public career was approaching the end.*[8]

Even though he had been assured by many that his position as superintendent was not in jeopardy, his political astuteness told him otherwise. Aware that there was now an opening on the board of administration, that of state alienist,* he began to lobby for the position.

This board of five members could have a maximum of three members from the dominant party, in this case the Democratic Party. Since the other two members had to come from the Republican Party, Dr. Zeller sought an appointment to this board. According to him:

> *I told the governor that as a superintendent, I came with the legal definition of the qualifications required of the alienist of the board and that I could qualify even more decidedly as a Republican. He said, If you will display half the energy as alienist I am told you have shown in politics I am sure your administration will be successful.*[9]

So on December 1, 1913, he assumed the position of state alienist; his replacement at the Peoria State Hospital was Dr. Ralph T. Hinton.

It was at this time that the training school received recognition from the State Board of Nurse Examiners. Now credit was allowed for the two-year program at Peoria State Hospital. The graduates of this program, after entering an accredited school and taking an additional nine months of training in surgery, obstetrics, and diseases of children, would be permitted to take the examination given by the board for the degree of registered nurse.

These competitive examinations were given by the Civil Service Commission yearly and determined whether or not an individual would graduate and be recognized by the commission as a graduate nurse. Those nurses who completed the program at the Peoria State Hospital were continually among the best in the state. Dr. Hinton, like Dr. Zeller, was also very proud of the school and its graduates' accomplishments. His satisfaction shows when he reported that:

> *In fact during both years of the biennium the graduating class, as a class, has ranked the highest among the State hospitals. The minimum grade received by any member of either class was 80%. In 1915 two of our class received respectively the second and the fifth honors, there being at that time sixty-five competitors. In 1916 ninety-four young women and young men of the State took the final examination, our class receiving the first, second, third, and fifth honors, there being at that time sixty-five competitors. In 1916 ninety-four young women and young men of the State took the final examination, our class receiving the first, second, third, and fifth honors.*[10]

Due to the school's success and staff's high expectations for those enrolling in the program, only those perceived as the very best were allowed to enroll. This was not always the case according to Dr. Hinton:

> *. . .formerly many entered the training, as it was called, for the want of something better to do and with no evident serious intent of purpose. The probability of just graduating and the receiving of a graduate's salary, was apparently all that was considered. These conditions, however, have been changed materially. Many applications are now received, but only those whose preliminary work and whose work on the wards have been satisfactory are permitted to enter the school.*[11]

In 1917, Dr. Ralph Goodner replaced Dr. Hinton as superintendent of the Peoria State Hospital. From this point forward the amount of official information regarding the nurses training program starts to dwindle. This does not mean that the program was no longer considered to be a vital part of Peoria State Hospital, but it was assumed that the stellar performance of the school and the students would continue.

* On November 1, 1905, the civil service law went into effect.

* An alienist is a specialist in mental disease.

Two years later, in 1919, Dr. Goodner reported that the program was reverting back to a three-year program. As a result of the extended program, the Illinois Board of Nurse Examiners allowed the program's graduates to take the examination for a degree as a registered nurse. The additional year had, perhaps, an unforeseen, affect on the program - the number of entrants diminished greatly.

The following year, in June of 1920, it was announced that, because of the new curriculum, the Training School of Nurses of the Peoria State Hospital was accredited by the Department of Registration and Education.[12]

From this point forward the amount of information regarding the training school seems to be minimal at best. The training school was not mentioned again for four years in the official reports filed, by either Dr. Goodner or Dr. Zeller, until 1924. There is no indication if the program was cancelled or if there simply was nothing much to report regarding it. In 1924 there was an apparent rebirth of interest in the school. Dr. Zeller reported the *". . .most essential feature of our work shows a gratifying revival."*[13] It was also noted that the 1924 graduation had stimulated a renewed interest in the training school.

This renewed interest apparently did not last long, and the school will again disappear from the annual reports. The school is not reported on again until 1931. At this time Dr. Zeller would merely mention, in the Annual Reports of the Department of Public Welfare, that the program would adopt the name of School of Nursing.[14]

Five years later, on July 1, 1936, it was announced that the School of Nursing would be discontinued as soon as the classes that were in progress were graduated. This school had been a mainstay of nurses training at the Peoria State Hospital for thirty years, and during its existence approximately one hundred ninety-nine nurses graduated. (This number was taken from the Twentieth Annual Report of the Department of Welfare, where it was stated that, *"the early records are not complete and this figure may not be accurate, however, it is a fair estimate."*) Out of these one hundred ninety-nine graduates, twenty-three were employed at this time at the Peoria State Hospital.

This was truly a watershed date for the Peoria State Hospital. Nursing and nurses training per se would never be the same.

In place of this highly successful three-year program, the new Peoria State Hospital School of Psychiatric Nursing opened its doors on October 1, 1936. The new school was to be affiliated with the Methodist Hospital School of Nursing in Peoria and the Brokaw Hospital School of Nursing in Normal. There were plans for future affiliations with the St. Francis Hospital School of Nursing in Peoria and the Graham School of Nursing in Canton.

This change was a result of the new ideas regarding nursing education. It was now thought, according to Dr. Irving Turow, the acting managing officer at the Peoria State Hospital, *". . .that the specialized hospital is no longer considered an ideal training center for the basic preparation of the nurse."*[15] A specialized hospital, such as the Peoria State Hospital, would now be utilized only for training nurses in specialized fields such as psychiatric nursing. Now, as part of the student nurses' undergraduate work at a general school, they would be given a two-month course of instruction in psychiatric nursing. The course was outlined by the Illinois State Nurses' Association, and would include the following:

Theory		Practice	
Psychiatry	20hrs.	Women's Acute Mental	2wks
Neurology	5hrs.	Men's Acute Mental	2wks
Psychiatric Nursing	30hrs.	Women's Hospital Service	2wks
Staff Conferences	6hrs.	Men's Hospital Service	2wks
		(Twentieth Annual Report, P. 334)	

The hospital did not expect to turn out a fully qualified psychiatric nurse in two months, but it was hoped that the course would generate sufficient interest in the student which would cause them to seek postgraduate instruction in the field.

Unfortunately, this did not happen. The state had not anticipated the shortage of qualified psychiatric nurses which occurred once the Peoria State Hospital School of Nursing ceased operation. The hospital no longer had an ever-continuing source of trained psychiatric nurses. Louis Allen, director of the Peoria State Hospital training school, reported that as a result, "...*the means of replenishing our rapidly diminishing graduate staff becomes increasingly serious.*[17] It was suggested that this shortage of psychiatric nurses would continue until sufficient numbers of general schools opted to include psychiatric nursing as a required part of their curriculum.

A survey, conducted by the Mental Hygiene Committee of the Illinois State Nurses' Association in 1935, to determine the demand for courses in psychiatric nursing was at best dismal. Of the one hundred and nineteen surveys sent out, only seventy-six schools responded, and of those only thirty stated any interest in arranging an affiliation with a psychiatric hospital. Later, each of the thirty which had expressed an interest in such an affiliation were once again contacted regarding a possible affiliation with a program such as the Peoria State Hospital's School of Psychiatric Nursing. Out of the thirty schools contacted only twelve responded. Seven of those who responded were negative, only five schools expressed any interest, and eighteen of those contacted did not even acknowledge receipt of the survey.[18]

In an effort to make a career in psychiatric nursing more desirable, salaries were increased for all nurses who were receiving less than $80.00 (including maintenance) per month. At the Peoria State Hospital, a new wing was to be built to house all of the nurses and it was to include modern conveniences for the comfort of the nurses. *"It is felt that these features, with the organization of a definite plan of staff-education, should attract nurses who have heretofore felt a desire to do psychiatric nursing but have not chosen the State mental hospitals mainly because of low salary and lack of opportunity for advancement,"* said Louise Allen.[19]

Louise A. Meyer, acting chief nurse, issued her report regarding the school of nursing on June 30, 1938. According to her, the new program was not progressing as well as hoped. Her report is so refreshingly honest, regarding the problems with the new program, it bears repeating in its entirety:

> *The affiliate course in psychiatric nursing is nearing its second year, and it is regrettable that the plan is not yet receiving the welcome which was anticipated. During the past year 31 undergraduates have taken advantage of the affiliation, and it is particularly pleasing to note that four of this number have applied for post-graduate courses in recognized schools of psychiatric nursing. Nurse educators plead patience, but it is extremely difficult to sit quietly by while the graduate nurse staff rapidly diminishes with no source of adequately trained psychiatric nurses for replacement. It must of necessity be years before the institution can realize its ultimate objective in the affiliate school.*
>
> *Why the delay of interest? The question thus far is answered by the general hospital by saying that the teaching organization of the State hospital is not on a par with that of the general hospital seeking affiliation in psychiatry. And this is a just criticism. The abundance of clinical material to be found in all State hospitals is of no value for teaching purposes unless correctly utilized. And proper utilization depends wholly upon the acquisition of a well prepared administrative and teaching personnel as well as adequate classroom and library facilities.*
>
> *The Peoria State Hospital School of Psychiatric Nursing has not received the welcome which was anticipated because the organization is lacking in the above mentioned essentials. The general hospital schools of nursing, with excellently prepared teaching and supervisory staffs, cannot afford to lower*

their standards by affiliating with a school of inferior organization. Thus the delay in interest shown. The general hospital is waiting for the State hospital to meet the requirements of the National League of Nursing Education relative to training school organization; while the State hospital is waiting for the general hospital to show sufficient interest in psychiatric affiliation to warrant the necessary improvements. The old question of which comes first, supply or demand, must be settled.

The National League of Nursing Education is responsible for all recommendations concerning the education of nurses and it is extremely gratifying to note that Psychiatric Nursing occupies a prominent place in the curriculum guide prepared by this organization. This guide book may be found on the desk of every administrator of nursing in this country as well as those in many foreign nations. It is evident therefore that affiliation in psychiatric nursing will soon be a required part of all nurses' education. It would indeed, be a great credit to the State of Illinois if its Department of Public Welfare would be the first in the country to shoulder the responsibility of preparing adequate facilities for affiliation in psychiatric nursing.

It is generally agreed that the school of nursing in any hospital may well be regarded as the hub of the institution, for out of the school emerges stimulation for all departments. The cultural tone of the institution with a school is greatly improved and the patients benefit directly through the specialized nursing care received. But just as the strength of the smallest wheel depends on its hub, so the reputation of the hospital depends on the sound organization of the nursing service.[20]

Four years later the school still had not grown a great deal. This lack of growth was viewed by some as a reflection of a poor program, but Dr. Irving Turow did not believe this to be the case. He claimed that:

". . .the course was built on a solid foundation, that which was laid by the Peoria State Hospital School of Nursing and whose high standards were outlined and maintained by Dr. George Anthony Zeller, Mary Bird Talcott, Hattie Levreau, J. Marion McNaughton, Alice Agatha Meehan, Rose Bigler and others. For that reason a solid structure must be planned with the same lofty ideals which characterized the old school of nursing and from which so many representatives have gone forth into the psychiatric field to champion the cause of the mentally ill."[21]

But the program which was established on October 1, 1936, never did fully meet the ever-expanding needs of the hospital. On July 1, 1944, it was decided to transfer the management of the program from the Peoria State Hospital to the Division of the State Alienist.[22] This change, along with the increased utilization of the affiliate hospitals for training, marked the end of an era. It is hard to imagine that the program envisioned by Dr. Zeller and his staff had come to an end. A program that, according to Dr. James Ward, caused:

. . .a large group of nurses from Southern Illinois came to the Peoria State Hospital in the early 30s and 40s, attracted by this new concept of treating the mentally ill. These nurses became the basis, the foundation for and the glue that held the nursing services to the solid base set by Dr. Zeller. This strong and uninterrupted program, based on the philosophies of Dr. Zeller, was considered one of the main reasons that the Peoria State Hospital became so widely known for its treatment programs.[23]

The Peoria State Hospital would continue to provide excellent training for the nursing profession and to be a vital part of the training for becoming a registered nurse. In fact, nurses were still receiving training at the hospital when it closed.

Chapter VIII

Women Attendants

"Women Attendants on Mens Wards, of which there is an overwhelming majority in this institution, should never forget that they are surrounded by abnormal minds." Dr. Zeller

By the time Dr. Zeller submitted his Fifth Biennial Report in 1904, his stamp was firmly imbedded on the Peoria State Hospital. Not being one to sit back and relax, he continually strove to make improvements at the hospital. More importantly, he sought to insure that the patients received the best care possible. As previously stated, Dr. Zeller, upon assuming control of the Peoria State Hospital, would immediately introduce some of the most controversial changes regarding the care of the mentally ill that the state had ever seen.

Another of Dr. Zeller's early and daring innovations was the implementation of women into the male cottages where they would provide the primary care for the insane male patients. He decided that it would be safe to place at least one woman attendant in each male cottage. He made this decision based upon a previous reclassification of the patients and evaluation of their needs which took place in 1906. There were few, if any, superintendents willing to take such a bold step at this time. What if one of the patients overpowered a woman attendant, physically assaulted her or, even worse, what if she were to be killed? The public and official outcry would have been immediate, and highly critical. The person who authorized such a catastrophic program would have faced the probable loss of their position and their reputation would, more than likely, be irreparably damaged as well. Dr. Zeller was willing to take such a chance; the results were immediate, and positive, much to the chagrin of some of his peers.

Dr. Zeller did not make such a move impulsively or without a great deal of consideration. Once he decided to introduce women into the male cottages, he chose to move cautiously. He slowly introduced the women attendants in small numbers into the male cottages. These first attendants were well aware of what the atmosphere was like in the male cottages due to their close relationship with the hospital, according to Dr. Zeller as they were *". . .invariably the wife of the attendant in charge."* [1]

Dr. Zeller, ever mindful of the innate danger of this program, made every effort to ensure the safety of the women in the cottages and the success of the program. He included in his Rules Governing the Conduct of the Illinois General Hospital for the Insane the following section:

Women Attendants on Men's Wards

Women Attendants on Men's Wards, of which there is an overwhelming majority in this institution, should never forget that they are surrounded by abnormal minds. They must never permit patients to lay hands on them, in kindness or otherwise. They must resent every familiar advance and at all times cultivate the respect of their charges. They will carefully develop inmates to do the necessary ward work, to run errands and will speedily discover in every cottage enough loyal and devoted inmates to come to their aid in emergencies. No women will remain alone in a cottage of men. In such cottages there will never be less than two women attendants assigned, whether by day or night and they are to govern themselves accordingly. [2]

This limited use of women in the men's cottages proved to be such a success that, by 1906, it was decided to extend the *"sphere of women over the milder men,"* and a woman was put in charge of one of the general dining rooms for men. There she would be responsible for supervising fourteen male insane helpers.

The employment of women in these previously male-dominated positions exceeded all expectations, and Dr. Zeller was quick to recognize the advantage of using women attendants. He commented that the success of the program was so profound that the *". . .superiority of women over men as attendants for the insane requires no defense from me."* [3] Ironically, even though the women had proven to be equal, if not superior in performing the duties of an attendant, they were paid less. The starting pay for a woman attendant was $18.00 per month, while her male counterpart received $25.00 per month.

The presence of a woman tended to further the illusion that this facility was a home, not a jail. It was the constant aim of Dr. Zeller to, *"restore individuality and remove from the surroundings of the inmate every suggestion of imprisonment."* [4] *"Their presence,"* he said, *"completes the final picture of home,"* which was still another step in bringing a sense of normalcy to the patient.

One of the first things that Dr. Zeller and his colleagues observed was that the patients tended to be more compliant when the women attendants were present and, as a result, it was decided to place even more women in the cottages. The introduction of women into these formerly all-male environments continued until, according to Dr. Zeller, *". . .we found the presence of the man embarrassing and he (the male attendant) was assigned to other duties, and the ward was given over entirely to women."* [5]

A direct correlation was soon observed regarding the patients' behavior and the arrival of women. It was apparent that coinciding with the introduction of the women attendants to the cottages, the men's habits improved, their appearances improved, their table manners improved and the neatness of their dress took a drastic change for the better.

At first, due to Dr. Zeller's sense of propriety, it was decided to rely upon only married or widowed attendants for this duty. With the dynamic success of the program there was an increased need for women attendants, and it was decided to offer these positions to single women as well. By 1906, there were eight hundred insane men under the direct care of women attendants, and only one cottage out of twenty-one still had male attendants. This particular cottage was home to *"one hundred and twenty-five of the most violent insane men to be found anywhere on earth."* [6] In this particular cottage, however, it must be noted, that even though there were men present, they were not in charge. They were there only to assist the female attendants who were now responsible for this cottage as well.

By 1908, the transformation was complete. Women were now in charge of every cottage in the hospital, and just two years later, in 1910, the Eight Biennial Report does not even make mention of the female attendants. In just four short years, the use of women in the male wards went from being quite controversial to being the conventional approach. Even though this major change in the care of mentally ill men took place rather rapidly, Dr. Zeller thought that this transformation, like many others, would, perhaps, have been even quicker if not for, *". . .that stumbling block to progress, precedent."*

Nurses and attendants responsible for the care of 800 insane men. Circa 1906

Chapter IX

Monuments and Memories

"Death must not come to be lightly looked upon even among these unfortunates and a due observance of the solemnity of the ccasion cannot fail to benefit the living." Dr. Zeller

The first patients would arrive by rail on February 10, 1902, and by June 30, 1903, there had been twenty-two deaths recorded at the Peoria State Hospital. This translates into a mortality rate of 3.23% or, on an average, 4.4 patient deaths per month. The statistics for the following year show that forty-six patients died there for a mortality rate of 6.3% or an average of 3.5 deaths per month. This may seem like a high number of deaths but, to be fair, there were extenuating factors that must be considered when evaluating their deaths. *". . .the average age is greater than that of the other asylums for the care of the insane since we receive only the chronic cases which have long been afflicted with insanity,"* reported Dr. Zeller in his Fifth Biennial Report in 1904 and, *". . .as we are not recruited from the ranks of the young and vigorous recent cases, our average age will always remain high."* [1]

These numbers would not change much throughout Peoria State Hospital's history. Reverend Eimo Hinrichs, who was the chaplain at the facility from 1963 until it closed in 1973, said, *"the hospital averaged about fifty burials per year during his tenure there."* Again, the seemingly high numbers of deaths can be, for the most part, attributed to the age and physical condition of the patients, not to their care.

The Peoria State Hospital was in operation for a period of seventy-two years, 1902-1973. It was over this relatively short span of time that 4,132 patients would die and be interred on the hospital grounds. This would mean that, on average, 57 people per year or five per month died and were subsequently interred there; however, this number does not take into account those who died at the hospital and were taken elsewhere for burial. The early biennial reports did give numbers as to how many deaths occurred, but the later reports do not contain such detailed statistics. This makes it virtually impossible to ascertain the total number of patients who actually died over this span of seventy-two years of time.

These statistics are not meant to be a reflection on the care of the patients, but to make a point that from the time the hospital opened until its closing in 1973 the death of patients was inevitable. Most of the deaths at the Peoria State Hospital can be attributed to natural causes, such as old age and physical illnesses but, sadly, others can be attributed to possible neglect, poor treatment and, in rare cases, murder.

Dr. Zeller was well aware of the fact that there would be deaths occurring at the Peoria State Hospital, and that not all of the deceased would be claimed by family and friends. In fact it has been estimated that forty percent of the deceased would go unclaimed. Coincidently, the last time the cemeteries are mentioned was in the Annual Reports of the Department of Public Welfare, June 30, 1930, filed by Dr. Zeller. From the very beginning every attempt was made by Dr. Zeller to show proper respect for those unfortunates who were interred at the Peoria State Hospital. It was as if there was a fear that any disrespect for the dead would inevitably lead to a disregard and unconcern for the living. It was with this in mind that Dr. Zeller would institute a short burial service and, for the first few years, he personally presided over the services.

After all, as Dr. Zeller later wrote:

. . .it is a very easy matter to have some sort of ritual at a burial and this is now the very general practice. A brief prayer, a recital of the short form of burial service while a few faithful and sympathetic employees stand uncovered at the side of the grave, while, in itself, perhaps only a matter of

routine, has an elevating influence upon the entire personnel. Very often some poor relatives are present and they go away with a greater respect for the public service and a feeling that the kindly ministrations of the state extend even to the grave. [2]

Dr. Zeller's sense of the propriety when dealing with the deceased came about partially as a result of his military service. One event, during this period of his life, had clearly made a lasting impression upon him. Apparently, he had drawn the ire of his superiors for the way he had conducted the burial of a young soldier who had succumbed to pneumonia. He said as a result of this experience that:

> *. . .I never permitted a corpse to be carried on a stretcher that is used for living persons and in conveying the sick from one of our cottages to the hospitals. I have more than once corrected the litter bearers who were carrying a sick man feet forward. A man is carried but once feet first and that is when on the way to the grave. Once, when a workman was fatally crushed, I had him placed on a stretcher and conveyed to the hospital. On the way, he died and I had the carriers reverse and carry him to the morgue, feet first. It seemed a minor thing but it impressed our force with respect to the living and the dead. It still persists. Our asylum cemetery contains three thousand graves and never a woman is buried without the presence of a female attendant and a nurse accompanies every woman's corpse that is carried from the hospital to the morgue. . . .* [3]

In 1909, Dr. Zeller issued his, "Rules Governing the Conduct of the Illinois General Hospital for the Insane Peoria Illinois." In this book of rules he included the following section dealing with the "Disposal of the Dead:"

> *. . .the disposal of the dead will be in the hands of the Pathologist. All bodies are to be properly prepared, awaiting the embalmer and most be removed to the morgue at once. Unclaimed bodies will be buried in the Institutional Cemetery and the short service will be invariably read at the grave. Where the deceased is a woman a Woman Attendant designated by the Chief Nurse must be present. Death must not come to be lightly looked upon even among these unfortunates and a due observance of the solemnity of the occasion cannot fail to benefit the living. Each grave must be marked with a numbered cement headstone and recorded in the plat of interments in order to make identification at any future time possible. A Soldier's Lot has been set aside for veterans of the wars and all such are to be buried therein and their graves bedecked on Decoration Day.* [4]

Degradation of the cemeteries

The cemeteries have long been and continue to be a source of controversy. Most of the controversy regarding the cemeteries relates directly to the lack of care and maintenance they receive.

By 1940 it was reported that the hospital, as well as the cemeteries, had been allowed to deteriorate. The initial response to the negative publicity by those responsible for the facility was to blame the previous administration. The incoming Democratic governor, John Stelle, and his director of Public Welfare, Archie Bowen, actively sought to lay the blame for the deterioration at the feet of their predecessors.

This seems somewhat strange as Stelle assumed office after the death of Henry Horner, who, while serving his second term as governor, died in office on October 6, 1940. John Stelle, also a Democrat who was serving as lieutenant governor, took control of the office of governor on October 6, 1940, and held that office until 1941. It may be true that the deterioration had started with the preceding administration, but the subsequent administration did little to alleviate the problems at the Peoria State Hospital. It must be remembered that Governor Horner was in office from 1933 to 1940; therefore, it could be surmised that the problems at the Peoria State Hospital were surely not entirely the fault of the previous administration. Also, Stelle served as the state treasurer from 1935 to 1937, and he was elected lieutenant governor in 1937. Surely, anyone in these positions would have some knowledge of the conditions at the various facilities controlled by the state, including the Peoria State Hospital.

Archie Bowen, in response to the negative publicity, told a reporter from the **Peoria Star** that, *"Governor Horner and I inherited from the neglect and indifference of the past many institutions sadly dilapidated and indecently overcrowded."* He further asserted that the stories regarding the cemeteries were a direct attempt at:

> *. . .malicious political libel the accusations and insinuations that he had neglected the burial of un-claimed bodies at the Peoria State Hospital as a result of which there are no records of such burials bodies have been lost and the burial ground in regrettable condition.*
>
> *The charges are without foundation, and appear to be some sort of a raid upon a Potters field in search of an issue.*[5]

Citing the ongoing work that was taking place at the hospital's cemeteries, Bowen sought to alleviate the public's growing concern about the Peoria State Hospital. Again, he sought to place the blame for the delays in action on others. This time he blamed the federal government, according to him, *"a WPA project for the complete restoration of the cemetery where three thousand unclaimed patients are at rest has been drawn up and is awaiting approval in Washington."*[6]

He did, to his credit, at this time institute the use of a new type of headstone to mark the graves. From this point on the individual graves would receive a headstone that, although still bearing the innocuous number, the stone gave the name, date of birth and date of death of the person interred there. In cases where the patients' identities and birth information was unknown, they were referred to as either Jane or John Doe. Prior to this, the graves were marked with a small insignificant numbered concrete slab. This essentially made everyone buried there, prior to this time, a virtual unknown.

Another charge that was leveled at Bowen was that the hospital had mishandled or lost bodies. He was adamant regarding these reports which claimed that the state had lost track of whom was buried there and, in some cases, had either lost or inadvertently switched the identities of some of the dead patients. It was his belief that the records were complete and intact from the very first grave to the present. The basis for this *"ghoulish and unwarranted attack,"* according to Bowen, came about due to the *"complaints of a woman that her mother had been lost."* He said that the woman's mother had been:

> *. . .committed in 1887 to the old Cook county insane hospital at Dunning and has been continuously in an insane hospital for nearly fifty-five years. She was transferred to Peoria State Hospital in 1906. Though a very disturbed disorganized and deteriorated patient she lived in Peoria State Hospital for more than thirty years and died at the age of seventy-seven years. Her name had been transcribed daily from one ward roster to another without an error in spelling and she went to her grave with her identity perfectly preserved.*
>
> *During this long period she was not visited by relatives. She had no correspondence. Mail directed to the address of the husband was returned by the post office.*
>
> *The state cared for her kindly, gently, tenderly and when she died a year ago this month laid her away with a Christian burial.*

A few weeks ago a daughter appeared to claim the body. She created a scene with her lamentations and abuse of the institution. She contended the body had been lost and she could never rest assured that the body given her was that of her mother. Even when she was shown the records and was assured that a card having her mother's name would be found within the casket she continued her abusive charges.[7]

These same accusations of neglect and mismanagement would arise again some forty-five years later. In 1985 Rick Baker wrote a scathing report on the conditions to be found at the now-closed Peoria State Hospital. His article, "Graves Without Bodies, a Hospital Without Pity," brought the poor conditions of the cemeteries to the public eye. In this story he reported as to what he and the security man at the facility found as they walked by one of the cemeteries. They discovered, during this walk, that a portion of one of the cemeteries had eroded into a deep ravine. This was more than likely Cemetery II, as it is the closest to a deep ravine and, to this day, shows the signs of erosion. When asked about the erosion and its close proximity to the graves, the security man replied, *". . .there are no bodies in those graves. There are no caskets. There are no urns filled with ashes. If there were, they'd be washed into the gully along with the stones."* [8]

Gary Lisman

Marker #1835 November, 2004. These pictures show just one of the many lost stones that have either washed away or wound up in one of the many ravines surrounding the cemeteriesas a result of vandalism. It is still there today nearly twenty years after Baker wrote his article.

There is another indication of the poor condition of the cemeteries that can be surmised from Baker's article. Apparently, the cemeteries suffered from an apparent lack of general maintenance and mowing. The following picture was taken in Cemetery III sometime in 1974. It is obvious that the weeds and brush had already started to overtake the cemetery, only one year after the facility had closed. It is hard to imagine what this area may have looked like when Baker wrote his article in 1984.

Cemetery III: Circa 1974

When Baker wrote this article he apparently could not find all the graves. In his article he wrote that, "*...the graves that simply identify people in the order they died from Body Number 1 to Body Number 3,124.*"[9] There are in fact 4,132 graves there. How was it possible for them to miss the other graveyard, and the other 1008 graves? One can surmise that the weeds and brush had more than likely covered them.

Grave number 3,124 is, in fact, the last of the larger headstones in Cemetery III. Starting with 3,125 the state had started using a flat stone that lay flush with the ground. Baker and the security man may have not walked very far into the cemetery and simply just did not see the flat stones. The picture to the right shows how easy this would be. Stone 3,124 is easily seen while stone 3,125 is hardly noticeable in this picture taken in November of 2004.

Gary Lisman

The stone on the left is stone number 3,124. The indentation on the right is the flat or flush stone number 3,125.

After the Peoria State Hospital closed, the care and condition of the cemeteries rapidly decayed and has become, what should be if nothing else, a source of embarrassment for the state. The lack of proper maintenance and care by the state for the cemeteries would continue for several years. By June of 1985, the degradation of the cemeteries was so appalling that only the most coldhearted among us would not feel a sense of shame at the condition of the cemeteries. Fortunately, the city of Bartonville has since taken it upon themselves to do what they can to maintain these cemeteries. They have done a creditable job of keeping the cemeteries mowed and cleared of trash and other debris. They have also made a concerted effort through their police department to keep vandalism to a minimum.

Unfortunately, though, the state continues to retain control of them and will not allow the city, or any concerned citizens or citizens' groups, to reset or refurbish the cemeteries. The cemeteries continue to deteriorate, and without some kind of intervention they will eventually be lost. It seems that Rick Baker was right when he wrote that, "*...the State wants this lingering nightmare torn down, and wants the Peoria State Hospital lobotomized from its memory.*"[10]

Lost Cemetery

One hesitates to include the following story regarding the possibility of perhaps another cemetery which may or may not be located on the grounds. The possibility of a "lost cemetery" has to be, for now, considered a myth due to the lack of tangible evidence to the contrary. Dr. William McNett, who has done extensive research at the Peoria State Hospital, may have been alluding to the possibility of a "lost cemetery" when he wrote about his Peoria State Hospital addiction. In his final remarks he claimed that, *. . .now I have information about another mysterious situation which I can't relate until further verification."* [11]

That story, like many of the others surrounding the Peoria State Hospital such as the "Graveyard Elm" or "Ed" and "Al," the two men who are reportedly haunting the Bowen Building, does warrant telling. Perhaps someone will come forward with a picture or some credible explanation for the strange and unexplained impressions that can be found only in one area of the hospital grounds.

Over the years, especially after the Peoria State Hospital closed, a disturbing story concerning the facility would surface. The rumor alluded to the possibility of a lost or secret cemetery located on the grounds. It was here that, some believe, there were patients who died from neglect, mistreatment, medical experimentation, murder and abortion, and were secretly interred.

Those who adamantly claim the existence of this cemetery, always refer to one area. This area was, and still is today, highly visible during the years that the hospital was in operation. This visibility, therefore, would make the use of this area as a secret cemetery virtually impossible.

Another problem with this notion of a secret cemetery is that nearly everyone associated with the hospital, the staff and patients alike, would have to be involved in such a cover-up. It is hard to imagine that out of the many thousands of individuals associated with the hospital, not one of them has ever come forward to give credence to this story.

The area in question does, however, show signs of some activity in years past. If one looks closely, there are numerous symmetrical indentations to be found there. These indentations are perfectly round and evenly spaced, indicating that they were certainly man-made. The source of these indentations may never be known. One could make a case that they are left over from the days when the grounds were extensively mined or, perhaps, it is truly a "lost cemetery."

Headstone Designs

The headstones utilized at the Peoria State Hospital are, for the most part, composed of six designs. There are, in addition to these six designs, a few privately purchased markers to be found.

Upon reading Dr. Zeller's short story "The Post Mortem Finding," I thought that this story could easily be attributed to one of the patients at the Peoria State Hospital. The last paragraph seemingly gave the location of the story's protagonist, Edward Callan's grave. Callan, according to Dr. Zeller's story, was interred in a grave located in the largest of the hospital's cemeteries and it was also marked with a rather distinctive stone. The stone was reportedly in the shape of a Maltese Cross. It was also said to be inscribed with the following:

Number 1461

QUEENS LANCERS

V.C.

Armed with this information I spent several hours in search of this stone. I finally came to the conclusion that this stone either no longer existed, or it had existed only in the mind and pen of Dr. Zeller.

I did, however, discover another interesting stone located in the same area where I had expected to find Callan's. It was in this area that a former patient Emily B. was interred. The story as to why she had a special marker amongst this sea of innocuously numbered stones was discovered in an Annual Report to the Illinois Department of Welfare, 1930, submitted by Dr. Zeller.

An Echo of the Armada

It is a far cry from the sixteenth to the twentieth century, from the days of Sir Francis Drake to the present - a long distance from Cape Finisterre to the Peoria State Hospital - but both time and space were eliminated when Emily B. died last year. She had regularly received a draft from London for twenty-five pounds sterling and when one came after her death we submitted to the superintendent of charities who very properly ruled that since it was a charitable gift it should be returned to the donor. This was done and we received an acknowledgement from the Royal Benevolent Institute expressing his appreciation of the attitude of the State of Illinois and conveying the information that our patient was the last surviving descendent of a British seaman who singally (sic) distinguished himself in the destruction of the Spanish Armada, in England's greatest sea fight, and that the crown has conferred the privileges of the British Seaman's Benevolent Fund upon any of his dependent survivors in perpetuity and that she was the last of the line. Three centuries of benevolence!

With Rupert Brooks she might well have said:

"If I should die,
Think only this of me.
That there's some corner of a foreign field.
That is, forever, England!"

She had a small balance in the trust fund which we were authorized to expend for a tombstone. The sculptors engraved upon it the coat of arms of the British Navy and a photograph was sent to England. We have romanced about our cemetery from time to time but monuments are visible of the truth of these statements.[12]

Gary Lisman

The most prevalent style of markers is one composed of a modicum of cement, just enough to hold them together, and pea gravel. Upon these stones all that can be found, where still legible, is a cold and impersonal number. Examples of this style can be found in Cemeteries I, II, and III.

Gary Lisman

The stones, top picture, are a variation of the original tablet stones in Cemetery IV. The picture above shows the traditional tablet style found in Cemeteries I, II, III and IV.

A portion of the first cemetery is dedicated to Civil War veterans. It is easily identifiable by the G.A.R. (Grand Army of the Republic) stone located in this area.

Grand Army of the Republic (G.A.R.) Stone

Many of these graves are marked by the traditional cement tablet but, in some cases, the graves are marked with a veteran's stone. There are a few newer veteran stones located in Cemeteries III and IV.

Veteran of World War I

Cemetery III contains the eight styles of markers utilized at the Peoria State Hospital to mark the graves. One will find a few military stones, a few privately purchased stones, and a few rectangular stones fashioned from sandstone, but the majority of the stones found there are the traditional tablet, the pointed tablet, the rectangular stone, the more classical looking cement marker and, finally, the flush with the ground marker. The twenty-three stones that are rectangular and appear to be made of sandstone seem out of place (similar to those in the picture). They appear to have been crafted off-site and they do not include an identifying number. These stones were used for less than a year from December of 1915 to April of 1916. From this point the stones revert back to the numbered cement tablet.

Starting in 1934 with grave number 2,326, the state changed the design again. This time the stones, although constructed of cast concrete, tend to humanize those interred there. These markers still have the innocuous number molded into them, but they also give the patient's name, date of death, and, where known, their date of birth.

Gary Lisman

The above picture is an example of the marker utilized from 1934 to 1948. This particular stone marks the remains of just one of the twenty-one John Doe's interred at Peoria State Hospital. The picture below shows the back of the same stone.

The state would once again change styles beginning in February of 1948, starting with stone number 3,125. These stones were designed to be flush with the ground. This change was, more than likely, made for economical reasons. First, this type of marker would be easier and cheaper to make. Secondly, by being flush with the ground, it made it much easier and faster to mow the area. Now instead of mowing by hand around the individual graves, one could mow continuously.

Sadly, the cemeteries located on the hospital grounds have continued to deteriorate, which makes the identification of many of those interred there difficult, if not impossible. One must wonder that Dr. Zeller would have to say about the conditions found at the cemeteries. A man who once wrote, ". . .*may we not hope that with a little more effort on our part and with a determination to mark each grave, we may so reduce the number of unidentified that a visit to an institution graveyard will be like a stroll through a community cemetery.*"

The state, in its own way, has contributed to the demise of the cemeteries and continues to ignore its responsibility to those who are interred there. Aside from the aforementioned care provided by the Village of Bartonville, limited by the state of Illinois, the cemeteries continue to deteriorate. According to Dr. William McNett of the Peoria County Genealogical Society:

> *Names and/or dates appear on only less than half the total 4,132 stones. Something that makes even more extravagant the facelessness of the dead is the fact that the State of Illinois will not release the vital statistics on these individuals. Although they say that it is a right of privacy not to release the names and dates, I feel that it is the public's and history's right to know.* [13]

Gary Lisman

One of the pictures depicting the neglect at the hospital cemeteries. Gary Lisman

Marker 4,132, for Walter K----, born in 1889 and died in August of 1973, is an example of the flush with the ground style that can be found in Cemeteries III and IV. This grave is significant as it is the last grave recorded at the Peoria State Hospital.

Gary Lisman

Cemeteries

Depending upon whom one talks to, there are anywhere from three to five cemeteries on the grounds of the Peoria State Hospital. Some claim that the Grand Army of The Republic (G.A.R.) cemetery, which is located next to the original cemetery, is Cemetery I. Others claim that these are two separate cemeteries. The other controversy over the number of cemeteries can be found in the areas marked III and IV on the map below.

There are some who would claim that the areas marked as Cemetery III and Cemetery IV are one cemetery since the only division is the road that separates the area in half. Others claim that the road divides the cemetery into two distinct areas, since the graves on the south side of the road are distinguished by a different style of headstone. For ease of description, however, it will be assumed that there are four cemeteries located on the grounds.

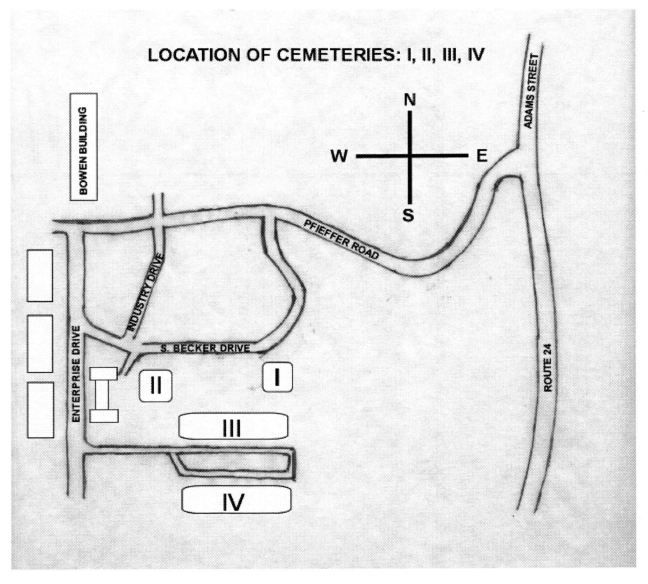

LOCATION OF CEMETERIES: I, II, III, IV

Cemetery I

Cemetery I contains the G.A.R. cemetery and the oldest of the graves located on the grounds. The veterans have not been completely forgotten as yearly, the American Legion of Bartonville places a small American flag at each of the graves on Memorial Day.

Left: Captain Holly Turner, U.S. Army, 82nd Airborne, placing flags on July 4, 2004.
Gary Lisman

Below: Flags placed on soldier's graves.
Gary Lisman

This area is made of twenty rows of graves and a total of 326 plots. The numbering in this area is somewhat erratic and hard to follow.

Nearly lost in the woods is the very first grave to be located at the Peoria State Hospital. Not only has the marker nearly disappeared from sight, the number that should be visible has also completely disappeared due to age, poor material and the weather. One of the more notable graves to be found here is that of Rhoda Derry (*217). Her tragic story was told in Chapter V.

Cemetery II

Cemetery II is somewhat hard to find, as it is hidden behind what was once the Pollak T.B. Hospital and is surrounded by some tall underbrush. The grave markers in this cemetery are similar to those found in Cemetery I. It is not known when the hospital started using this cemetery. There are only three markers on the site, out of 532, that contain any information and these markers were all privately purchased.

The first grave there is number 336. Grave 350, which was privately purchased, gives a date of death as 1907. So it is probable that this site was first used either in late 1906 or early 1907.

It has been long suspected that this site contains the grave of, arguably, one of Peoria State Hospital's best known patients, "Old Book." The location of his grave was disclosed in an article by the Peoria Journal Star on Sunday, June 30, 1974, and, shortly thereafter, the stone covering this grave was taken.

The story of Manual Bookbinder, or "Old Book," has been told so many times that the truth and the myth of the story are hard to differentiate. There are some who claim that "Old Book" never existed at all and there are others who would claim otherwise. His story and the myth that surrounds him is detailed in Chapter XV.

Gary Lisman

Cemetery II. It is believed that Grave 713 is where "Old Book" was buried.

Cemetery III

Cemetery III contains 1,842 individual graves. This cemetery, as earlier written, contains several markers similar to those to be found in Cemeteries I and II. One will, however, find eight different styles of markers in this area. There is in this area a larger model of the original numbered stones; these have a pointed top, which contain only a number and no other pertinent information.

At the east end of Row 10 there are twenty-three stones (December 1915 to January 1916) that are made of sandstone. These are the only stones of this type found in any of the cemeteries.

The hospital changed to a different style of marker beginning in 1934. These new markers formed ". . .*rows of well organized large, clearly readable stones*" which, according to Dr. McNett of the Peoria County Genealogical Society, "*stand in sharp contrast to those in the earlier cemeteries.*" [14] The stones, however, are anything but well organized. Rows 1-6 contain this new style of marker but, if one walks north, one will find the new style in Rows 20-24. Even with this lack of continuity, the newer markers are a great improvement. These markers provide one with not only the person's name but the date of their death as well. It is in Row 1 that one will find the last style of marker used at the facility. These stones are flush with the ground for ease of maintenance, and, like the larger markers, it is possible to ascertain the name and date of death from them. Regrettably, the flush stones have, for the most part, been lost due to settling and the growth of vegetation, which tends to cover them over time.

Cemetery IV

Cemetery IV lies directly south of Cemetery III and contains six long rows with a total of 901 gravesites. The markers in this cemetery are also flush with the ground and many of these markers have become difficult, if not impossible, to find. According to Dr. McNett, *"...if a visitor happened to try to locate a specific grave (only an infrequent happening), the odds would be against him/her. Probably two to three inches of sod and clover cover a high percentage of stones. Several dozen are almost a foot deep, and some are nearly two feet deep."* [15]

Last Grave

It was on December 18, 1973, that the last remaining nineteen geriatric patients at Peoria State Hospital were slated to be transferred. They were to be sent to the Galesburg Research Hospital about eighty miles away from the only home some of them had ever
known. Among this group was Walter K., but he would not make the trip. Walter died on August 8, 1973, and would become the last patient to be interred at Peoria State Hospital.

Walter K.'s death and the transfer of the remaining eighteen patients marked the end of the Peoria State Hospital. All that can be found on the grounds, to remind one of what was once there, are a few rapidly decaying buildings and the cemeteries. The hospital as it stands today, like those interred there, is mostly forgotten. What a sad epitaph for what was once such a proud institution.

Chapter X

Treatment and Therapy

"Long ago they lowered insane persons into snake pits; they thought that an experience that might drive a sane person out of his wits might send an insane person back to sanity." Mary Jane Ward

The beginning of the treatment of the mentally ill is impossible to decipher. In fact, as Dr. Mark D. Altschule wrote, *". . .the treatment of mental disease quite possibly began when the human population of the earth increased from one to two."* [1] During the Stone Age it is believed that holes were drilled in the skull to release the demons within. Later, people relied heavily upon amulets and charms to ward off the demons. Around 500 B.C. herbs, such as hellebore (veratrum album), were being used to treat melancholia. Ingestion of the herb apparently caused convulsions and, once the convulsions had passed, many patients went into remission. Blood letting, or venesection, came into use during the time of the Byzantine Empire. This dubious practice was still being used in the nineteenth century.

Punishment, either corporal or mental, was used extensively in the treatment of the mentally ill for many years. The idea behind this treatment was to drive out or kill the evil spirit that was believed to have taken possession of the psychotic person. Along these same lines Dr. Zeller often remarked that *". . .a reputable textbook published late in the eighteenth century declared that after all, severe and repeated flogging is the best treatment for the insane."* [2]

Hermann Boerhaave of Holland (1688-1738), considered by many as one of the most renowned medical men of his time, thought that melancholia was a disease caused by "black juices." By spinning the patient long enough and fast enough, approximately 100 revolutions per minute, they were rendered unconscious and the "black juices" were removed. One proponent of the spinning chair, or the centrifuge, claimed that *"when patients are unruly. . .it never fails to be physically and morally beneficial,"* but added, *"that it was not effective when the patient was in a furious state."* [3]

J. B. Steward, the author of <u>Practical Notes on Insanity</u>, after having tried the treatment himself, called the treatment barbarous. He claimed that, *". . .unless tried, it is quite impossible to conceive the suffering produced by it."* As a result of his experience with the centrifuge he was convinced that, *"this was a remedy which would be tolerated in no disease but insanity."* [4]

Others, such as Benjamin Rush, thought that mental illness was caused due to congested blood in the brain; therefore, if a patient was placed in the spinning chair, the congested blood would be dispersed.

Two different examples of the "Whirling" or "Spinning" Cage are show on the next two pages:

Another form of early shock treatment employed during the early nineteenth century was the so-called "Bath of Surprise." In this treatment, the patient was unwittingly dropped into a tub or vat of cold water. Early depictions of this eerily resemble a public execution by hanging. One can only imagine the terror felt by the person receiving this treatment. Unaware of what was awaiting them, they were, in some cases, blindfolded and led up a set of stairs to be suddenly dropped into cold water.

"WHIRLING CAGE"—an old time device for calming mental patients

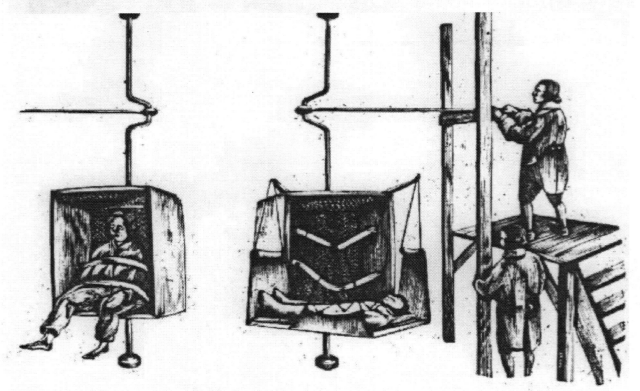

"The O'Halloran Swing & Hammock for the Insane." The upright swing was used to calm an unruly patient while the horizontal swing was used to treat insomnia and to induce sleep.

According to the Illinois Department of Mental Health 1970 Annual Report these:

. . .forms of treatment seem incredible today. For example, in one form of treatment, doctors and attendants would jump up and down with all their weight on a patient who was spread-eagle on the floor. This was supposed to drive out the madness.

Less bizarre but still no more therapeutic, were such practices as the cold needle shower, hydrotherapy in which patients were immersed in cold or hot baths for long periods, insulin shock in which a patient was maintained in a coma for one or two hours, Metrazol convulsive therapy in which camphor and oil were used to produce epileptic-like convulsions.

If you feel it is inhuman to restrain an overactive patient with chains, you can always use the sulphur and oil treatment as was practiced for a while. These two substances were injected into the muscles of the patient's arms and legs. They caused excruciating pain if the patient moved. It was guaranteed to keep anyone quiet.

The performance of a lobotomy operation was another means of treating patients. Two holes were drilled in the skull and the nerve fibers cut. The result was a dramatic reduction of psychotic symptoms. But also the patient became immature, shallow, complacent and lacking in self-awareness. The procedure is seldom used today except in the most extreme cases. Was this a procedure from the dark ages? In Illinois 96 lobotomies were done in one institution between 1953 and 1955.

The list of such well meant atrocities perpetrated on a helpless patient population in the name of treatment is long and varied. But in 1955 with the discovery of the psychotropic drugs, a dramatic change in the character of institutions for the mentally ill took place. At the time the discovery of the tranquilizers was considered a major miracle. Today, such chemicals have wide spread use in the hospitals and in the community. [5]

Prior to the establishment of state facilities specifically designated for the care and treatment of the mentally ill, the prognosis for recovery was dismal at best. The mentally ill were, for the most part, housed in the almshouses or jails. It was not the intent of these facilities to treat those housed there, but to remove them from society as their actions, in many cases, were disturbing to the public. Treatment, such as it was, was for the benefit of the staff and society, not for the patient.

There were numerous forms of treatment and therapy utilized at the Peoria State Hospital during its seventy-one years of operation. Some were quite successful and others not so successful. From the very beginning, Dr. Zeller and his staff sought to discover and employ new and innovative treatments. Many of these treatments were still being used when the facility closed in 1973. Not all of the therapies developed and utilized at the Peoria State Hospital are included in this book. For example, an innovative treatment for alcoholics was developed by William N. Becker, supervising psychologist at the Peoria State Hospital. In 1955, he developed a program to treat alcoholism in which he incorporated the insulin coma therapy with a medical/social/psychological educational approach. This program was not only innovative but quite successful as well. As a result of this success, he was asked to present his findings at various conferences, not only in the state but throughout the United States and Europe as well. According to Dr. James Ward, *"William Becker was asked to present at conferences such as the one in Frankfurt, Germany. . .at the International Congress at the Goethe University in Frankfort, Germany, from September 6-12, 1964. A paper describing the Peoria Alcoholism Treatment Program was presented to the International Association of Alcoholism Programs in Portland, Oregon. The Peoria State Hospital treatment philosophy soon became a widely accepted model for alcoholism treatment programs."* What follows is a brief summary of some of the treatments that were utilized over the years to treat the insane mind at the Peoria State Hospital.

Color Therapy

Color treatment was one of the first methods of therapy employed at the Peoria State Hospital. In an effort to improve sanitation at the facility, paint was applied to the walls and ceilings in many of the buildings which housed the patients. Since the buildings were already scheduled to be painted, it was decided to test the patient's reactions to specific colors in their surrounding environments.

At this time there was a theory that the use of primary colors would have a calming effect upon the mentally ill. By 1904, seven of the cottages, home to four hundred patients, had been painted with the color scheme of violet and blue. There was insufficient data available to Dr. Zeller for him to reach any conclusive theories as to the effectiveness of primary colors upon his patients when he submitted his biennial report in 1904. He did, however, note that *". . .the effect upon the visitor is pleasing and the atmosphere of the wards is restful to the extreme."* [6]

Dr. Zeller also described his observations as to the effects that red light had upon a group of female workers in his Fifth Biennial Report. It had been discovered at a film developing establishment which had their female employees working under red glass that the women were inefficient due to what was described as "hilarity" amongst the workers. Once these women were removed from this red atmosphere, their attitudes became more solemn, and the work improved immensely. [7]

Based on the findings at the developing establishment it was decided to take one cottage and paint the walls red, install red carpet, and use red incandescent globes with red shields. It was into this atmosphere they then placed a number of despondent and melancholy female patients. After two years in this environment it was noted that there was a growing cheerfulness and contentment amongst this group of patients. [8]

It was also observed that the color blue tended to be soothing to the patients. As a result, most of the cottages were now painted in blue tones. One cottage was not only painted blue, it had blue linoleum carpet and blue lights with blue hoods. Here it was claimed that the *". . .entire atmosphere is filled with the blue ray, and its effect is most pronounced."* [9]

A variation of the color therapy was the absence of all color, or the black room. The black room was initially utilized to test the effects of complete darkness upon the extremely violent. The room had a black floor, a black bedstead, black walls and black curtains.

The effectiveness of the room was first observed shortly after the Peoria State Hospital opened for patients in 1902. It was at this time that the decision was made to place one of the hospital's most violent women patients, suffering from recurrent mania, in it. Not being entirely sure of the outcome of this proposed treatment, a great deal of caution was exercised. A physician was placed in charge and a nurse checked her respiration every thirty minutes. These extra precautions were not, according to Dr. Zeller, done because they feared danger, but because *". . .the suggestion that a patient was to be placed in a black room caused a shudder to pass through the force, and extravagant forebodings of the outcome were made."*

It was observed that once in the black room the patient soon went to sleep. Three days later her condition was greatly improved and she was returned back to her cottage. Once the success of this initial treatment was confirmed it became common practice to place patients, though to be suffering from hysterical insanity, in the black room. [10]

Phototherapy

In 1909, as part of a vacation trip to Europe, Dr. Zeller noted that *". . .we had been experimenting with phototherapy and had ten sun parlors of ruby, violet, chrome or opal glass. There was little literature on the subject, and I thought something might be learned by visiting the Finsen Light Institute in Copenhagen, Denmark."* [11] *"Dr. Zeller, recognizing that in the treatment of the deranged mind the patient was entitled to every agency that might in the slightest degree exert a beneficial influence"* and *". . .while no great claim is made for phototherapy, the experiment is considered well worth while, being both harmless and inexpensive."* [12]

Phototherapy was first used at the Peoria State Hospital in the operating room. Here, incandescent bulbs of violet, ruby, canary or amber and white were in use for specific purposes. The ruby or red light was believed to lessen inflammatory conditions. The blue or violet, according to Dr. Zeller, *"seems to possess a germicidal as well as anesthetic action, and in a case of advanced tuberculosis of the hand subjected to its influence there has been a marked improvement. It is also being tested extensively in the field of dermatology."* [13] As a result of the observed germicidal and anesthetic qualities of the different colors, a solarium utilizing colored glass panes was built in conjunction with the tent colony for the treatment of tuberculosis.

The canary light was thought to be relaxant and they had some success in treating patients with spasmodic conditions. Based on these observations, it was decided to test the effects of the canary light in the epileptic wards. The white light was considered a counter irritant and stimulant. Dr. Zeller cautioned that prolonged use of white light was apt to burn the skin; therefore, if a prolonged use was indicated, it was advisable to cover the exposed part with a thin asbestos mat. [14]

Note the "Ruby Solarium" in this tuberculosis tent colony.   Alpha Park Library

Two years later, in 1908, Dr. Zeller was asked to submit a report as to his conclusions regarding the effects of color upon the "diseased mind." [15] It is safe to say that he was cautiously optimistic. In his report he wrote that:

> *I have been exceedingly reticent in claiming beneficial results. The whole subject of phototherapy is yet in its infancy and even the literature is meager. I do not wish to add to it unpreparedly, but I do wish to say that something has benefited these patients beyond the power of the pen to describe. They have been brought here in many instances in the wildest stage of maniacal excitement and with no other treatment than exposure to the violet or amber ray of the leucodescent lamp have speedily recovered and always and invariably without narcotics, without imprisonment and without mechanical restraint. Not only the acute but the chronic patients have improved beyond measure and our institution partakes of the nature of a village with its two thousand inmates contented and happy and engaged in a variety of labor extensive as to bring our per capita cost of maintenance far below the allowance.*
>
> *Some influence has calmed these excited minds and perhaps the same influence has cheered up the depressed and has changed despondency into contentedness.* [16]

Photo and color therapy would be utilized at the Peoria State Hospital through the first part of the twentieth century. The Peoria State Hospital's ongoing belief in the relevance of these therapies resulted in the installation of four thousand different colored window panes, with numerous color incandescent lamps as well.[17] *"It even had resurgence,"* according to Dr. Joe Mehr and *"in the early 1970s, when seclusion rooms or time out rooms and some jail cells were painted in a particular shade of light pink because it was supposed to have a calming effect!"* [18]

Hydrotherapy

Dr. Rebekah Wright, noted specialist in hydrotherapy and the author of <u>Hydrotherapy in Hospitals for Mental Diseases</u> published in 1932, defined hydrotherapy as *". . .the remedial use of water in any of its forms -- ice, liquid, or vapor, internally or externally."* [19]

The effects of hydrotherapy, or continuous bath, have been known for thousands of years. The ancient Egyptians, Hebrews, Greeks, Persians, and Hindus all used water in the treatment of various diseases.[20] Perhaps the first wet-sheet pack was performed by a Chinese doctor several centuries before the birth of Christ. He prescribed, *"one hundred affusions of ice-water, each followed by wrapping in a linen sheet."*[21]

The New Way

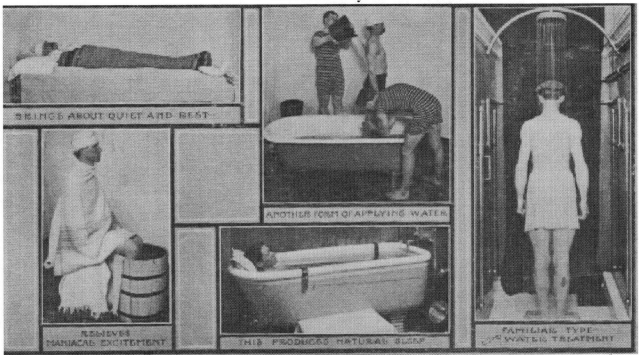

Sir John Flayer, in the late eighteenth century, described how wet sheets and blankets could be used to induce perspiration and sedation.[22] Philippe Pinel, chief physician at the Hospice de la Salpetriere, was, perhaps, the first doctor to systematically employ them to treat the mentally ill.

By the late nineteenth century, the use of hydrotherapy to treat the mentally ill had gained many supporters. "Between 1890 and 1900, physicians Frederick Peterson, H. W. Mitchell, G. W. Foster, and E. C. Dent," according to Dr. Mehr, *"reported on the use of hydrotherapy with people with mental illnesses and published widely."*[23] It was the sedative and calming effects of the treatments which caught the imagination of Dr. Zeller and many others who were responsible for the treatment of the mentally ill. The 1907, Illinois Bulletin of Public Charities contained the two following pictures showing how care for the mentally ill had evolved through the use of hydrotherapy.

Early in 1905, the Peoria State Hospital installed its first continuous bath in their ward for violent women. The tub was designed so a patient could be left indefinitely in any depth of water. Dr. Zeller reported that the success of the treatment was, *". . .gratifying and has caused the staff to wish many times that this was a receiving hospital, in order that its extension would be justifiable and a greater field for its application presented."*[24]

There were at least twenty-five different applications or therapies associated with hydrotherapy, with each treatment designed to treat a specific disorder.[25] It was believed by Dr. Rebekah Wright that there were fifteen conditions or disorders which could be relieved by hydrotherapy:

(1) Delirium, (2) psychomotor excitement, (3) agitation, (4) insomnia, (5) cerebral congestion, (6) arterial hypertension, (7) vasomotor paresis, (8) gastric disturbances, (9) intestinal disorders, (10) suppression, retention of incontinence of urine, (11) autointoxication, (12) visceral congestion, (13) pain, (14) faulty metabolism, and (15) inanition. [26]

The Old Way

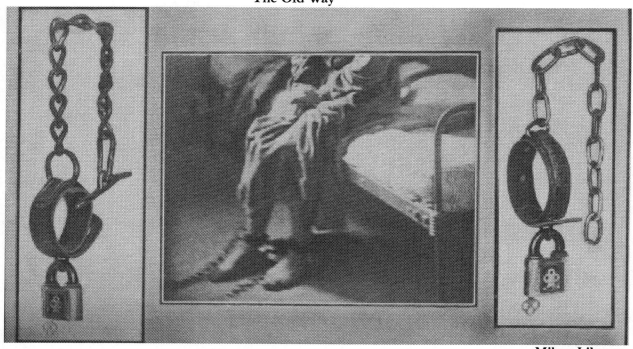

The Peoria State Hospital reported by 1919 that they had the specially trained personnel needed and equipment to offer the following types of treatment: Hot, cold, wet, dry and neutral packs, continuous, Turkish and Russian bath, Scotch, revulsive and many other douches; electric light cabinet treatment, massage and other appropriate methods. [27]

Hydrotherapy had become firmly entrenched as the preferred method for treating the disturbed mind at Peoria State Hospital by 1919. Through the use of hydrotherapy, it was now possible to halt the use of all forms of restraint and seclusion at the hospital. Dr. Ralph A. Goodner, the managing officer at Peoria State Hospital, wrote that *"...the more hydrotherapy that is used, the more we are convinced of its unrivaled supremacy over all other means of treating certain mental symptoms, and the conviction becomes stronger all the time from the results obtained and its widespread application."* [28]

The following table, taken from the 1919 Illinois Department of Public Welfare, shows just how extensively this form of treatment was being used at the Peoria State Hospital.

BATHS

Continous	992	Spray (Alternating)	119
Foot	40	Spray (Graduated)	98
Local (hot & cold)	63	Spray (Needle)	17,231
Pail Pour	39	Tub	80
Shower	21,775		

FORMENTATIONS 381

MASSAGE

Local (hand, arm, spine, etc.)	7,457	Scalp	8
Swedish	760	General	54

PACKS

Hot Blanket	5,944	Wet Sheet	30,341
Local	54		

MERCURIAL INUNCTIONS 234

RUBS

Alcohol	51	Oil	1,250
Cold mitten friction	5	General Centripetal	144
Cold towel	5	Talcum Powder	12
Wet Sheet	26	Salt Glow	530

SHAMPOO

Swedish	126
Hair	10

TOTAL **87,818**

Strangely, with all of the hydrotherapy treatments being administered and its perceived usefulness in treating the mentally ill, hydrotherapy will not be mentioned again until 1949. Then it was reported, by Dr. Richard J. Graff, that three hydrotherapy units were now being used at the Peoria State Hospital. It would be interesting to know how many people were employed just to administer these treatments. Using the 1949 statistics, when 1,263 patients received 26,612 treatments requiring 51,260 treatment hours, one could certainly assume that a large specially trained staff would be required.

Another example of the growing reliance upon hydrotherapy at the Peoria State Hospital can be seen using the same statistics. It had taken 14 years, from 1905 to 1919, for the Peoria State Hospital to administer 87,818 treatments or about 6,272 treatments per year in 1919. By 1949 the hospital was administering about 4.24 times more treatments per year for 26,612 treatments per year.

The discovery of psychotropic drugs in 1955 resulted in dramatic changes, not only in the institutions responsible for the care of the mentally ill, but in the methods used to treat the mentally ill. It was now possible to treat patients in shorter, more intensive programs instead of relying upon the long-term custodial care previously available.

By 1961, the use of tranquilizers had supplanted hydrotherapy as the primary method of treatment. *"Hydrotherapy,"* according to Dr. Ernest S. Klein, superintendent, *"was still considered to be a valuable method of treatment.*"[29] This is evident in the number of hydrotherapy sessions administered that same year. It was reported that a total of 12,771 hydrotherapy treatments were administered to 1,352 Peoria State Hospital patients in 1961.[30]

The following pictures depict but just a few of the hydrotherapy treatments administered at the Peoria State Hospital.

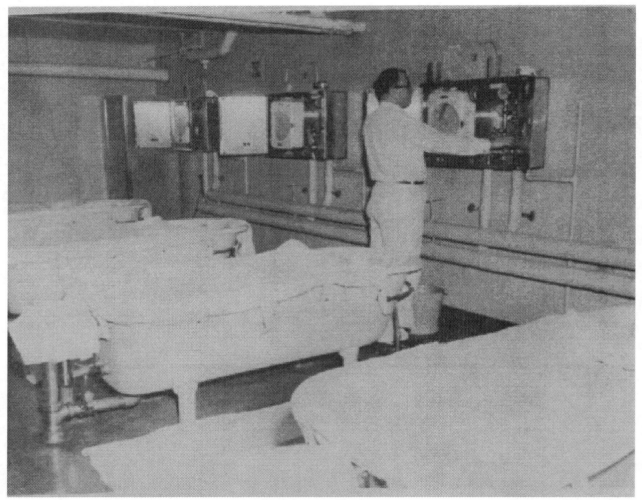

Continuous Bath   **Alpha Park Library**

The hydrotherapy tubs shown were used at the Peoria State Hospital for the continuous or prolonged bath. These baths, according to Dr. Rebekah Wright, could be administered for:

". . .hours, days, weeks, or months. Some patients are soothed and kept comfortable by baths of short duration (two or three hours), given two or three times during each twenty-four hours. Daily baths of six or eight hours' duration are frequently administered to excited patients. In some hospitals daily continuous baths of eighteen hours duration are given. Some very disturbed patients are kept in the baths without removal for periods of two or three weeks.[31]

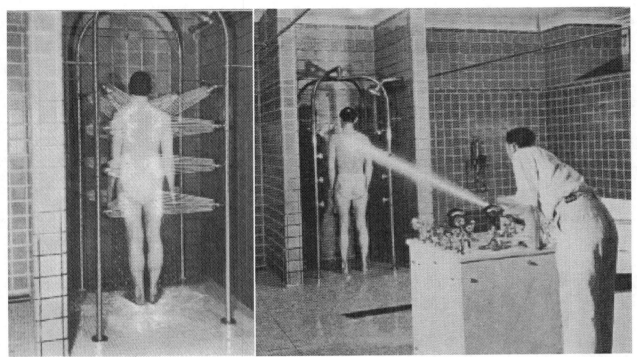

The Needle Spray   **The Fan Douche**   **The Abraham Lincoln Library, Springfield**

Douches and showers were treatments which involved the spraying of water through a single jet or many jets against the body. The volume, pressure, and the temperature of the water varied upon the patient's needs and the hydrologist directions to the attendants.

The Jet Douche   **The Abraham Lincoln Library, Springfield**   **The Rain Douche**

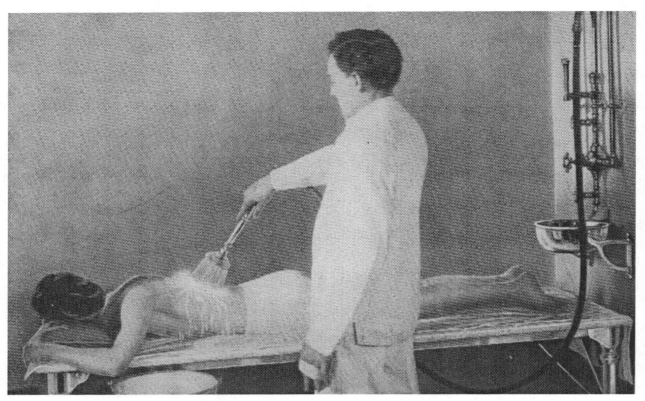

The Swedish Shampoo   The Abraham Lincoln Library

The Swedish bath or shampoo was considered a therapy, but it also allowed for the patient to receive a thorough cleansing as well. Dr. Wright described the Swedish bath in this way:

> . . .*the shampoo frees the body of exfoliating epithelium and odors clinging to hirsute areas. The millions of ducts, commonly called pores, opening upon the surface from the sweat and sebaceous glands are cleansed of accumulated material, sebum and bacteria of decomposition. The friction dislodges the grease and dead epithelium. An immediate effect of the shampoo, followed by an affusion with clear water, is a feeling of well-being, the whole organism refreshed.* [32]

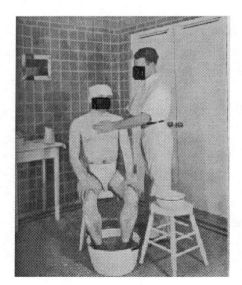

The salt glow is when the entire body was given a rub of salt. This resulted in what best can be described as a *"vivid glow."* [33] Dr. Wright recommended this treatment for all, *"frail patients with psychoses who need gently stimulating tonic baths for the improvement of the circulation, elimination, and nutrition."* It was also supposedly *"of value in the treatment of anemia, nephritis, diabetes, and the convalescent stage of morphinism."* [34]

The Salt Glow
The Abraham Lincoln Library

The Wet Sheet Pack   **The Abraham Lincoln Library**

The wet pack was extensively used at the Peoria State Hospital. It was administered to 30,314 patients in 1919 alone. This therapy basically involves the patient being tightly wrapped in sheets and blankets. It was usually administered to those patients who were exhibiting excited, violent or destructive behaviors. To many this treatment would appear to be nothing more than a way to punish or restrain a patient.

The treatment did limit the movement of the patient when correctly administered, but it was not prescribed as a substitute for restraint, punishment or seclusion. In fact, about three-fourths of those patients would become quiet and fall to sleep shortly after the wrap was applied.

Insulin Shock/Coma Therapy

Insulin shock was first introduced by Austrian psychiatrist Manfred Saskel in 1933. Insulin, which had been discovered in 1922, was being used to treat those suffering from anorexia. One of the effects of this treatment was a general improvement in the physical and mental state of those receiving the treatment.

Saskel, while working in a private German clinic, decided that, perhaps, insulin would also ease the symptoms of those suffering the symptoms of withdrawal in the treatment of morphine addiction. By mistake, he administered too large of a dose in several of his patients which resulted in them going into a coma. Once the patients were revived, it was observed that they seemed to be less agitated than before.

Based on his observations, Saskel tested the treatment on schizophrenic patients with some initial success. It was discovered, though, that many of those who showed improvement often became ill again. This led some to conclude that, perhaps, the intensive care received by the patients while in the special insulin wards was the reason for the positive results, not the insulin shock.

Saskel continued his experiments and refined the treatments at a private clinic in Austria and, in 1934, published his results.[35] Although the initial acceptance by the medical community was not immediately forthcoming, by 1939 the treatment was being widely used. In Illinois, according to Dr. Joseph Mehr, *"Elgin State Hospital was the first of the Illinois hospitals to use the new insulin shock therapy, and adopted it in 1937."* [36]

Peoria State Hospital started making preparations for the implementation of an insulin coma therapy ward the following year. In October of that year there was a clinic given at the hospital by a Dr. Abraham Low.* The following is excerpted from the notes of that clinic given by him:

> *Lately it has been proposed to treat dementia praecox patients with the so-called Insulin shock. The treatment has been heralded in fat headlines with the result that hopes and expectations have been aroused far beyond reasonable possibilities of fulfillment. I shall try to give you an outline of the treatment and its realistic promise but, mindful of the offensive and harmful ballyhoo of the press publicity, I shall stress its limitations rather than its merits.*

> *Let me tell you first that at the present stage nobody has sufficient experience to make an authoritative statement. I began treating patients with Insulin shock early in November last year, and probably was the first in Illinois to use it. I mention this point not in order to establish a priority claim but merely to emphasize that if anyone is qualified to make pronouncements on the value of the shock therapy, we at the Psychiatric Institute are.*

> *Nevertheless, the press statements have issued from sources other than the Institute. I claim as much if not more experience than anybody else in the state. Yet, my experience covers only 13 cases to date. The originator of the treatment, Dr. Saskel of Vienna, has in close to four years accumulated an experience with over two hundred cases to date. Anyone who is at all acquainted with the complexity of dementia praecox knows that even an experience of two hundred cases is insufficient for final conclusions. Let me tell you that the physicians who either contacted the press or permitted the press to contact them have violated the plain principle that no one must offer himself as an expert in a field of which he has only the experience of a beginner. And the newspaper advocates of the Insulin shock were as much beginners as I still am.*

> *The unfortunate result of this newspaper campaign was that the public started a rush on the state hospital. The superintendents of the state hospitals found themselves in a very distressing situation. It is a standing rule the wisdom of which is obvious that state hospitals must not apply therapeutic methods without adequate experience and equipment. In this instance, the public raised an insistent demand for a treatment for which the state hospitals lacked both experience and equipment.*

> *I shall describe the salient points of the shock treatment. The patient is given daily an increasingly larger dose of insulin until finally he goes into coma. The coma is then maintained for from one to two hours. During this coma stage anything from a cardiac collapse to plain passing out may happen. The danger is obviously not negligible. Physicians and nurses must always be on the spot ready to meet an emergency that may arise at any moment. It is a general rule that not more than three or four patients should be treated at the same time. One physician and one nurse are about able to meet the emergency possibilities of three or four patients. These patients will on an average require about two months of treatment. For the period of two months then ten physicians and ten nurses will have to spend the greater part of the day at the bedside of these forty patients. If you consider that the majority of our hospitals are staffed with less than ten physicians you realize how utterly chimerical* is the demand that the state hospitals adopt this method of treatment at the present time.*

> *There is no doubt but the treatment is effective. Its effectiveness does by no means coincide with the fairy tales published by the newspapers. However, the conclusion is warranted on the basis of present experience that the Insulin shock is superior to anything we have seen so far. I will only make the qualification that another shock treatment, the metrazol shock, seems to be superior to the Insulin*

*Chimerical existing only as the product of unchecked imagination; a fantastically visionary or improbable.

* This information was taken from the Peoria State Hospital's monthly newsletter, "Asylum Light." It did not give Dr. Low's official position, or where the "Institute" in which he worked was located.

shock. However, at present I have only experience with about two dozen cases treated with metrazol. If the metrazol treatment should be found, after sufficient experience with it, to live up to its present expectations I will not hesitate to commend it as the logical means of treating patients in state hospitals. It is inexpensive and does not make an excessive claim on the time of physicians and nurses.

To sum up: Years ago dementia praecox was generally considered a malignant, hopeless condition. With the newer treatments, there is good reason for hope that medical effort will be able to make a sizable dent in the yearly toll of this scourge. However, at the present still lacking, and while an attitude of hopeful conservatism is well justified, enthusiastic expectations ought to be discouraged. [37]

There is very little information as to how extensively insulin therapy was utilized at the Peoria State Hospital. It is known that the Peoria State Hospital had two insulin wards for both men and women by 1938, and that the treatment had become a "routine therapeutic procedure in suitable cases." [38] The last reference to insulin in the public records was reported in 1954. At this time, insulin was mentioned not as a therapy per se, but strictly as a treatment for the diabetic patient.

This seems somewhat strange as William N. Becker, a supervising psychologist at Peoria State Hospital, would develop a widely recognized treatment program at the Peoria State Hospital. He discovered that his patients were *"more amenable to treatment upon being revived from their induced comas."* With this in mind, he developed a treatment program utilizing the insulin coma in conjunction with a medical, social, psychological, and educational approach to treat his patients.

Electroconvulsive Therapy

One of the most common and widely used of the convulsive therapies was the electroconvulsive therapy, or ECT. In this procedure a patient receives an electrical shock when current is passed through the brain to trigger a seizure. It is still not fully known as to why this treatment works, but it is thought that the seizure causes the brain's chemistry to be altered.

The first ECT was performed at the Peoria State Hospital shortly after the equipment was installed in September of 1942. Once installed, the equipment was used nearly every day from that point on according to Dr. J. H. Ellingsworth, the managing officer at Peoria State Hospital.[39] There is no record available as to exactly how many ECT treatments were given but, according to Dr. James S. Ward *"the 40s and 50s were characterized by frequent administrations of this treatment."* [40] This leads one to believe that the number of treatments must have been in the thousands.

For most, the thought of ECT treatment conjures up the image of Jack Nicholson receiving an unwanted and unnecessary ECT in the 1975 movie "One Flew Over the Cuckoo's Nest." This was not an accurate portrayal of ECT's today, but the early ECT's could be extremely painful and dangerous. In early treatments, patients were not administered any type of anesthesia or muscle relaxants, which in some cases, resulted in broken bones.

Early proponents of the treatment used it to treat almost every type of "disorder" including depression, mania, schizophrenia and even homosexuality and truancy. This indiscriminate use of the ECT, according to Dr. Joseph Mehr, led to:

"...the greatest travesty of the ECT era when the inappropriate long-term use of ECT by some physicians virtually every day on chronic patients who could not benefit from it, and who suffered cumulative side effects of probable memory loss from thousands of applications of the ECT. Things such as that did unfortunately happen in the 1950s and 1960s in some state hospitals." [41]

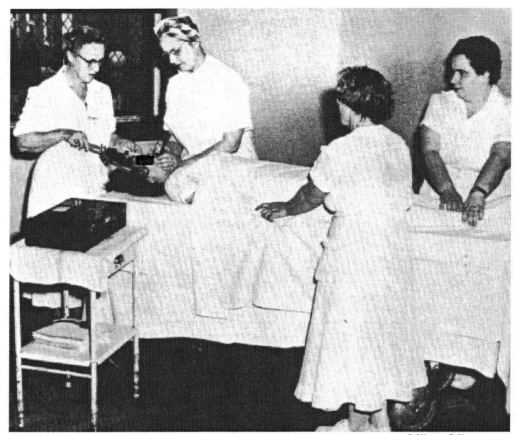

Lobotomy

The lobotomy is, perhaps, the most controversial and feared form of treatment ever to be performed on the mentally ill. The lobotomy is a procedure which involves invasive surgery to the cranial area where the nerve fibers connecting the frontal lobes to the thalamus are severed.

It was around 1890 when a German researcher, Friederich Golz, began seeking a brain surgery that could be used to improve, if not cure, the mentally ill. He found that if he removed portions of a dog's temporal lobes, they tended to be calmer and less aggressive. Based on Golz's findings, Gottlieb Burkhardt, the head of a Swiss mental institution, attempted a similar procedure on six of his schizophrenic patients. The surgery did have a calming effect upon four of his patients, but the other two died.

In 1935, Antonio Egas Moniz of Portugal developed the idea that some forms of mental illness were caused by an abnormal sort of stickiness in nerve cells, which caused the neural impulses to get stuck, which in turn caused the patient to repeatedly experience the same pathological ideas. He had no real evidence to back up his theory, but he further surmised that, if the nerve fibers causing this stickiness could be destroyed, the patient should improve. So, in November 1935, Moniz attempted his first psychosurgery. In this first attempt, the patient received alcohol injections to the frontal lobethrough holes drilled in the skull. This procedure was performed on six more patients when it was decided to sever the nerve fibers connecting the frontal lobe to the thalamus.

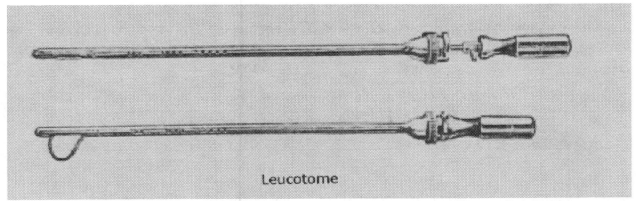

Leucotome

The "leucotome" was designed by Egas Moniz to perform the lobotomy. It was an instrument with a retractable wire loop which was later replaced with a steel band, which he used to cut six cores in the white matter of each hemisphere.

In the United States Walter Freeman, a neurologist, and James Watts, a neurosurgeon, started doing lobotomies using the techniques developed by Moniz. Freeman would eventually develop what was known as the "ice pick" lobotomy. In this procedure he would insert an ordinary ice pick above each eye, utilizing only a local anesthetic, and then, using a mallet, he would drive it through the thin bones, move it back and forth like a windshield wiper destroying the nerve connections.

The following account cannot be verified, but the description is similar in nature to several others regarding Dr. Freeman and his procedure. Apparently, in 1940, Patricia Derain, a student nurse at the University of Virginia witnessed a lobotomy performed in an amphitheater on the campus.

> *As each patient was brought in, Dr. Freeman would shout at him that he was going to do something that would make him feel a lot better. The patients had been given electroshock before they were brought in; that's probably why he yelled at them. The shock was the only medication they received, he gave them nothing for the pain; no anesthesia, no muscle relaxant.*
>
> *After the patient was placed on the table, Dr. Freeman would clap his hands and his two assistants would hold up an enormous piece of green felt the color of a pool table. That was the photographic backdrop. Dr. Freeman would direct the placement of lights so that each operation could be photographed, and he checked carefully to be sure that the cameraman was ready, that they had a good angle showing Dr. Freeman with his instrument, that there was no shadow to spoil the picture. His main interest during the entire series of lobotomies seemed to be on getting good photographic angles. He had each operation photographed with the ice pick in place.*
>
> *When all was ready, he would plunge it in. I suppose that was part of his surgical technique, if there's a technique for such surgery. You probably have to plunge it to break through the back of the eye socket. He lifted up the eyelid and slid the icepick-like instrument over the eyeball. Then he would stab it suddenly, check to be sure the pictures were being made, and move the pick from side to side to cut the brain.*

There are many horrific stories to be found regarding the lobotomy. Two of the more infamous cases are Francis Farmer and Rosemary Kennedy. Francis Farmer was an eccentric actress who was admitted to a psychiatric hospital and found herself the recipient of a lobotomy, even though she was not actually mentally ill. Rosemary Kennedy, sister to John, Robert, and Edward Kennedy, was given a lobotomy when her father complained about the mildly retarded girl's interest in boys.

The actual benefit or harm of the lobotomy will probably never be really known. Fortunately, the lobotomy was only occasionally attempted at Peoria State Hospital, and it never was a frequent or popular form of treatment. *"The complications resulting from this therapy were significant,"* according to Dr. James Ward, *"and led to its banishment."* [42]

Occupational and Industrial Therapy

Occupational therapy was supposedly used to provide patients with some employable life skills for use once they were discharged. Industrial therapy, like occupational therapy, was, in theory, designed to help the patient but, in reality, it had minimal therapeutic value other than keeping the patients active. Patients were regularly assigned to the kitchens, the grounds crews, the farms, the housekeeping staff, or the powerhouse. This would not change until 1951, when it was decided to coordinate the two programs. From this point on a patient's work assignments on the grounds were to be made according to the individual's therapeutic needs rather than the institution's maintenance demands. [43] The following pictures depicts a few of the various activities associated with industrial therapy:

The mangle room. A mangle was a somewhat dangerous machine used to press laundry - Domestic Building. Circa 1904

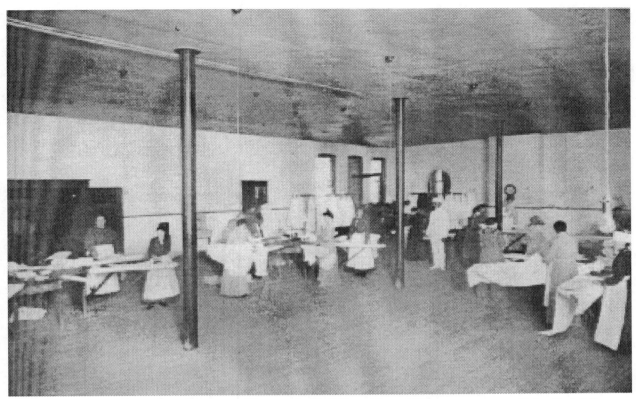

Ironing room Domestic Building Circa 1904   **Alpha Park Library**

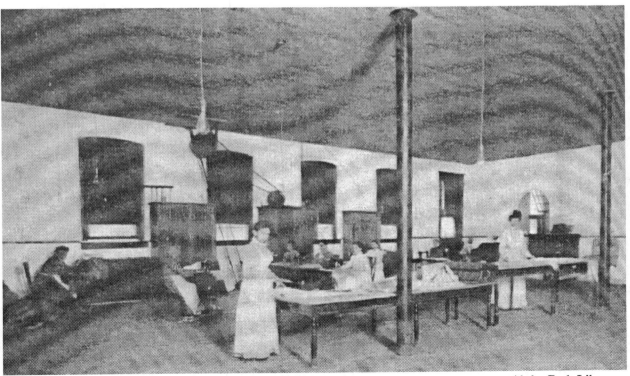

Sewing room Domestic Building. Circa 1904   **Alpha Park Library**

89

Wash Room through which more than three million pieces of laundry pass annually - Domestic Building. Circa 1904

The bakery with rotary oven. Domestic Building. Circa 1904

Patients with food carts delivering the day's meals. Circa 1904   Alpha Park Library

The Industrial School in which 105 old ladies were employed at needle work.   Alpha Park Library

Employees and patients at work laying the pavement on the main street at Peoria State Hospital. The building on the left is the Domestic Building and the Building on the right is the Bowen Building.

When Dr. Zeller filed the Seventh Biennial Report in 1908, industrial therapy had become one of his favored programs. He now believed that through industrial therapy it was possible for many of his patients to develop a sense of self-worth and purpose; including those who had previously been deemed incapable of performing any sort of work. The therapy also provided the hospital with many needed and useful products.[44] The commissioners were in agreement with Dr. Zeller on this, and reported to the governor in 1908, that the *". . .universal employment of the patients in both useful and pleasant occupations has resulted to a great extent in vanishing unrest as well as promoting mental and physical betterment."*[45]

By 1919 the two therapies at the Peoria State Hospital had become one and the same. While it was true that the patients were learning "life skills," most of their work involved work that was directly related to the daily and economical operation of the hospital.

The report filed by Dr. Ralph Goodner, the managing officer at Peoria State Hospital in 1919, does give some rather amazing numbers concerning the employment of patients. His report barely touches on the therapeutic value of these programs but is extensive regarding the economical value of them to the Peoria State Hospital.

Between the years 1918 and 1919 the patients at the Peoria State Hospital produced the following:

Ladies' dresses	11,187	Ladies' corset cover	193
Ladies' nightgowns	4,379	Ladies' dress skirts	68
Ladies' petticoats	6,199	Ladies' apron	417
Ladies' waists	69	Men's gloves (pairs)	118
Sunbonnets	124	Men's night shirts	2,973
Ladies' drawers	2,746	Men's shirts	2,769

In addition to this the patients produced:

> *. . .in the flat work, such as sheets, towels, pillow-cases; etc., we made 39,227 pieces. In the tailoring department 418 woolen and 1,181 khaki pairs of trousers, 44 duck coats and 45 khaki storm coats, lined with discarded blanket material were made. We also have three weaving machines making rag rugs and carpets and shoe repairing departments here employing patients, supervised by one employee.*
>
> *The gardener employs 55 and the farm 50 male patients. Many others, male and female, are employed in the laundry, kitchen, dining rooms, boiler and engine rooms, coal detail, lawn, painting, carpentry, etc. Counting the patients employed in a field of activity, that is, labor saving and useful and more or less specialized, that engages the patient more or less during a reasonable and usual number of a patient's daily working hours, we total 781* (there were approximately 2,135 patients at the hospital during this period of time) *patients employed. This number is aside from the patients engaged on cottages and wards doing chores, some domestic work, running rubbers and food carts, working at odd times on details and ward gardens. If all these partially employed were credited, it would roughly approximate two-thirds of our patient population.*[46]

When dealing with the utilization of patients to perform certain tasks budgetary concerns may have been the driving force, rather than the well-being and treatment of the patient. It is hoped that these patients' needs were the primary factor when assigning them work throughout the institution. One does have to question the program when extensive use of patient labor appears to be primarily budgetary. A good example of this appears in the 1920 Administrative Report under the section dealing with repairs and improvements. Dr. Goodner stated that:

. . .under this heading we will refer only to some of the more extensive improvements and repairs made.

A general shop was badly needed. Our mechanical departments were scattered and some of them housed in poorly lighted and ventilated unsanitary basements. The shop we built is of cement block construction. The blocks were made and practically all of the construction done by patient labor. It is one-story, 100 feet long and 40 feet wide, with an 8-foot concrete unloading platform the entire length. The building is sub-divided into shops for the mechanical force with a central stock room where supplies are issued on requisition. Provision has been made for additions to house other departments, now separate, needing better and more commodious quarters.

The nurses' home has been generally overhauled and painted two coats, both inside and out, and the old wooden steps and landings on the west side replaced with concrete.

The brick road pavement on the main street of the institution grounds was re-laid over a distance of 1,200 feet in length and 14 feet in width. This was a very necessary work and was done with patient labor, under the supervision of one employee. [47]

Occupational and institutional therapies would continue to be a mainstay of "treatment" at many state hospitals until the mid 1960s. The statistics as to how many patients were actually involved in this therapy when it was halted is unknown. It is believed that as many as 35 percent of the patients were assigned jobs related to industrial therapy at this time.[48]

The utilization of patient labor to perform tasks directly related to the daily operation of a mental health facility came to an end when federal peonage* laws were enacted in the 1960s. These laws required that the patients would be paid a wage equal to the federal minimum wage at a prorated rate. Apparently, the state decided that they would not pay wages to the patients, and chose to hire more non-patient full-time employees.[49] This seems somewhat strange as the state was going to have to pay for this work regardless of who was performing it and, more importantly, if the patients were truly benefiting from the therapy, why stop affording the patient the opportunity to avail themselves of this therapy.

*Peonage is defined as the use of laborers bound in servidtude because of debt, or in the case of the state hospitals the use of patients, not because of debt but due to their mental illness.

Chapter XI

Unrelated Conditions and Treatments

The Peoria State Hospital not only treated mental illnesses but a wide variety of physical maladies and ailments as well. Three unrelated conditions which were treated at the hospital were tuberculosis, pellagra, and epilepsy. The doctors and staff treated many other conditions and ailments also, but these three are significant to the history of the Peoria State Hospital. With the exception of pellagra, many of the patients would arrive at the hospital already suffering from one or more of the other two conditions.

Tuberculosis

Tuberculosis is defined as a highly variable communicable disease of humans and some other vertebrates caused by the tubercle bacillus, and is characterized by toxic symptoms or allergic manifestations which, in humans, primarily affect the lungs.

By 1906, tuberculosis had become the leading cause of death at the Peoria State Hospital. From June 30, 1905, to June 30, 1906, sixty-four patients succumbed to tuberculosis. The high numbers of patient deaths led to Dr. Zeller's taking action in hopes of controlling and curing the incidence of tuberculosis at the Peoria State Hospital. It was decided that the best approach to solving this problem would be to segregate the consumptives* in porch colonies. This decision was made based on Dr. Zeller's firsthand observations of Dr. Pettit's tent colony for consumptives in Ottawa, Illinois. While

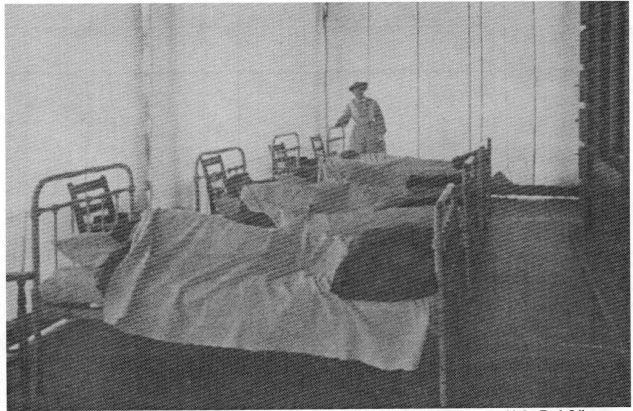

Alpha Park Library

Beginning of fresh air treatment for consumptives. Enclosed porch at South Bartonville, the Illinois General Hospital for the Insane. Circa 1905

*Consumptive was the term used to describe those patients suffering from the effects of tuberculosis.

there, he became convinced that such a program of isolation and fresh air would be beneficial to his patients. He was of the opinion, *". . .that our insane asylums were really disseminators of the germ; that the presence of consumption of the crowded wards was exposing the non-tubercular inmates to the disease."* [1]

The first colony at the Peoria State Hospital consisted of a large porch on one of the newer cottages being enclosed with a heavy canvas, and a doorway by which the patient would have access to the toilet rooms. The canvas was installed so that it could be rolled up in fair weather and strapped down in cold weather.

It was into this environment that Dr. Zeller placed six consumptives, some of whom were in the advanced stage of the disease. These six would spend the entire winter of 1905 in this colony. *"The effect,"* according to Dr. Zeller, *"was soon apparent. The fresh air and nutritious diet promptly resulted in a gain in weight and the subsidence of the hectic fever."* [2] The success was clearly evident, according to Dr. Zeller, as he reported that of the six patients isolated, *"a number of them are still alive to testify to the efficacy of the outdoor experiment."* [3] It is not known exactly how many of the six patients survived.

Based on the apparent success of the porch colonies, it was decided to erect an extensive annex to each of the hospitals. These annexes were described as a wall tent eighteen feet by twenty-four feet, to which a number of nine foot by nine foot canvas houses were attached, all of which were connected by means of a covered passageway. The largest of the tents was provided with a wood stove, and it was proposed to keep sixteen consumptive women and ten consumptive men in the tent colony throughout the winter of 1906. [4]

Interior view of the larger eighteen by twenty-four foot tents.   Alpha Park Library

Tent colony for consumptives. Annex to the women's hospital. Circa 1906   Alpha Park Library

One of the many individual tents.   Alpha Park Library

By 1908 the success of the tent colonies had led to further expansion of the program. There were a total of one hundred and four patients now being housed in the tents. This meant that five percent of the hospital's patients were housed out of doors.[5]

The first main tent colony, located between 4B and 1A. Circa 1907   **Alpha Park Library**

By removing the critically ill from the tents it was now possible to provide "curative and prophylactic care" to the patients housed there.[6] Based on the success of the tent colonies it was decided to erect a permanent structure strictly designed for the care and treatment of the consumptives; so, in 1909, the state legislature appropriated $6,000 for the erection of a small hospital strictly for the care of advanced consumptives.

The tents, by 1912, were also being used, not only to treat the consumptives, but convalescents and semi-invalids as well. These patients would, according to Dr. Zeller, *". . .profit by this mode of life no less than the consumptives."*[7] Strangely, this seemingly successful program is apparently abandoned for unknown reasons shortly thereafter, and there is no further mention of the tents in the biennial reports.

The reason for the demise of this program may have been directly related to Dr. Zeller's leaving the Peoria State Hospital. Dr. Zeller was replaced at the hospital in 1913 by Dr. Ralph T. Hinton. It is not clear if Dr. Hinton did not share Dr. Zeller's enthusiasm for the tents or if newer treatments had become available. In either case, the program seems to have halted upon Dr. Zeller's departure. It is evident from later photographs that the tents, like the zoo, under Dr. Hinton's and Dr. Ralph Goodner's respective superintendency, were allowed to deteriorate and, at some point in time they were abandoned. This deterioration can be seen in the following picture.

One of the abandoned tent colonies at Peoria State Hospital.   **Alpha Park Library**

Tuberculosis would continue to be a problem at the hospital. In 1937, a survey was started under the direction of Dr. M. Pollak, superintendent of the Peoria County Tuberculosis Sanitarium. The study would run from October 1, 1937, through December 22, 1939. In the course of this study they examined 2,129 patients in residence, 666 newly admitted patients, and 448 employees. Out of the 2,129 resident patients it was found that 2,016 or 94.69% of them had positive reactions to their tuberculin test. Of the 666 newly admitted patients' tests, 537 or 80.64% of them had positive reactions. The employees fared somewhat better, but the results would still have to be considered alarming at best. They tested 448 employees, with 257 employees or 57% of them testing positive. [8]

Upon further investigation it was discovered that, of the patients who tested positive, the odds of them contracting tuberculosis while at the Peoria State Hospital increased in accordance with the length of their residence. There was an insufficient amount of data collected for Dr. Pollak and his commission to make any correlation between the length of employment and the increased incidence of tuberculosis among the hospital staff. It was, however, discovered that, of those employees tested, one-half of them had developed the disease after five years of service. [9]

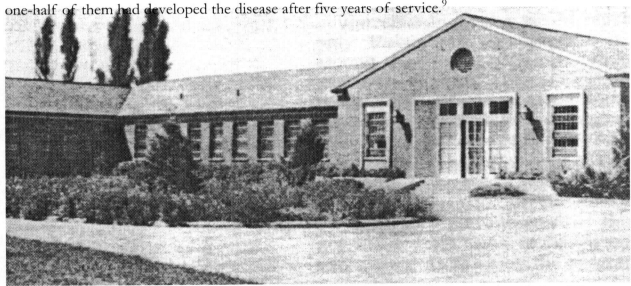

Pollak Hospital Treatment Center for tubercular patients.　　　　　**Milner Library**

In 1949, Pollak Hospital and Infirmary Building was built to care for patients with tuberculosis.

Pellagra

Pellagra had suddenly appeared in the summer of 1909, and would virtually disappear just three years later. Dr. Zeller estimated that pellagra had afflicted approximately 500 patients and had resulted in the death of 150 of them.

The outbreak did cause a great deal of trepidation when it was first diagnosed. It was sometimes referred to as Italian Leprosy, which led many to fear that a contagious disease had emerged. It was soon found to be noncontagious due to the fact that not a single nurse or attendant contacted the disease, even though they were constantly engaged in dressing the extensive and active lesions of those patients so afflicted. [10]

The first case of pellagra appeared at the Peoria State Hospital August 7, 1909. The reason for this sudden outbreak, in 1909, was never discovered. Actually, the disease was initially misdiagnosed by Dr.

Zeller and his staff. He wrote in his autobiography that on this morning:

> . . .a staff physician asked me to accompany him to the bedside of a patient suffering from extensive scalds. Examination showed that both his feet had been submerged in boiling water. The skin was blistered and discolored well above the ankles. He was in delicate health and we felt that he could not survive the shock. He suffered no pain and could give no account as to how the scalding took place, neither could (or would) the nurse. He died the next day and we promptly notified the coroner who made a searching investigation and the jury censured us not only for carelessness but for failure to fix responsibility upon any one person. Within a few days, another 'scalding' occurred and then another and within a week 20 more, followed by 250 cases during the summer.
>
> We immediately consulted our library and in Manson on Tropical Disease, we found that we had an outbreak of pellagra, known as Italian Leprosy and ascribed in Italy as due to the use of maize or American corn as a principle diet. We had dismissed the nurse in compliance with the recommendation of the coroner's jury and she had gone home, a heartbroken girl conscious of her innocence, a victim of mistaken diagnosis. I immediately notified her of her reinstatement, without prejudice, but she proudly declined the offer and I not only apologized to her at this late day, but wish to impress the reader with the danger of condemning any accused person upon purely circumstantial evidence. [11]

It would be easy to blame Dr. Zeller and his staff for this outbreak of pellagra at the Peoria State Hospital. While it was true that the disease was first diagnosed at Peoria State Hospital, pellagra appeared in many other parts of the country and state as well, about this same time. Illinois was the fifteenth state to report the disease, and ten additional states would soon follow in reporting an incidence of pellagra.[12]

The Illinois Commission to Study Pellagra, established in 1909 after several cases of pellagra had been diagnosed at the institutions for the insane at South Bartonville, Elgin, and Dunning, defined pellagra as:

> . . .an endemic trophoneurotic skin disease occurring among the squalid and destitute, due to chronic poisoning with diseased or fermented maize, and affecting chiefly the cerebro-spinal and digestive systems. It usually occurs in those between 30 and 50 years of age. It always begins in spring, and the lesion appears on the parts of the body exposed to air and light (face, neck, back of hands and feet). It consists of an intense, rapidly extending erythema, bright red, livid or brown in color, with much swelling, and causing violent burning or itching. The spreading edge of the patches is much elevated and generally darker than the central portion. There are marked nervous and generally symptoms, insanity, mania or melancholy being common. [13]

Simply put, pellagra is a dietary disease.

The picture on the next page was included in the report submitted by the Illinois Commission to Study Pellagra in 1909.

Notice the line of demarkation between the black, that looks like sunburn on the hands and the white natural skin just above the wrist. The photograph is of a group of insane men at the South Bartonville institution, showing pigmentary deposits under the skin of the hands, seen in the chronic form of pellagra.

The Illinois Commission to Study Pellagra found that the disease could, in all likelihood, be corrected through *"the correction of dietary inequalities."*[14] As a result of the commission's recommendation, the hospital started to provide the patients with a better diet and, as a result, they witnessed a steady subsidence of the disease.

The fact that the incidence of pellagra declined with the introduction of better nutrition among the patients raises the question -- What was different, or had changed in the patients' diet at this time which would cause the outbreak? Since the outbreak in Illinois was, for the most part confined to three state hospitals located in Bartonville, Elgin, and Dunning, it would seem logical that there must have been some change to the patients' diet which led to this sudden outbreak.

The following pictures were taken at the Peoria State Hospital between 1909 and 1914, to show the effects of pellagra in different stages.

Left: Man with pellagra on his hands.

Right: Woman suffering from a pellagra outbreak on her neck.

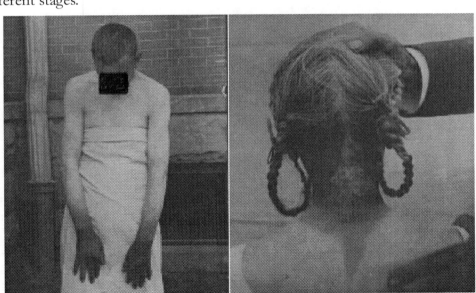

Alpha Park Library

Pellagra would disappear as suddenly as it had appeared in 1909. There had been 250 cases of pellagra reported at the Peoria State Hospital from August of 1909 to July of 1910, resulting in 93 deaths. Thirty-four deaths were attributed to pellagra in the Eighth Biennial Report, filed in July of 1910. The Ninth, Tenth and Eleventh Biennial Reports each show three deaths due to pellagra. The last death attributed to pellagra was reported in 1916.

Epilepsy

Epilepsy is a neurological condition that makes one susceptible to seizures. These seizures are brought on by a brief electrical disturbance in the brain. Epilepsy has been reported for thousands of years, and the seizures were thought to be a form of mental illness. Sadly, for many years insane asylums, prisons, jails, and poor houses were the only places where epileptics were segregated - not treated. It was not until 1908 that the State of Illinois would seek to develop colonies for the treatment and care of epileptics. It was then that the Board of State Commissioners of Public Charities recommended that $435,000 be appropriated to establish colonies, for what they called insane epileptics, at Anna, Watertown, Bartonville, and Jacksonville.

They presented a picture of a six-year-old girl as evidence of the need for these facilities. The following picture has been altered and the name of the little girl has been omitted out of respect for her. According to the commission:

> . . .*a pitiful and forceful argument for a colony for improvable epileptics is presented in the case of 6-year old Helen ----, -----Street, Springfield, Illinois. A picture of the epileptic child, tied with a rope in the home of her parents. Mr. and Mrs. ----, is used as a frontispiece to this report. She has had epileptic seizures for four years. For that period of time she has been restrained as shown in the picture. During a seizure, when she had escaped on one occasion she fell into a pond and would have drowned, but for a timely rescue. Her case was brought to the attention of the State Board of Charities, which,*

as the State has no epileptic colony, secured the admission of the child to the Asylum for Feeble-Minded Children at Lincoln on January 25, 1909. She was placed under careful observation for ten days. During that period nine grand mal seizures were observed, eight at night and one in the day. Scientific treatment for epilepsy was then begun. The seizures apparently ceased. The child, previously wild and intractable, was sent to school, where she was making excellent progress at last reports. The chances for improvement are considered "very favorable so long as the convulsions can be relieved by treatment." Perhaps this child will be cured and eventually become a working member of society and an economic asset to the State instead of an economic liability, as she is at present.[15]

Even though the state was taking steps to establish an institution for the care of epileptics, *"it was decided to test the advisability of concentrating the afflicted class."* [16] So, a separate epileptic colony was established in 1906 at the Peoria State Hospital. Prior to this it was believed that, of the eighty patients with epilepsy, *". . .the epilepsy and the insanity both vary so widely in degree that it is impossible to classify them otherwise than with reference to the mental condition. It is impossible, therefore, to designate certain cottages for the exclusive care."*[17] At this time, two cottages were set aside for the exclusive use of epileptic patients, one for female and one for male patients.

Right: An Argument for an Epileptic Colony.

Here is a 6-year-old epileptic girl as she was treated out of necessity at home. She was tied like an animal. The State Board of Charities secured her admission to the Lincoln School for Feeble Minded Children as the State has no place for such an unfortunate. She is receiving both book and manual education and her seizures apparently have ceased under proper diet and other treatment.

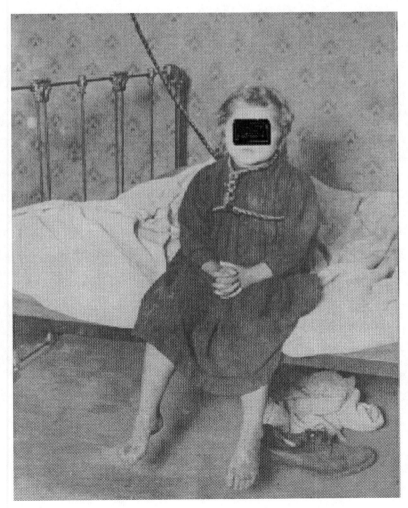

Milner Library

Billiard table in Day Room of male cottage for epileptics.   **Alpha Park Library**

Within these cottages, a physician was assigned to treat them with *". . .reference to dietetic, industrial, hygiene, moral, medicinal and social influences."* The patients according to Dr. Zeller:

". . .care for their own cottage, look after their own dining room, and even the sick are cared for in a dormitory of the cottage. These are the only cottages caring for their own sick. The beds are lowered to within a few inches of the floor and no accidents have occurred. The sixty-two epileptic men are cared for night and day by women attendants. The ferocity an epileptic is supposed to exhibit after recovery from a convulsion has proven to be a myth. We find the epileptic returning to consciousness an extremely irritable individual and much confused, but our people have observed the principle of non-resistance to such a degree that no quarrel can arise and such a patient quickly regains his normal state. The inmates have been brought to a high state of efficiency in caring for each other, and the moment a patient falls his companions are at his side, one loosening his clothes and the other placing a pillow under the head of the victim.[18]

There are no further entries in the biennial reports regarding the care of epileptic patients at the Peoria State Hospital. It is unknown when or if treatment for those with epilepsy changed beyond the separate cottages. It is also unknown as to when or if those patients with epilepsy were transferred or released from the Peoria State Hospital.

Chapter XII

The Young and Helpless of Peoria State Hospital

"We do not ordinarily think of mental illness as a common affliction of childhood." Governor Adlai Stevenson

A great deal has been written about the care and treatment of the adult patient but, what about the child who was also in need of help? Obviously, there were children in dire need of care as evidenced by this letter from a beleaguered father to Dr. Zeller:

Esteemed Sir and Friend -

I have a boy who is deaf, dumb and blind and insane and also helpless. His mother has died and left he and I and one only daughter. Now I am in such a situation as I can't provide for my family of us three and take care of him. Is there any way by which I can get him in your institution? What means would I have to go about to get him there? I would rather keep him if I could, but I can not and feel that my state should help in this matter as I am a native born of Illinois and have stood by her laws and did all in my power as a citizen to make her glorious. Now is the time for her to help me in my hour of distress if she has any help for me. Please advise me what to do. [1]

This boy, age unknown, was perhaps the first child admitted to the Peoria State Hospital and, even then, it took the intervention of the governor to get him admitted. *"No door could be legally opened for this unfortunate case"* according to Dr. Zeller, *"and even in this instance the aid of the Governor had to be invoked."* [2]

The early records of the Peoria State Hospital do not indicate as to when children were first admitted. They do, however, show that for a two-year period, from 1904 through 1906, there were two deaths recorded for patients under the age of twenty. For ease of description, it has been arbitrarily decided by the author to refer to those patients twenty years old and younger as children; therefore, one can safely claim that there were children housed at the Peoria State Hospital since 1904.

Apparently, by the time that the Eighth Biennial Report was published, 1910, something had changed in the state laws regarding mentally ill children. There were now several children housed at the Peoria State Hospital. At this time, the youngest patient there was an eleven-year-old female; the oldest patient there was a ninety-four-year-old female, and the median age for patients was fifty-two years. The following chart is a partial representation of the patients at the hospital and deals only with those patients under the age of twenty when they were admitted:

AGES	MALE	FEMALE	TOTAL
11		1	1
12	1		1
13	-	-	-
14	-	-	-
15	-	-	-
16	1	1	2
17	4	6	10
18	9	2	11
19	8	5	13
20	8	7	15

Children and their special needs are never specifically referred to until 1951. Due to this fact, one should not assume that this was a new phenomenon. These children existed, but there was now a growing awareness of them and their needs.

As a result of this growing awareness, it was decided to convert the dairy farm into a children's center. The dairy farm, which had supplied milk for the Peoria State Hospital since it opened, was no longer needed. By 1951, Peoria State Hospital was able to buy an adequate supply of milk from the community.

This facility would be used strictly for the care and treatment of prepsychotic and psychotic children ranging in age from six to fourteen years of age.[3] This new unit would be known as the Grace Abbott Children's Center, in honor of Grace Abbott (1878-1939), one of the early leaders in the field of social work for children. She began her career in service to children at Hull House and various Chicago organizations that were also working to protect the rights of children. In 1921, in recognition of her commitment to children, she was appointed as Chief of the United States Children's Bureau by President Warren G. Harding, a position she held until 1935. At that time she returned to Chicago to be a professor of public welfare administration at the University of Chicago.[4]

The Grace Abbott Children's Center was located about one and one-half miles northwest of the main hospital. It would be dedicated on October 8, 1951. It was at the dedication ceremony that Governor Adlai Stevenson stated that:

> . . .we do not ordinarily think of mental illness as a common affliction of childhood. Yet emotional disturbance due to a variety of adverse environmental factors is not at all uncommon among children. The psychotic child (as opposed to the mentally defective child under care at Lincoln or Dixon) may have a perfectly normal mental capacity, or even an above-normal mentality. His breakdown may be temporary and subject to early correction through intelligent treatment and a wholesome emotional environment.[5]

Also in attendance at the dedication was Edith Abbott, Grace Abbott's sister. While expressing her gratitude in behalf of her family, she declared of the facility that ". . .the great thing is that it's hopeful; it is a place to cure children, not a place to confine them."[6]

Milner Library

This is an early picture of the farm colony which would be converted into a facility for the treatment and care of children. Once refurbished in 1951 it would be known as the Grace Abbott Children's Center. Circa 1913

*This picture and the others in this chapter, regarding Abbott Center and 4-B, are of rather poor quality as the originals first appeared in an open house magazine and were of poor quality also.

Abbott Children's Center in 1951.   **Alpha Park Library**

The new facility had a riding stable which had been established through a donation of four horses and saddles by V. J. Mueller of Peoria. There was also a two-acre stocked lake where the children could fish, boat and swim as well. Plans were made to erect a quonset- type building which would contain two classrooms and a gymnasium.[7]

The first patients were transferred there on November 19, 1951. By June 30, 1953, there would be a total of twenty-four children (8 girls, 16 boys) housed there ranging in age from seven to fourteen.

Four years after opening, in 1951, Abbott Center had made many improvements. There was now a resident psychologist, experienced in child psychology, and a qualified psychiatric social worker on staff. There was also a full-time social worker assigned to the facility and a registered occupational therapist on hand.

The Grace Abbott Children's Center quonset building housing school classrooms and a gym.

The children's center was the recipient of a children's library on April 15, 1951. The books were donated by the Cosmopolitan Club of Peoria, and they had also committed to making further donations of books from time to time.

Children's Hour at Abbott Center.

Story time at Unit 4-B.

A volunteer service was responsible for bringing special entertainment to the Grace Abbott Children's Center. As a result of their efforts, in 1955, Fran Allison of television fame (Kukla, Fran, and Ollie) entertained not only the adult patients but the children as well.

Kukla, Fran and Ollie. Circa 1949

Peoria Public Library

That same year, Duncan Renaldo, the "Cisco Kid," made an appearance at the facility. Later that year, the Arthur Murray Dance Studio made an appearance. They gave an exhibition of ballroom dancing and lessons to those in attendance.[8]

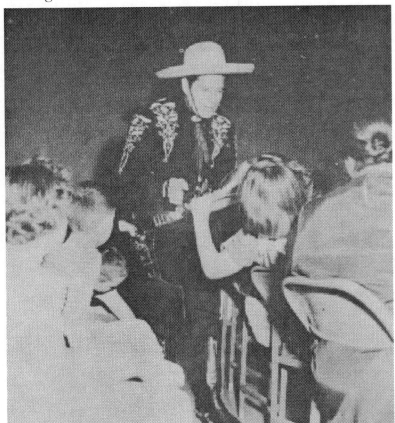

The "Cisco Kid" visits the children at Abbott Center. Circa 1955

Alpha Park Libary

109

Four years later, Curt Flood, outfielder for the St. Louis Cardinals, would also join the list of celebrities to visit the hospital.

Danny Thomas would visit in 1959, and provide a variety show for all of the patients. (See Memories - Our Billy Boy)

Let's talk baseball! A group of boys in the adolescent unit at Peoria State Hospital give rapt attention to Curt Flood.

Alpha Park Library

For the young girls a collection of dolls was donated by a teacher-volunteer at the Grace Abbott Children's Center. A group of Peoria women and Peoria beauticians would dress and style the dolls' hair. *"Making this collection,"* according to Dr. Ernest Klein, superintendent at Peoria State Hospital, *"one of the best dressed in the country."* 12

Volunteers dressing the dolls.   **Milner Library**

A survey was conducted in 1957 in all forty-eight states to see what was being done for children by a committee under the direction of Dr. Otto Bettag, director of the Illinois State Welfare Department. The survey provided them with some rather startling statistics. They found that, nationally, children under the age of nineteen made up about 1% of the mental hospital population, but very few states offered any form of specialized treatment for them. In fact, Illinois was but one of thirteen states to provide specialized treatment programs for children. Illinois had two facilities for the treatment of patients under the age of eighteen, the Grace Abbott Children's Center, located at the Peoria State Hospital, and the Healy School, located in Chicago. The problem was that these two facilities could not come close to treating and caring for the 306 children that were under state care at various facilities throughout the state. Perhaps even more startling was the fact that these 306 children represented only 20% of the children in Illinois that were in need of treatment.[9]

It was not unusual at this time, the mid 1950s, to find children, especially teenage boys, housed with the adults at the Peoria State Hospital. In an effort to alleviate this problem, it was decided to renovate a cottage on B-row specifically for adolescent boys and their needs.

The Grace Abbott Children's Center provided treatment to thirty children, and the renovated cottage on B-row would double the hospital's capacity, accommodating thirty-five adolescent boys. It is not clear as to why boys outnumbered girls at the Peoria State Hospital, but as a result of this disparity, there was no mention of plans for the renovation of a cottage for girls at this time, or at any later time.

The renovation of the cottage on B-row was completed at a cost of $43,730 and on April 15, 1958, eight boys, ranging in age from eight to seventeen, were relocated there. The younger patients came from the Grace Abbott Children's Center, while those fifteen and over came from several of the adult cottages. The ages of these patients seem odd since the cottage was initially supposed to house only teenage boys. There is no explanation given as to why this occurred.

When the staff at the Peoria State Hospital was asked by Robert Nelson, a reporter for the **Peoria Journal Star**, how the treatment at the newly-renovated cottage would differ from the past, he was told by Charles Launi, director of the Grace Abbott Children's Center, that it was *". . .a separate facility. There will be only children there. The program will be geared for them."* He was also told that *". . .the treatment becomes radical merely by changing the physical setting,"* by Arthur Zetterberg, a child psychologist at the Peoria State Hospital.[10]

Nelson went on to report that:

> *They believe the new surroundings will create a completely new attitude. Four-B, the remodeled ward, has been redecorated in cheerful colors. There will be curtains at the window, cloths on the table, silverware by the plates. The patients will eat family style. For some, this will be a big change.*
>
> *Upstairs, the patients will sleep - for the most part - two to a room. There are some four-bed rooms, too. Before, some of the youngsters have slept in dormitories with adult patients.*
>
> *Meals will still be brought in from the central kitchen, but there is a modern kitchen in 4-B. Patients can have between-meal snacks.*
>
> *The unit will be staffed by a psychiatric aide, a dietary worker, the physician and consultant who now serve Abbott Center, a part-time psychologist, a part-time social worker, a full-time activities therapist, and a full-time school teacher. Volunteers also will help with the education program.*[11]

Activities for the children were further expanded in 1958. These activities now included field trips to various points of interest in the Peoria area, fishing trips, swimming at the YWCA, picnics, and cook outs.

4-B Unit, located on the grounds, was used for boys 8-17 that had emotional problems. Circa 1955

Boy Scout Troop 241 was established in 1959 for the teenage boys. Previously, the boys had been affiliated with troops in Bartonville, but now they had their own charter, which is unique in mental hospitals. One of the highlights for these boys was the three-day "camporee" held away from the grounds.[13]

Boy Scouts of America, Troop 241, camping on the grounds.

Milieu therapy would replace individual psychotherapy at the Grace Abbott Children's Center in 1961. Milieu therapy can be defined as a type of treatment wherein the patient's social environment is manipulated for their benefit. One type of this treatment is the therapeutic community, like the Grace Abbott Children's Center, in which patients stay at a residence where they lead a highly structured life.

In 1963, more changes were made in the children's treatment and training programs. One was for boys and girls, six through eleven years of age, the other for adolescent boys. Now:

> . . .*regular weekly meetings were held for the parents of these children under the direction of the superintendent. Parents were encouraged to speak freely regarding problems relating to their own relationships as well as those with the children and hospital. The discussion groups increased in size and the response was enthusiastic. Plans are carefully made for the patient to return to the family and community as soon as it is psychiatrically sound.*[14]

A supervisor of special education services was added in October of 1964 to coordinate the program for corrective, developmental, remedial and therapeutic educational experiences. As a result, the children now enjoyed periodic shopping trips for small groups; a physical fitness class and a program, utilizing volunteers, was developed to give the adolescent boys experience in socializing with girls near their age. For the smaller children, a play room was now available for their enjoyment.[15]

Over the next three years life would not change much at the Grace Abbott Children's Center or for the teenage boys housed in 4-B, but on September 18, 1967, eight children were transferred from the Grace Abbott Children's Center to the newly opened children's unit at the Zeller Zone Center in Peoria, Illinois. The four remaining children were scheduled to be transferred to treatment facilities back in their home communities or discharged.[16] This movement of these twelve young patients, in many ways, was the harbinger of things to come at the Peoria State Hospital.

Chapter XIII
Peoria State Hospital: A Small City

"Only a very few give much thought to the internal management of insane asylums. Casual visitors are impressed with the stately buildings, elaborately furnished reception room, smooth lawns and formal gardens, but with that their interest ceases."

Dr. George A. Zeller

The Peoria State Hospital was much more than just a mental health care facility; it was a small self-sufficient community. Aside from the patient cottages and hospital units, there were numerous other buildings on the grounds as well.

Aerial View Peoria State Hospital: Circa 1970.   **Alpha Park Library**

The facility included:

Power Plant	Fire Department	Laundry
Tin and Paint Shop	Butcher Shop	Commissary
Carpenter Shop	Bakery	Garages
Security Unit	Business Offices	Public Health Unit
Machinist Shops	Pharmacy	Beauty Shop
Shoe Repair Shop	Dental Offices	Barber Shop
Post Office	Medical Clinics	Gardens and Farms
Switchboard	Electrical Shop	General Stores
Mechanical Stores	Nurses Quarters	Laboratories
Hospital	Chapel	Library
Clothing:	Doctors' Housing	Cemeteries
Supply Store		
Sewing Room		
Mending Room		

Meeting the medical needs of the patients was no small task but, the difficulty of meeting their daily needs is hard for most to imagine.

Perhaps, the following statistics will show just how large an undertaking it was to efficiently run the Peoria State Hospital. From June 30, 1905, to June 30, 1906, the powerhouse consumed 19,128 tons of coal to provide heating and electricity. By 1952, the hospital's consumption of coal had risen to sixty tons per day or 43,800 tons every two years. The ice plant was producing 274 tons of ice per year. The dairy produced 18,756 gallons of milk. The farm produced approximately 56% of the meat consumed at the hospital.

The farm and garden colonies produced:

Article	Measure	July 1904 to June 30,1905	July 1,1905 to June 30,1906	Total for two years
Potatoes	Bushels	800	545	1,345
Turnips	Bushels	1,200	840	2,450
Tomatoes	Bushels	1,100	1,819	2,919
Onions	Bushels	162	197	359
Beans	Bushels		108	108
Beans, green	Bushels	323	421	744
Beets	Bushels	484	328	813
Carrots	Bushels		41	41
Peas, green	Bushels	174	256	430
Lettuce	Bushels	245	279	524
Cucumbers	Bushels	378	10	388
Cress	Bushels		2	2
Spinach	Bushels		7	7
Radishes	Dozen	7,509	8,562	16,071
Onions, green	Dozen	3,334	4,311	7,645
Sweet corn	Dozen	700	904	1,604
Rhubarb	Dozen	464	2,458	2,922
Cabbage	Pounds	68,000	36,380	104,380
Corn	Bushels	2,000	775	2,775
Oats	Bushels	860	1,562	2,422
Rye	Bushels		150	150
Hay	Tons	35	45	80
Straw	Tons	8	20	28
Millet	Tons		6	6
Fodder	Shocks	1,500	660	2,160
Pumpkins	Number	900		900
Tomatoes, canned	Gallons	1,250	1,682	2,932
Sour kraut	Barrels	93	6	99

It has proven to be an impossible task to obtain pictures and exact locations for all of the buildings and facilities that were once located on the grounds of the Peoria State Hospital. For example, according to Dr. Zeller's Annual Report to the Illinois Department of Public Welfare filed in 1922, it was decided to erect an "Auto-Tourist Camp" on the grounds.

This is the only entry in these reports regarding the auto-tourists' camp. This facility, like many others, has disappeared.

Dr. Zeller noted that:

> In changing the front entrance, a hitherto, neglected and unused corner of the grounds was made accessible. Its adaptability as a park became apparent and it was decided to place it at the disposal of auto-tourists as well as a recreation camp for our patients. Camp stoves were built, a hydrant installed and every convenience that a properly equipped camp should have.
>
> More than 1,800 of our patients had an outing there this summer. They were taken in relays of 200 and each group spent the entire afternoon there, supper being prepared on the camp ovens and served on the lawn.
>
> The camp became popular with tourists before it was ready to be occupied. No part of the institution is visible from the site and the presence of these visitors has not interfered with any of our activities. On the contrary, many pleasant expressions of appreciation were heard and the visiting tourists went on their way with a kindlier feeling toward the state. There is enough fallen timber on our premises to keep the camp supplied with fuel perpetually.
>
> As an experiment in public welfare, it is well worth observing and it quite conforms to the good roads program which Governor Small has done so much to promote. It can easily be abandoned if found to be an embarrassment. [1]

Later reports do not tell exactly where the "Auto-Tourist Camp" was located or when it was discontinued, but it did exist. Apparently no pictures of this campground are available and there is very little written information, as well. This lack of tangible evidence gives one an idea as to the difficulty encountered when trying to document all of the facilities that were once part of the Peoria State Hospital.

In an effort to give one a visual image of the hospital grounds, the following map and key shows the locations of many of the buildings that were once and, in some cases, still are located at the Peoria State Hospital. Corresponding with the map and key, there is also a brief description of the individual buildings and, where possible, a picture of that building.

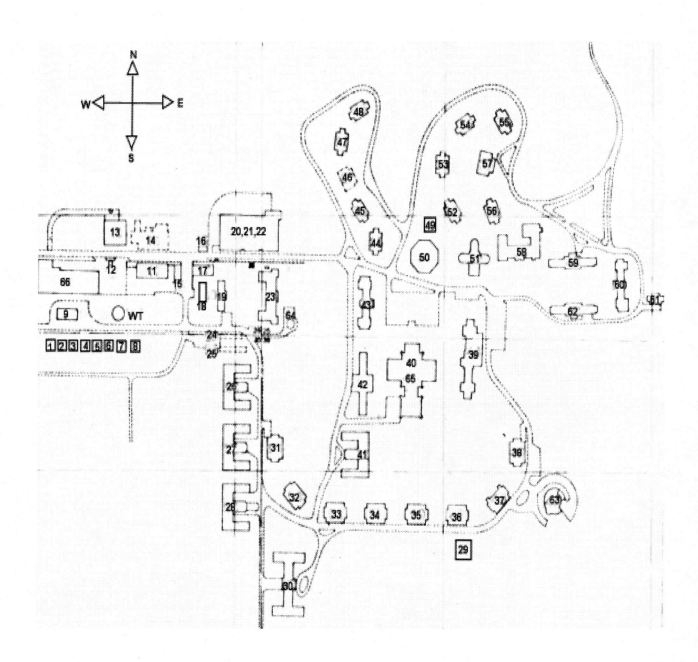

1-8. STAFF COTTAGES
9. FIRE HOUSE & GARAGES
10. TRUCK GARAGES
11. GENERAL STORE BUILDING
12. SCALE HOUSE
13. POWER HOUSE
14. OLD POWER HOUSE
15. CHIEF ENGINEER'S OFFICE
16. SAFETY & SECURITY
17. CRAFT SHOP
18. STORAGE SHEDS
19. CLOTHING CENTER
20. LAUNDRY
21. SEWING ROOM
22. DINING ROOM, KITCHEN, & BAKERY
23. BOWEN BUILDING
24. GARAGE #2
25. GARAGE #1
26. D-1
27. D-2
28. D-3
29. MECHANICAL SHOP & GARAGE
30. POLLAK HOSPITAL
31. C-8
32. C-7
33. C-6
34. C-5
35. C-4
36. C-3
37. C-2

38. C-1
39. ZELLER HOSPITAL
40. ACTIVITY BUILDING
41. B-1
42. B-2
43. B-3
44. B-4
45. B-5
46. B-ROW DINING HALL
47. B-7
48. B-8
49. GARAGE #3
50. PATIENT SERVICE CENTER
51. MICHELL BUILDING
52. 1-A
53. 2-A
54. 3-A
55. 4-A
56. 5-A
57. A-ROW DINING HALL
58. KNOWLES BIGLER RESIDENCE
59. TALCOTT HOSPITAL
60. STONE COTTAGE
61. VETERAN'S COTTAGE
62. LEVITIN HOSPITAL
63. AUDITORIUM
64. SUNKEN GARDEN
65. LOHMAN HALL
66. MECHANICAL SHOP & GARAGES

(1-8) Staff Cottages: Buildings one through eight were single-family houses for the doctors. Some of them were torn down prior to the hospital's closing in 1973, but four of them were moved to another location in the Village of Bartonville. These four houses are now being utilized as rental property.

(9) Firehouse and Garages: Building number nine was erected in 1899 and served as a firehouse and garage facility. The firehouse held one truck and two offices. The rear portion of this building was divided into ten single-stall garages. This building is still standing and in use today.

The fire truck pictured was purchased in 1956.   Milner Library

Firehouse 2005.   Gary Lisman

Over the years the Peoria State Hospital's fire department would extinguish several fires on the grounds and in various buildings, most of which were minor. In 1964 there was, however, a major fire at the hospital which destroyed an activities building. No one was injured, but the loss was estimated at $100,000.

(10) Truck garages: (No picture available) The truck garages were razed sometime before 1973.

(11) General Store Building: This building was built in 1899. It had three floors. Located on the first floor was a butcher shop with three large walk-in coolers.

General Store Building   Alpha Park Library
One hundred and fifty working patients occupied the second and third floors. Circa 1906

Scale House 2005.   **Gary Lisman**

(12) Scale house: This building was located near the powerhouse and was used mainly to weight coal trucks. It is in disrepair, but still standing.

(13) Powerhouse: This building is sometimes referred to as the new powerhouse. It was built in 1949 to replace the old outdated one. It is still standing but in disrepair. The powerhouse consumed, on average, one carload of coal per day to meet the electrical and steam needs of the hospital.

New Powerhouse. Circa 2001   **Melody Bridges**

(14) Old Powerhouse: The old powerhouse was built in 1899. It supplied electricity and steam for the Peoria State Hospital until 1949 when the new powerhouse was built. According to Dr. Richard Graff, superintendent, the hospital changed its service from DC to AC current once the new powerhouse was operational in 1949. [2]

Old Powerhouse. Circa 1906   **Alpha Park Library**

Peoria State Hospital Mechanical Force, 1912. These men were responsible for the powerhouse.

Powerhouse Pump Room. Circa 1906

(15) Chief Engineer's Office: (No picture available.) This building was razed.

(16) Safety & Security: (No picture available.) This building has been razed. It was built in 1899.

(17) Craft Shop: (No picture available.) This building has been razed.

(18) Storage Sheds: This building was built in 1899. It had an unloading dock in front with storage rooms in the back.

Storage Shed. Circa 2001
Melody Bridges

(19) Clothing Center: This building was built in 1919. It has been refurbished and is being used as a Masonic Lodge.

Clothing Center 2005.   **Gary Lisman**

Clothing Store 1997.   **Melody Bridges**   **Clothing Store 2001.**   **Melody Bridges**

(20, 21, 22) Laundry, Bakery, Kitchen, and Employees Cafeteria (Domestic Building): This building was built in 1899 and remodeled in 1964. It has been allowed to a deteriorate to a condition where it will have to be razed in the near future.

Domestic Building. Circa 1899   **Alpha Park Library**

Domestic Building 2001.   **Gary Lisman**

Domestic Building 2004.
Gary Lisman

(23) Bowen Building (Nurses' Residence):

The Bowen Building was built in 1899 as a nurses' residence. Due to a shortage of space in the cottages women patients were housed there for a time. It was remodeled in 1967 and was used for offices. This one building still stands as a proud but broken edifice of what once was one of the best mental health facilities in the country.

Alpha Park Library

Picture, taken around 1902 shows some of the insane women who were temporarily housed in the Bowen Building in the early 1900s.

Bowen Building.   Circa 1902   **Alpha Park Library**

Bowen Building one hundred years later, 2002.   **Gary Lisman**

Bowen Building. Circa 2000   **Lisa Helms**

(24,25) Garages: (No picture available.) Buildings were razed.

(26, 27, 28) D-Row: These were dormitory buildings and were built in 1939. They were built in an E-shape, with the center of the buildings containing a kitchen and dining area and a general activity room. The wings on either end of the buildings contained open-style dormitory rooms. 1-D and 2-D were male dormitories and 3-D was a female dormitory.

One of three dormitories in D-Row.   **Gary Lisman**

(29) Mechanical Shop & Garage: (No picture available.) The buildings have been razed.

(30) Pollak Hospital: Pollak Hospital was built in 1949 as a separate hospital to treat patients with tuberculosis. The northern wing was for female patients and the southern wing was for male patients. It was named in honor of Dr. Pollak, superintendent of the Peoria County Tuberculosis Sanitarium, who did extensive research on the incidence of tuberculosis at the hospital in 1937.

Milner Library

Pollak Hospital. Circa 1954   The Pollak Hospital was built to accommodate 100 patients.

Pollak Hospital. Circa 2002   **Melody Bridges**

(31, 32, 33, 34, 35, 36, 37, 38) C-Row: C-row consisted of eight buildings. 2-C to 7-C were male wards. 8-C and 9-C were female wards. 5-C, 6-C, and 7-C were "open" wards. Open wards were wards where patients were allowed to come and go freely. These cottages were built around 1904. The bricks used to construct C-Row were red as opposed to the yellow bricks used on A-Row and B-Row. All of the buildings that made up C-Row have been razed.

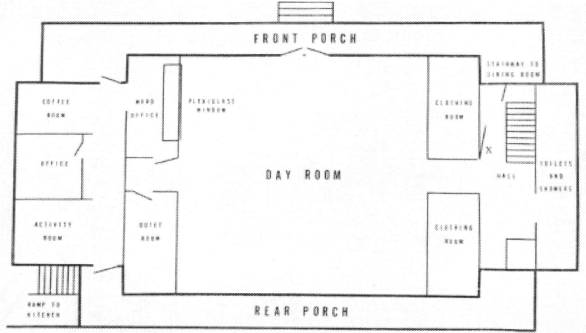

Basic floor plan for the cottages on C-Row.   **Alpha Park Library**

Alpha Park Library

Ward 8-C is one of four cottage-type wards which comprised the Peoria State Hospital's mental retardation unit.

(39) Zeller Building: The Zeller building was built in 1937 and, in 1956, a centralized morgue and postmortem room adjacent to each other were located there. This was actually a major improvement. Previously, the postmortem room was located in the basement of Talcott Hospital and its equipment was deemed to be antiquated and inadequate. The pathologist had to perform autopsies in various mortuaries throughout the city. The morgue was formerly located in the clinic room in the basement of the Zeller building directly across the hall from the kitchen.[3] A new surgical wing was added in 1965. This building has been razed.

Zeller Hospital Building.   **Alpha Park Library**

(40) Activity/Therapy Building: This is one of the more modern buildings located on the grounds. It was built in 1966 to replace the former activity building, Lohman Hall, and was built on the same site. Lohman Hall was named after Dr. Otto Lohman, who organized the public health services at the hospital. In addition to a gymnasium there were several multi-purpose rooms there also.

Activity Building: 2005   **Gary Lisman**

131

(41, 42, 43, 44, 45, 46, 47, 48) B-Row: Buildings 41, 42, and 43 were one-story structures. Building 41 was built in 1925 and utilized as a geriatric dormitory. Buildings 42 and 43 were built in 1915 and utilized as female patient dormitories.

Buildings 44, 45, 46, 47 and 48 were all part of the original hospital and were built in 1900. The bricks used to build them were yellow, as opposed to the red bricks in C-Row. Buildings 44, 45, 47 and 48 were all cottages; whereas, building 46 was a dining hall. The dining hall was eventually closed and one-half of it was used for therapy and recreation. The other half was used for arts and crafts. All of the cottages and the dining hall have been razed.

This picture is of 3-B. It is the dormitory style building still in existence, 2005.   Gary Lisman

Alpha Park Library

Around 1952, a Pilot Alcoholism Treatment Unit was located in 5-B (Building 45). The primary purpose of the unit was to both treat the alcoholic and to do research. The main objective was to find the most effective method for the care and treatment of the male alcoholic in state institutions.

Left: 5-B. Circa 1952

Above: Typical of the cottages found on B-Row. Circa 1902   **Alpha Park Library**

(49) Garage: (No picture available.) This building has been razed.

(50) Patient Service Center: This was an octagon-shaped building which was built in 1909. It was remodeled in 1966 and, again after the hospital closed in 1973. This building contained a commissary, barber shop, and a beauty shop, among other things.

Melody Bridges   **Gary Lisman**

Patient Services Center. Circa 1967 and 2002

133

(51) Michell Building: This building has been razed. The Michell building was built in 1899 as the administration building. This building was eventually named in honor of Dr. George W. Michell, an assistant physician at the Peoria State Hospital and lifelong friend of Dr. Zeller. Dr. Michell left in 1910 to start a private institution in Peoria for the care and treatment of the mentally ill. He and his wife are interred next to Dr. Zeller's family at Springdale Cemetery in Peoria, Illinois.

Michell Building. Circa 1902   **Alpha Park Library**

(52, 53, 54, 55, 56) A-Row: A-Row, like B-row, was built in 1899 and, except for its location on the grounds, the cottages are virtually indistinguishable from the cottages in B-Row. All of the cottages in A-Row were utilized by female patients.

**Right: Typical Cottage, A-Row.
Circa 1904**

Alpha Park Library

134

(57) Dining Hall, A-Row: This building was built in 1899, and is still standing today.

Dining Hall, Row-A. Circa 1902 Note the Michell Building in the background and the cottage on the right.

Dining Hall 2005.   Gary Lisman

(58) Knowles and Bigler Residences: This building (although it had two names, it was actually one building) has been razed. It was built in 1910 as a personal residence building and expanded in 1937. Bigler Residence (student nurses' home) was named in honor of Rose Bigler, one of the chief nurses at the Peoria State Hospital from 1923 to 1933. Knowles Residence (staff house) was named in honor of Dr. Henry Knowles, who was superintendent at Peoria State Hospital, from 1951 to 1954.

(59) Talcott Hospital: This building has been razed. Talcott Hospital was built in 1908 on the site of the original castle-like building which was never used. It was a male infirmary with 108 beds. Talcott Hospital was named in honor of Mary Bird Talcott, a former chief nurse and Spanish American War veteran. She was instrumental in developing the nurses' training program at the Peoria State Hospital.

Talcott (left) and Levitan (right) Infirmaries. Circa 1908   **Alpha Park Library**

(60) Stone Cottage: (No picture available.) This building has been razed. Stone Cottage was named in honor of Dr. Esther Stone, a female psychiatrist, who served 42 years with the State Welfare Department, most of that time at the Peoria State Hospital.

Stone Cottage was an active treatment unit for newly admitted patients who were in need of quick and intensive treatment. It was a coeducational unit, housing 17 women and 12 men. The offices of the Psychology department were located in this building.

This facility was equipped to provide both electric and insulin shock therapies. There were also hydrotherapy units, but they were apparently not used. Mary Fran Buehler claimed that, *". . .they are not needed. The intensive treatment program has kept the patients from becoming disturbed enough to need the calming effect of hydrotherapy."* [4]

(61) Veterans' Cottage: The Veterans' Cottage served as a meeting place for the many veterans who received treatment at the Peoria State Hospital. This building has received extensive renovation and is in use today.

Veterans Cottage. Circa 1955   **Alpha Park Library**

Veterans Cottage 2005.   **Gary Lisman**

(62) Levitin Hospital: This building, like Talcott Hospital, was also built in 1907 and later razed. These two buildings are virtual mirror images of each other.

Levitin Hospital was named after Dr. Emil Levitin, a Peoria psychiatrist, an early member of the medical staff and part-time clinical director at Peoria State Hospital. It had beds for 78 female patients.

The two architect's drawings below are of Levitin, but Talcott looked exactly like this also.

Architect drawing of Levitan Hospital. Circa: 1905.   Milner Library

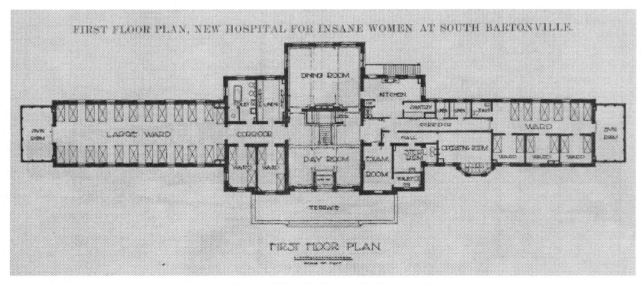

Floor Plan for Levitan Hospital   Milner Library

(63) Auditorium: This building was built in 1969. It is in use today.

Auditorium 2005.   **Gary Lisman**

(64) Sunken Garden: When Peoria State Hospital opened for patients in 1902 there was a lake in front of the Bowen Building. The lake served as a picturesque place for the patients, staff, and visitors to relax but, more importantly, it provided the hospital with a ready supply of water in case of fire.

Bowen Building and lake. Circa 1902   **Alpha Park Library**

It is not clear as to when or why the lake was drained and replaced with a sunken garden. The lake may have been gone as early as 1907, when the __Peoria Star__ ran an article about the Peoria State Hospital and mentions a pedestal that was known to have stood for many years in the sunken garden. It is known, however, that the lake was gone by 1930; because in 1930, Dr. Zeller reported that a miniature golf course, for the entertainment of the patients, had been laid out on the sunken garden.

This undated photograph shows two patients walking in the sunken garden.   **Alpha Park Library**

(65) Lohman Hall: (No picture) Lohman Hall was named in honor of Dr. Otto Lohman, who was responsible for organizing one of the public health services at the hospital. It was razed in 1966 and, on the same site, was replaced with a new activity center which also included a gymnasium. These buildings are in use today.

(66) Mechanical Shop and Garages: This building was built in 1969 and is in use today.

Mechanical Shop and Garages.   Gary Lisman

When the Peoria State Hospital closed in 1973 there were 47 buildings standing on the grounds; of these, 33 were part of the original complex built between 1899 and 1910 and three others were over fifty years old. By 2005 nearly all of the original buildings are gone. Had action been taken sooner, perhaps, more of these historically significant buildings could have been saved. Hopefully, the preceding pictures and brief descriptions will give one a glimpse of the grandeur that was once the Peoria State Hospital.

Chapter XIV

The End of an Era

"The history of 20th century psychiatry mirrors the national experience. There have been heroic people and there have been scoundrels. The high strides taken in the century -- especially the last half will undoubtedly be multiplied in the 21st century. It should be of great interest to review in a hundred years." Dr. James S. Ward

"State Hospital Here, 'Obsolete,' To Close," was the headline carried by the Peoria Journal Star, on September 19, 1972. This announcement did not come as a surprise to most. The closure of the Peoria State Hospital had been rumored for many months. Governor Richard B. Ogilvie had finally made the inevitable official.

One might ask what had led to the obsolescence of the Peoria State Hospital. There is no one defining reason, moment, or event which led to the closing of the Peoria State Hospital in 1973. The closing was a combination of several things. Starting in the early 1950s, there were new innovative concepts and ideas implemented regarding the care and treatment of the mentally ill. New drugs were being discovered and utilized to effectively treat patients who had once been relegated to long term, if not perpetual, treatment at a state hospital. There were budgetary restrictions; the Peoria State Hospital was an old facility with most of its original buildings still in use. The 1960s saw the emergence of community-based programs. As part of the community-based agenda, Illinois developed what was called the "Ninety Minute Program*." Also, the Peoria State Hospital was the recipient of a scathing investigatory report, in 1973.

The closing of the hospital had been recommended to Governor Ogilvie by a Citizens Task Force from the Peoria area. This group, led by Robert A. Jamieson, president of Security Savings and Loan Association of Peoria, studied provisions of mental health services in the area in detail. They found that the state assisted community-based services, along with the Zeller Zone Center, had made the Peoria State Hospital obsolete. Although this was true, there were other factors which affected this decision as well.

The hospital's patient population had been on a downward spiral since the mid 1960s. At its peak, there were nearly 3,000 patients at the hospital. By 1965; this number had fallen to 2,300 and, by September of 1972, there were only 600 patients on the premises.[1] A year later, there were only 280 patients there. Only five buildings were being utilized, the Zeller Acute Hospital, the Pollak Rehabilitation center, Geriatric Wards D-2 and D-3, and the Comprehensive Geriatric Treatment Ward B-3. In actuality, the Peoria State Hospital had become a nursing home, albeit a nursing home for the mentally ill.

The following story about Archie G., is a good example of this phenomena:

No Letters, Visitors in 55 Years:
FETE HOSPITAL: FORGOTTEN MAN ON 100TH BIRTHDAY

A "forgotten man" who has spent 55 years as a patient at Peoria State Hospital without a single visitor or letter yesterday became the center of a flood of attention and honor on the occasion of his 100th birthday.

Wheeled into a flower-banked room, Archie G. was suddenly confronted by a group of nurses, volunteers, and visitors singing "Happy Birthday."

A new light came into his pale eyes as they rested on a huge cake bearing 100

* In 1964 the Illinois General Assembly passed a bill for $150 million to building and staff seven regional zone centers. It was called the "Ninety Minute Program." No citizen in the state would be more than ninety minutes away from acute psychiatric care.

candles and a pile of over 80 congratulatory cards.

G. seldom speaks, but his lips repeated the words "thank you" over and over again, barely audible over the gay music of a piano played by Mrs. Thomas Pinkerton, of the hospital volunteer corps.

There was a birthday package to unwrap, too, and the delighted old man eagerly unwrapped it to find a pair of soft slippers. He was equally pleased at the dollar bills enclosed with some of the cards, spending money he can use when the commissary cart comes around.

Afterward, he and the cake were paraded through the ward upstairs, where fellow patients also sang "Happy Birthday." The candles were lighted and all 52 patients on the ward were served cake and fruit punch.

Without assistance, the honored guest stepped from the wheel chair to return to his bed, first kneeling in prayer as he often does at the bedside. He feeds himself, takes his own baths, was recently discovered scrubbing the bathroom floor of his own volition.

Archie G. was 45 years old when he entered the hospital in 1903, a year after the institution was opened. He was admitted on June 15, his birthday that year, coming from Taylorville. At that time he had sisters in Cotvallia, Oregon and Cooper, South Dakota, show the records, but they are believed long since dead. In all the years he had no greeting or visitors from the world outside.

SUNDAY PARTY occurred because Mrs. R.J. Sherwood of East Peoria, one of the volunteers who go to the hospital weekly to entertain and talk with the patients, noticed on G's bed card the birth date 1858. Incredulous, she checked the office records, then suggested that there be a birthday party. Church people in East Peoria, Creve Coeur and Pekin, told of the birthday, sent cards.

Mrs. L. Bramlet, another volunteer, got the gift of slippers and saw to it that there was a birthday cake decorated and donated by the Melvin Bakery.

In charge of the event was Mrs. Helen G. Mayers, director of volunteer services. She pointed out that it is unlikely that any of today's 2,395 patients will remain so long at the hospital, because with present treatment methods and drugs many of them stay such a short time that volunteers hardly have a chance to know them.

G. is the oldest patient at Peoria State Hospital, but two others younger than he is have been there longer, being admitted in 1902, the year the hospital was opened.

The occasion was a new experience for husbands of volunteers, who accompanied their wives to the hospital for the first time and helped with the party, some of them choking up so on the "Happy Birthday" that they could not go on singing.[2]

On November 18, 1980, Dr. James Ward gave a speech on the history of mental illness and part of it dealt with the closing of the Peoria State Hospital and the geriatric patients. The following excerpt comes from that speech.

There was an interesting study that we did when I came in 1965 - the average length of stay at Peoria State Hospital at that time was 12 years. Twelve years of people getting very, very good care - excellent care. And, when we closed the institution in 1973, at that point in time, the average length of stay for every patient at Peoria State was 20 years. So, there really were some very "long timers." There were other developments on the horizon back in the 60's that made Peoria State - made its fate rather *doomed. One was Medicare/Medicaid - came in 1965. I know that when I came to town in 1965 - that it cost $212.00 to go to the County Nursing Home. It cost $50.00 for the relatives to put their relative in Peoria State. There was absolutely no doubt about where they would go because the care of Peoria State was excellent care. So in fact they even had more opportunities at Peoria State than they would ever have at the county nursing homes. We were not terribly discriminate about who would go because usually the decisions were financial decisions - the decisions were that the geriatric population went to Peoria State or went to the State Hospital. Before long, we took numbers and found out that 40-50% of the population were people who were geriatrics - not people who were in active treatment programs. Well, then Medicare/Medicaid came in and nursing home care was possible, under these bills. So people did not go to the State Hospital. Then, the state itself, began to have the preadmission examination. Which we still have, as a matter of fact. We had to demonstrate that the person who was over 65 years of age is in need of state hospitalization because of symptoms that are mental symptoms. And so the population - at least the admissions - of geriatrics went down and down.*

In the 1950s a new family of drugs were found to be extremely effective in the treatment and reduction of many of the symptoms associated with mental illness. The discovery of chlorpromazine* (Thorazine) was thought by many to be the elusive "Magic Bullet," a drug which would cure severe mental illness. [3] Chlorpromazine was followed by other drugs which were touted as cures for depression, mania, and anxiety. With the advent of these drugs, many patients who had been unresponsive for decades were now being helped.

Dr. Otto Bettag, the director of the Illinois Department of Public Welfare, reported to the American Psychiatric Association's Midwest conference, held in 1956 at the Galesburg State Research Hospital, that:

> *Tranquility induces better patients' living conditions. Furniture and TV sets can now be set up on wards of formerly combative patients who would have destroyed such items before the drugs were used. The drugs have also reduced the need for electro-shock treatment and have virtually abolished hydrotherapy, water packs, or sprays. Because of these new drugs the patient discharge rate in Illinois mental hospitals is the highest in history.* [4]

This does not mean that the patient population was immediately reduced, but it was the precursor of a new era. Even though the effectiveness of these new drugs was proven, many in the mental health care field were slow to change. Once it was found that these antipsychotic medications tended to make a psychotic individual more amenable to psychotherapy, there was a rapid expansion in their use. *"This combination of antipsychotic drugs and on occasion the addition of psychotherapy,"* according to Dr. Joseph Mehr, *"would begin a reduction in state hospital population that would gather momentum from broader social changes. Over the next decades the term deinstitutionalization would be coined to characterize the systematic depopulation of the state hospitals."* [5]

For example, patients who at one time were considered extremely difficult if not impossible to reach on a personal level were now being successfully treated. The **Peoria Journal Star**, in April of 1958, ran an article by Frank Barry about the successful use of one of these new drugs to treat the mentally ill at the Peoria State Hospital. He reported that a new drug, Vesprin*, was being used, resulting in dramatic changes on a large group of female patients. According to him the drug:

*Chlorpromazine:a phenothiazine used as a tranquilizer to suppress the more flagrant symptoms of psychotic disorders (as in schizophrenia).
*Vesprin made by the E.R. Squibb & Sons, was administered orally in tablets of 10, 25, and 50 milligrams three times daily. Squibb claimed that Vesprin was at least twice as potent in controlling psychotic manifestations as Chloropromazine. Dr. Joseph Marcovitch, medical assistant superintendent at PSH, claimed that the side effects were fewer with Vesprin than those experienced with other tranquilizers.

. . .allows the patient to be approached for training purposes and eventual rehabilitation without promoting a state of lethargy and apathy. The hospital's grimmest building always has been Ward 9-C, a maximum security ward.

It houses 70 seriously agitated women. Six weeks ago it took some measure of courage to visit the place. Today, after its occupants have been taking the Vesprin pill for that time, 9C is a place of peace and unremitting quiet. [6]

It is obvious that the advances in pharmacology had changed the face of mental health care and treatment. These new drugs were used to effectively treat many patients who had once been considered hopeless. Now the need of a lengthy or, in some cases a lifetime stay at a facility like the Peoria State Hospital, was no longer needed. This led to dramatic reductions in the population at the Peoria State Hospital and other similar facilities, not only in Illinois but throughout the country as well.

By the mid-1960s, facilities used solely for the care of the mentally challenged, such as the Lincoln and Dixon state schools, were becoming extremely overcrowded. Since the population at state mental hospitals like the Peoria State Hospital was rapidly declining, it was decided to establish mental retardation units at the hospitals. These units would be the focus of a later investigation at the Peoria State Hospital. Being cognizant of the changes that were rapidly occurring in the care of the mentally ill, the Illinois General Assembly, in 1964, passed a bill that would fund the building and staffing of seven regional zone centers. At the heart of this bill was the "Ninety Minute Program."

The care and treatment received at the zone centers was quite different from the care and treatment that was available at the large state hospitals. Facilities like the Peoria State Hospital operated under the theory that the "rest cure" lay in remote, country institutions. Fine custodial care was given. Restitution followed prolonged exposure to fresh air, rest and reduced responsibility and expectations. Unfortunately, discharges were few, the hospital's population continued to grow and many of the patients would never leave. In fact, if you were admitted to the Peoria State Hospital before 1920 there was an eighty percent chance that you would be buried there. By 1972, the average stay there was measured in decades. In stark contrast to this, the average length of stay at the Zeller Zone Center* was just three weeks.[7] This is not an indictment of the care given at the Peoria State Hospital; patients did receive excellent care and treatment there. It is merely meant to show that mental health care and treatment had changed.

The Illinois Investigating Commission gave a report to the Illinois General Assembly which virtually ensured the hospital's closure on December 18, 1973. The Commission concluded that, "It would appear that the announced phaseout of Peoria State Hospital during the next year may be an unavoidable necessity." [8]

The physical condition of the Peoria State Hospital was another reason given for its closing. The Peoria State Hospital had been virtually neglected for several years and it was now in need of major repairs and renovation to make it a viable option for those in need of long-term care. It would have required the allocation of millions of dollars in order to make the Peoria State Hospital a viable facility. Although the buildings appeared outwardly to be in relatively good condition, their interiors were, in many cases, antiquated. Most of these buildings and facilities had been in operation since its opening in 1902 and did not meet the requirements needed for patient care and safety.

For example, the cottages had dormitories on the second floor, where the patients slept, with only two means of egress. One was a stairway to the hall adjoining the day room and the other was an exterior fire escape. It was estimated that, in the event of a fire, perhaps five of the twenty-five patients normally housed there could successfully negotiate their way down.[9]

*Zone IV. This zone consisted of seventeen counties in the upper Illinois River valley centered in Peoria, its largest city. It was here that the Zeller Mental Health Center was constructed and opened in 1965.

Alpha Park Library

Patients usually slept on the second floor. In the event of a fire it was deemed highly unlikely that most patients could be safely evacuated down the steep fire escapes.

Furthermore, hard use and poor maintenance had exacerbated the deterioration of the buildings. The report to the Illinois General Assembly in 1973 stated that:

...the physical facilities used by the Mental Retardation Unit at Peoria State Hospital have been sorely neglected for the last several years, possibly since the very establishment of the unit in 1969. As mentioned above, the four ward buildings were dirty and in poor repair. Even simple painting and replacing of floor tiles have been neglected. Worse still, the unclean environment is a breeding area for diseases and contagion. [10]

The following pictures and captions were taken from the State of Illinois Legislative Investigating Commissions' Report:

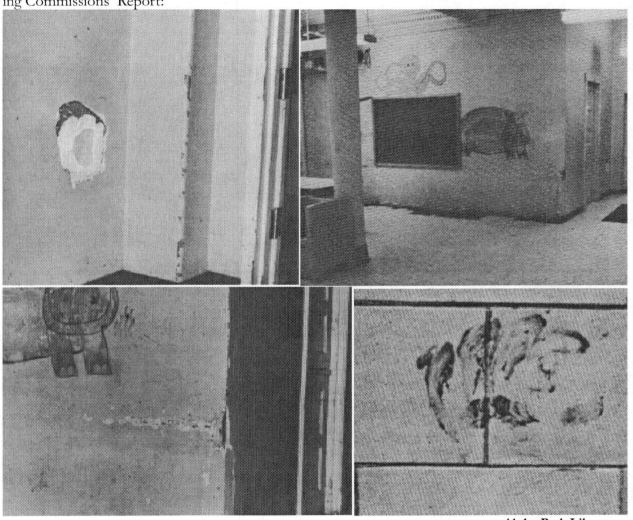

Alpha Park Library

All four pictures were taken in Ward 8-C's dayroom. The picture on the top left shows a hole that was caused by Odell Y., who kicked through the plaster with his bare feet. Odell Y. is suspected of having beaten Jerome S. to death. Ward personnel indicated that their request for repairs and maintenance had been fruitless. The picture on the lower left shows the deteriorated physical plant. Paint and plaster have been chipped, and feces smears are clearly visible. The black areas on the floor of the top right picture were the aftermath of places where tiles had been pulled up by the patients and never replaced. The lower right shows excrement on the walls. In general the floor and walls were filthy. The entire building had a strong odor of urine and excrement.

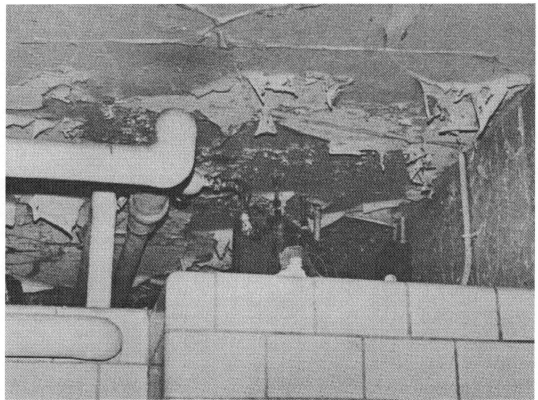

Left: Physical deterioration of the ceiling in the picture on the left is noted, with the peeling of paint and plaster.

Another concern of the Commission was the lack of personal effects and privacy allowed the patients:

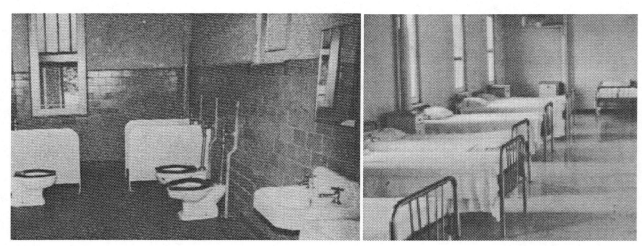

Open toilets such as those pictured at the left were common among the mental retardation wards at Peoria State Hospital. Some staff members were of the opinion that such impersonal facilities were dehumanizing to the patients and had a deleterious effect on programming efforts. Although cleaner than most other areas of Ward 8-C, the same lack of privacy was apparent in the patients' dormitory. Commission investigators also noted feces smears, urine soaked bed clothing, and a large pool of vomit next to one bed.

148

The physical condition of the facility was bad enough, but the Commission was extremely alarmed by the condition of the patients in these buildings. They found that *". . .many of the patients exhibited large open sores on their bodies which no doubt frequently became infected by the patients' fetid surroundings."* [11]

The end of the Peoria State Hospital was all but finalized in the summer of 1972. It was at this time three patients would suffer tragic deaths, which was the death knell for the Peoria State Hospital. As a result of these deaths, "House Joint Resolution 146*" was adopted by the seventy-seventh General Assembly. This resolution originally called for an in-depth investigation into the *"brutal and vicious beating of Jerome S.*, a mentally retarded patient at Peoria State Hospital,"* which occurred on May 2, 1972, and ultimately caused his death. [12] Before the commission could begin its investigation on June 21, 1972, a second patient was struck on the head with a chair by another resident and died the following day. The Commission was in the process of studying these two deaths when another patient would die. This patient died on August 30, 1972, of spinal meningitis, which has been caused by a severe and chronic ear infection. It was reported that his ear infection was *". . .neither detected nor treated by the hospital's medical staff despite frequent requests by the ward personnel for medical attention for L."* [13] It would be a mistake to blame the closing of Peoria State Hospital solely on the deaths of these three patients in a relatively short period, but they certainly hastened the hospital's demise. (To see a copy of the letter written by the Illinois Investigating Commission to the General Assembly in February of 1973 regarding their findings at Peoria State Hospital. See Appendix V).

Although these deaths were certainly tragic and may have been preventable, the grim reality is that patients had died due to, what may be referred to as, unnatural causes. It would be unfair, however, to insinuate that these were the first or only patients to die under suspicious circumstances. The first such death occurred on October 19, 1903; it was on this date that Thomas H.* would die due to a savage beating that he supposedly suffered in an encounter with two male attendants. It must be noted that neither of the two attendants was indicted for the death by the Grand Jury. What actually transpired during this encounter is, therefore, known only to the two attendants and those patients who may have witnessed the struggle. What is known is that Thomas H. suffered greatly as evidenced by the coroner's testimony before the Grand Jury on October 23, 1903:

> *. . .the marks on the body are of the worst description. On one side of the neck is a large black mark, black, discolored, and of the color of putrid liver, evidently the result of a fearful blow. The balance of the trunk of the body is simply covered with black and blue bruises that look as if they might have resulted from terrific blows with a club or kicks from a heavy boot or shoes. If they were in one place the aggregate would cover the bottom of a good sized dishpan. The back, the sides, the stomach, the region of the vital organs are simply hammered and beaten into an unrecognizable mass. Discoloration has set in, and did set in immediately after the awful assault. The body looks as if it might have been run through some gigantic milling machine. How any man could have lived three hours after such an assault is incomprehensible.* [14]

---

*House Joint Resolution 146 was adopted by the General Assembly on June 27, 1972. The resulting investigation led to a scathing report regarding PSH. Portions of this report have been excerpted for use in this book but the names of the patients involved have been omitted. The omissions were made out of respect for the patients' right to anonymity. It is a matter of Public Record and is available at many libraries for those who wish to ascertain a copy.

*It has been decided by the author to omit the full names of the patients. For those so inclined the full name can be found in the Report of the Illinois Legislative Investigating Commission - Peoria State Hospital, which was submitted to the Seventy-Seventh General Assembly on June 27, 1972.

*The death of Thomas H. was extensively reported on in the Peoria Journal. Again, out of respect for the patient's right to anonymity and privacy, his full name was not used.

Perhaps, we had indeed come full circle, the following scene described could well have come from an earlier time and place. This scene was, in many ways, eerily reminiscent of the conditions that the Peoria State Hospital was meant to alleviate. It was being reported in 1972 that:

> . . .when our staff investigators first visited the hospital they went to Ward 8-C to examine the site of the S. beating. The first sensory impression they received was the stench of urine and feces that is think in the air. The walls and floors were dirty. The walls were badly in need of plaster and paint. Some walls were punctuated by large gaping holes, and flaking paint and plaster. In some areas, floor tiles were ripped up creating crevices where dirt and filth accumulated. On virtually all the walls there were traces of excrement which had been smeared by patients who had "acted out." Even the patients themselves were part of this grim setting as they wandered about aimlessly, dressed in torn, dirty clothing or not dressed at all. There was virtually no opportunity for patients to find privacy, because there were no drapes or partitions of any sort between beds or toilets. Throughout most of the day the patients were simply herded into the large open day room where there was little for them to do but wander about, occasionally antagonizing or assaulting one another.[15]

Furthermore, in 1904 Dr. Zeller was happy to report that Peoria State Hospital had virtually abolished the use of narcotics to control patients. In 1972, however, the use of sedative drugs was once again being used to control patients at Peoria State Hospital. Witnesses claimed:

> . . .that the policy of the medical staff and the administration of the hospital was to maximize the use of sedative drugs to keep the mentally retarded in a state of perpetual tranquilization. Virtually every mentally retarded patient received some form of sedative every day. These drugs were used as "chemical straight jackets" to keep the patients from evincing any form of hostility or aggression whatever.
>
> This over-medication led to several unfortunate results, according to witnesses who testified at our public hearings. Since patients were heavily sedated, they were slow to respond to therapy. Worse, many skills taught to them while drugged were not retained when the tranquilizer wore off and the person returned to a drug-free state.[16]

The fate of the Peoria State Hospital was a foregone conclusion once the Illinois Legislative Investigating Commission reported their findings to the General Assembly in February 1973. So, on December 18, 1973, the last eighteen geriatric patients were transferred to the Galesburg State Research Hospital. The end had come to one of the country's finest mental health hospitals.

First administration building at Peoria State Hospital, named the Michell Building after Dr. George W. Michell. Dr. Zeller called him his "most valuable aide." Dr. Michell stood with Dr. Zeller in administering his reforms, i.e. taking away the restraints. When this building was razed the corner-stones were saved and are now a part of the Peoria State Hospital memorial park.

View from the Bowen Building (also known as the employees building) with A-row on the left and the Michell Building on the right. Circa 1902

Michell Building on the left, A-row cottages in the center, A-row dining hall on the right. Circa 1902

Three cottages on C-row. Circa 1902

A-row on the left and the Michell Building on the right. Circa 1902   Alpha Park Library

Staff in front of the Michell Building. (Dr. Zeller on the left in uniform.)   Alpha Park Library

Cottages and lake under construction. Circa 1902   Alpha Park Library

Cottage with a canvas enclosure for tuberculosis patients   Alpha Park Library

Hillside near the bottom of the hill leading up to the hospital.

The steps in 2002 a hundred years after the first patients walked up to the hospital.

The steps as they were in 1946.

A-row cottage. Circa 1902 **Alpha Park Library**

Industrial Reeducation: The caption with the original picture claimed that: **Alpha Park Library**
"Before its advent these patients had spent years in imprisoned idleness."

Business Office. Circa 1904
From left to right: Jim Sexton (bookkeeper), Renny Sapp (supervisor), Dr. Burham (assistant super-intendent), James Conway (chief clerk), Dr. George Michell (medical staff).

Assembly room in Sunnyside Cottage. (Note the piano on the right). Dr. Zeller reported in 1904 that "The firm of Lyon & Healy, very kindly presented us with three old square pianos of superior quality. There being no fund for the purchase of musical instruments this gift was peculiarly accept-able. Our day rooms are so large that a square piano is a distinct ornament, and every cottage can muster a few players."

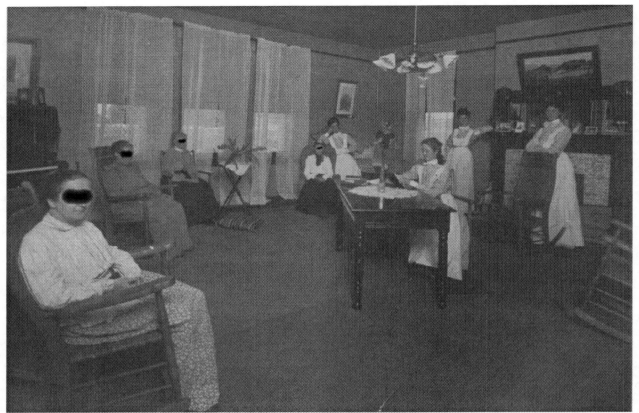

Reception room in nurses' quarters. (This picture, like many others, show   Alpha Park Library
the gratings on the windows, most of which Dr. Zeller had removed by 1905.)

Nurse on duty in a day room.   Alpha Park Library

Each of the eight new cottages had a similar day room. Circa 1902   Alpha Park Library

Institutional Library.   Alpha Park Library

General kitchen located in the domestic building. The kitchen produced up to 20,000 meals daily. Circa 1906

General kitchen in the domestic building. Circa 1906

Bread Room located in the Domestic Building. Circa 1905   Alpha Park Library

The bakery -- it required at least ten barrels of flour daily to produce bread for the Peoria State Hospital. Circa 1905

Women dining in one of the cottages. Circa: 1906   Alpha Park Library

Meal time in one of the men's dining halls.   Alpha Park Library

Dining Hall, Domestic Building.

Sunny Side Cottage dining room, (Note screens on windows).

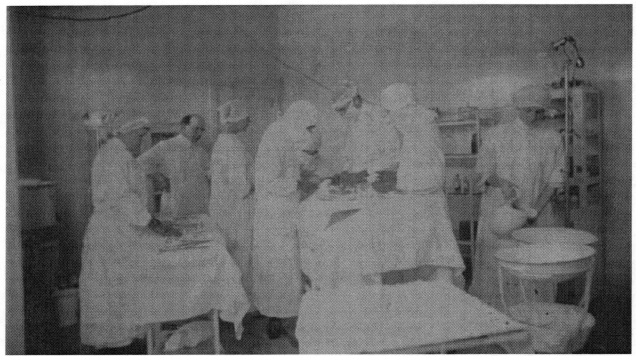

The original picture listed the names of the individuals shown; unfortunately some of the names were impossible to decipher. From left to right: Elizabeth Robinson (head nurse) Dr. McLie--, Dr. Ric--(lady doctor) Dr. Levitin, Dr. Brock (administering ether).

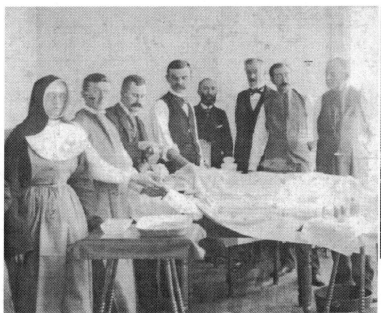

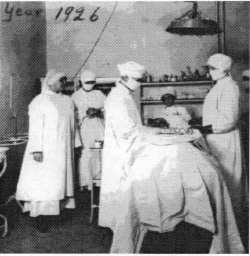

Surgery, 1926.

Surgery at Peoria State Hospital. (Note Dr. Zeller in the center of the picture.)

Talcott Hospital on the left, the Stone Cottage in the center, and
Levitin Hospital on the right. Circa 1905

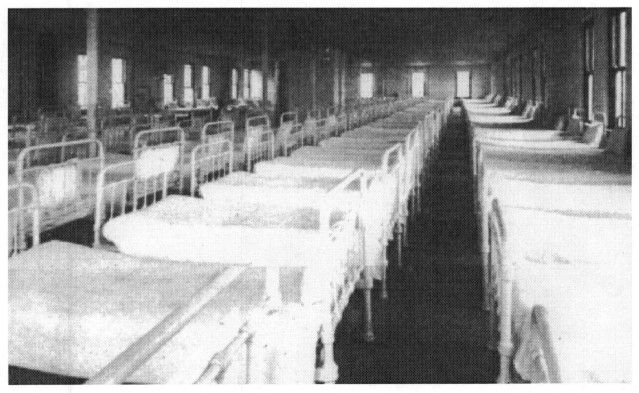

Largest Dormitory -- 150 beds.

Peoria State Hospital Orchestra   **Alpha Park Library**

Horse Barn -- it was later converted into a firehouse and garages.   **Alpha Park Library**

Utica Crib   Gary Lisman

Restraining chair. (Some chairs of this type had a hole in the bottom with a pail placed below so that patients could be restrained for long periods of time.)
Gary Lisman

This page and the next page -- various forms of restraint on display in Dr. Zeller's office. Among the items displayed were shackles, leg irons, handcuffs, mangles, ball and chain, leather muffs, mitts, anklets, wristlets and the infamous "bed saddle." All were abolished by Dr. Zeller.
Alpha Park Library

Above -- So-called "humane restraints" consisting of the canvas camisole or "straight jacket," the "blind sleeve dress," and the "straight suit."

Left: Leather restraints.

Right: Shackles, chains and irons.

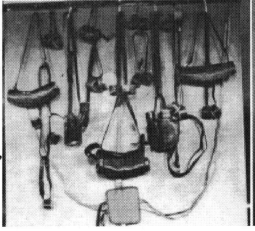

Alpha Park Library

Memorial to Dr. Zeller. It stood in front of the Zeller Hospital, above, at Peoria State Hospital until the facility closed. (The stone is still located on the grounds, but the plaque has disappeared.)

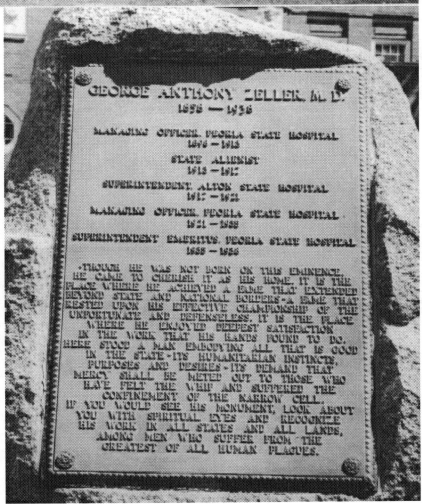

Bowen Building (also known as the employees' building. Circa 1902   Alpha Park Library

Bowen Building 2002.   Gary Lisman

Above: Artist's drawing of the future Zeller Memorial Park which is to be located on the grounds of the former Peoria State Hospital.

The Zeller Memorial Park gazebo as it stands today. Note the cornerstone on pillar on the right. This was taken from the Michell Building, the first administration building, when it was razed. The finishing touches will be added, including a miniature Peoria State Hospital in the middle of the gazebo, to be built by the Industrial Arts classes of Limestone High School.

General Contractor -- Phil Schindler and Sons

Chapter XV

Asylum Romances

Dr. George Zeller is widely known for his work with the mentally ill, but he was also a prolific writer. Over the years he wrote many fiction stories. These stories almost always lead one to believe that he got his inspiration from some special patient or incident which occurred at the Peoria State Hospital. Dr. Zeller added to the mystery by not telling the reader if his stories were indeed works of fiction. He left it up to the reader to decide, if he or she believes, that these were works of fiction or nonfiction. One thing that is known, though, is that his short stories are enjoyed by almost all who read them. J. Christian Bay, a literary critic and librarian at the John Crerar Library, dubbed him the "Kipling of Illinois" and swore that Kipling himself enjoyed reading Dr. Zeller's stories.[1]

The Illinois Department of Welfare published nine of Dr. Zeller's stories in a book titled "A Series of Asylum Romance," in 1919. Three of his stories that may be attributed to Dr. Zeller's experiences at the Peoria State Hospital have been selected. The stories selected are as follows: "The Genealogist," "The Graveyard Elm," and "Fainting Fanny."

Within the records regarding the history of the Peoria State Hospital, one will only find records regarding infants or births on two occasions. The first report of babies at the Peoria State Hospital was in the Sixth Biennial Report of the Commissioner, Superintendent and Treasurer of the Illinois Asylum for the Incurable Insane at Peoria on June 30, 1906. Under the heading of "Illicit Parentage" Dr. Zeller wrote:

On April 23 the superintendent of the Edgar County almshouse brought us five patients, among them a woman. Her appearance aroused the suspicion of the ward physician, and a consultation revealed advanced pregnancy. The facts were at once communicated to the Governor, the State Board of Charities and the officials of Edgar County. The Governor immediately made a demand upon these officials for a searching investigation, with the object of fixing the responsibility for this outrage upon a defenseless, dependent and defective woman. She was given every attention and on May 4, thirteen days after her arrival here and nine months and nine days after her arrival in the Edgar County Almshouse,

she was delivered of a healthy female child. She has never shown cognizance of the child, and as she is of a violent and destructive disposition she had to be separated from it. The child is being reared by a graduate nurse and is developing splendidly and appears to be normal in every particular. The case attracted wide publicity at the time, but the State Board of Charities promptly cited the facts and quoted our correspondence, and instead of censure the institution received credit out of the affair. It is to be regretted that the identity of the father was never established.[2]

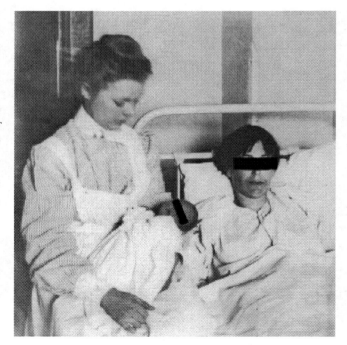

The picture on the right was taken around 1905 at the Peoria State Hospital. It is possible that this is the patient and child referred to in Dr. Zeller's 1906 report.

Alpha Park Library

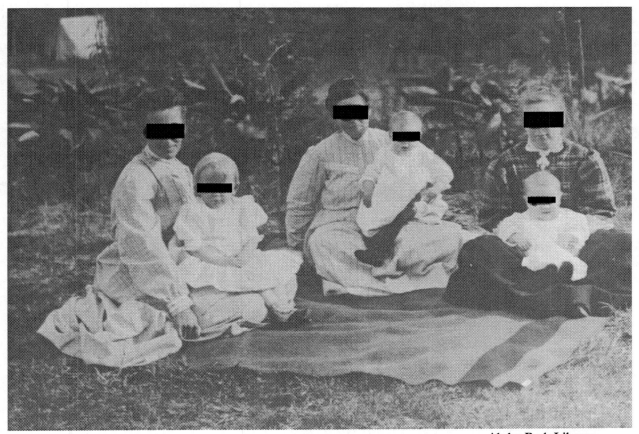

The picture above was taken around 1907 at the Peoria State Hospital and clearly shows three babies such as those described in Dr. Zeller's 1908 report.

Two years later, on July 30, 1908, Dr. Zeller filed his Seventh Biennial Report of the Illinois General Hospital for the Insane at Peoria. He included a section concerning three babies. The following is the last official mention of infants and the Peoria State Hospital.

> *Although an insane asylum is not considered the abiding place of babies we have three. One girl born here seventeen days after the mother's admission is now two years old and two other children both brought in the arms of their insane mothers are a year old. They have endeared themselves to the entire force and their removal, which is inevitable, will be considered a calamity. It is sad commentary of the conditions surrounding the insane that all three children are illegitimate, although the parentage is in no instance traceable to a state institution. Their development is being watched with keen interest and they will soon be placed in surroundings that will take away the sting that a latter knowledge of the paternity would entail.[3]*

Perhaps these babies were the inspiration for the following short story written by Dr. Zeller; especially the baby girl which was born at the hospital. One will find references to Rhoda Derry whose story is well-documented. Dr. Zeller also utilized his military service and his experiences in the Philippines in the writing of this story, much of which can be found in his autobiography.

Most will, certainly, appreciate the irony of this story which rivals that found in any tale written by O'Henry.

The Genealogist

A GENEALOGIST is naturally one who is a student of ancestry and heredity. Of late years, enthusiasts in that line have come to be known as eugenists, whether their studies pertain to the human race of the animal kingdom.

Well, I happened to be thrown into intimate relationship with one of the kind and our friendship has continued unbroken through more than a human generation.

In the late eighties, while prospecting in Arizona, I learned that Lieutenant Culbertson was excavating an ancient Aztec village which he appropriately named El Pueblo de los Muertos, a term which seemed ponderous enough to me at the time but which, after my sojourn in Spanish speaking countries, translated itself very clearly into "The City of the Dead."

Lieutenant Culbertson was a real explorer and he had with him a large force of Mexican laborers under the direction of American foremen and he was liberally backed by the funds of an eastern society for ethnological research.

Here is where I first met the genealogist; not the lieutenant -- far from it. That individual was a practical man and as much at home with greasers, muleskinners, cowboys, ranchmen and rustlers as with the stately dames and profound scholars who made up the society which provided the means for his explorations.

The camp on the mesa had tents, mess houses, kitchen and cooks as well as a lot of swearing teamsters who were constantly covering the desert trail in escort wagons hauling away crated trophies and returning with camp supplies. Such an outfit, far removed from the beaten paths of travel much needs to have a doctor and, naturally, looked him up. He seemed much pleased to meet one of his professions and I was doubly so for that reason he not only welcomed me heartily but invited me to share a generous meal which my long hike caused me to anticipate with unusual heartiness.

Outside his tent, a sweating olla hung in the broiling sun and I stepped out and drank a quart of water so refreshing as to take away the taste of the alkali stuff which I had been gulping down from water holes the past week.

A sweating olla is simply the primitive people's refrigerator. It cools its contents by the evaporation of the water which exudes through the pores of the burnt clay of which it is made. The hotter the rays of the sun, the quicker it cools. Put that same water in a glazed jar and it will become as hot as the enveloping atmosphere.

But I have said nothing about the genealogist and could not until I drew the camp chair up to the mess table opposite Dr. Vender. I soon discovered that he was one.

The full blood Apache Indian boy who waited upon us brought in a can of baked beans mixed with bacon.

"A Bostonian never forsakes his native dish even in the desert," I observed.

He replied: "Why should he? There is nothing quite as good as New England fare unless it be New England people. If you will look in the commissary you will find a stock of desiccated codfish put up in five pound tins. It makes a man feel out here as if he were eating a meal in the shadow of Faneuil Hall."

I told him that the country owed much to Boston, not only because it was the cradle of liberty but because of the culture that had radiated from it and, wishing to impress my appreciation of his hospitality, I said that no better example of a refined people's influence could be shown than the presence in this out of the way place of cultivated men preserving their standard of living in the midst of most primitive surroundings.

This opened up the subject of heredity and descent and I became a willing listener to his thorough presentation of the subject. He seemed to be an epitome of all the blue books and "Who's Who" of all New England.

I tell you, "that the influence of our people has endured because we are of the pure strain. We have not gone outside of our intellectual circles to select wives and husbands and the result is that we excel in mentality. You may drop a New Englander wherever you please and he will always land on his feet and his offspring will maintain the traditions of the family. Look at the Adams, the Wilcotts, the Harrisons, and the Edwards and, in fact the descendants of all the signers. They have not deteriorated in a single instance and their names loom large in every history of our country. That is because they have not intermarried with the plebian stock that is pouring into the country from every foreign land."

I listened to the doctor with marked attention. We are both young and I, who could boast only of a birth and bringing up on the prairies of Illinois, whose father came from the foot of the Bavarian Alps and whose mother was a native of Nancy, the ancient capitol of Lorraine, naturally looked with awe upon this splendid descendant of the "Pilgrim Fathers."

I recalled now, during my course at the state university, we looked upon a sophomore of Yale or Harvard as in every way superior to even our professors and I wondered why my wealthier classmates were wasting their energies here when they might just as well have been getting a real education in the east and at the same time rubbing elbows with the elite of the land.

Ah, the disillusionment that time works! Looking back over the vista of years, I now see those plodding fellow students of the fresh water college holding the very highest positions in the affairs of the nation, conspicuous in finance, in political life, in architecture, in agriculture, in literature and in art.

It so happened that my subsequent activities dealt largely with mental derelicts and the position I filled gave me free access to public charitable institutions. There I quickly learned that mental alienation makes no distinction as to class. Insanity is just as apt to push the electric button and enter the mansion of the rich as to rap on the door of the poor man's novel. The ranks of the insane in our public institutions are recruited from every condition and station in life. It would be deemed a sacrilege were I even to hint as to the number of members of leading families that I have seen and known among the mentally afflicted.

But my associations were not altogether with the mentally bereft. Official life threw me frequently into the company of the leaders of the state and nation and I am free to say that in spite of what I know of the bar sinister across the mental escutcheons of many of their families, my admiration for their noble qualities, keen intellect, high ideals and unflinching patriotism has never for a moment been shaken by the knowledge that came to me in confidential or at least in a professional relation.

But I am writing of a time when these things were unknown to me. Courtesy alone would have barred me from taking issue with my host but I had no occasion to differ with him. He had a family tree that extended without a broken twig from Plymouth Rock to the Arizona Mesa. We, of the middle west, were as of yesterday in comparison with him. He did not intimate as much but in the presence of such a blue blood who showed the aristocrat even in his camp surroundings, one naturally felt it. One supreme satisfaction I got out of the specimens that were being unearthed was the thought that here were the remains of Americans who antedated his forbears. And what inter-marriage had finally brought them to was another thought which impressed itself upon me as the excavations began to reveal the ruined walls of what had once been the capital of a prehistoric people, while all around lay implements and ornaments indicating an advanced civilization and an art not unlike that of the Egyptians.

I did not see Dr. Vender for many years and when we did meet, it was under circumstances almost as strange as in the first instance.

We were not wholly out of touch with each other in the interval. He settled down in a growing western city and I saw his name in the press occasionally as he continued his steady advance to the head of his profession. I envied the city that had as its leading physician a man of his polish and attainments and family tree and felt sure that at some time in his professional activities he must have found time to at least lecture on eugenics, conduct a mental hygiene clinic or instruct a class of anxious mothers or a group of adolescents as to the safeguards to be observed in selecting a husband or wife. These matters would never be left to chance in a circle in which Dr. Vender moved. No wedding could be considered complete unless the bride and groom had previously handed to the minister a hygienic certificate procured from a complacent family physician who, on either side, knew the contracting parties sufficiently well to relieve them of the embarrassment of submitting to an examination. He was the very soul of the uplift.

Ten years after our first meeting, the fortunes of war brought us together again. He went to the Philippines with the first expedition as a major in the National Guard of his state and I followed a year later as an officer in the newly organized national volunteers. Although he was attached to headquarters, I did not get to see him upon landing for the reason that I was promptly ordered to join an expeditionary force that was on the point of embarking for the Camarines. I thought it was to be a sort of excursion, but I remained almost two years participating in that time in the initial invasion, the taking an garrisoning of the towns, martial law and, finally, the establishment of complete civil government.

Dr. Vender ranked me one grade by reason of his previous service, but I felt that if the authorities could half appreciate his qualifications they would have made him at least the surgeon general of the islands.

I often came across his name in official reports and we were all conscious of the splendid record he was making. When I was finally relieved from field duty and ordered to Manila, he met us at the wharf and his hearty greeting atoned for all of the hardships we had endured in the provinces.

He was not alone in extending the glad hand. The fellows at headquarters are wonderfully kind to one just in from the line, as we called it. They somehow felt that they had been favored in having at their disposal the fine old mansions, the splendid Spanish garrisons and the hotel and club life of the capital while we had been subsisting on the commissary supplies sent down on the inter-island transports and sleeping in improvised quarters in nipa shacks and abandoned convents. In keeping with the customs of the service, they acted as though the best would be non too good for us. A seat at the officers' mess was ours, a card to the army and navy club was promptly made out and a "muchacho" was placed at our disposal with instructions to look after our every want and provide us with the most comfortable bed in the staff house. All this, of course, while we were seeking permanent accommodations.

My pleasure at again being in Dr. Vender's company may well be imagined. Instantly the intervening years were swept away and we were again a Casa Grande on the Arizona mesa. We took a small table in the corner of the mess room and while the Tagalog waiter was loading it with viands and we were consuming them almost as fast as he set them down, the doctor tried to draw me out on my experiences and observations among the Bicols and the Negritos of the southern provinces where I had been stationed. I told him that was a long story and that he would eventually be detailed for duty in the outposts himself and would, with the knowledge of ethnology, quickly learn more than I could tell him. This immediately afforded an opening for his hobby and he was not slow to avail himself of it. He promptly began to exhibit the usual fault of the white man in failing to see the native Filipino any latent talent for self government of ultimate improvement.

"I tell you, the stock is not there; the foundation does not exist. They are a race of islanders barely emerging from savagery. They have no intellectual ancestry."

I told him that in my two years in the field I had come into intimate contact within many alcaldes, gubernadorcillos, ex-officers of the insurrecto forces, native merchants and other members of leading families whose mind reflected study and whose homes displayed a refined and discriminating taste and, given the opportunity, these people could quickly establish and securely maintain a stable government.

He seemed to think this might become a possibility after a hundred years of guidance by men with pedigrees such as hi possessed.

I told him that when the memory of the insurrection became sufficiently remote to remove present day prejudice, the historian would accord a high place to some of the native leaders, that the generalship of Emilio Aguinaldol in the insurrection against the Spaniards and his final and successful stand at Biak-na-Bato was one of the very finest examples of leadership; so, too, was the influence of the martyred Rizal, whose book, *Noli Mi Tengere*, had started and kept alive the revolution, and the Dr. Rizal would forever live in the memory of these people as a true patriot and would take rank along with the martyrs of other lands who had kindled the flames of liberty in the hearts of their countrymen.

I didn't want to talk. I wanted to be the listener. I had simply acquired a lot of folk lore, gained a knowledge of Spanish and a smattering of several dialects while he knew all these and was a master student of our own tongue and an interpreter of the highest qualities of our own people as well.

As my stay in the capital was prolonged many months by an outbreak of Asiatic cholera in which we were both assigned to active duty, we were both assigned to active duty, we were destined to see much of each other. After dinner, which in spite of army regulations he persisted in calling it, he insisted that we go to the theater. As I had seen nothing even resembling a show for twenty-three months, I gladly accompanied him. It was an all round vaudeville, including a skit based on campaigning in the provinces. Moving pictures had not yet reached the islands but the illustrated song was in full favor. The hall was suddenly darkened, a singer came forward with the spotlight centered upon him and he proceeded very plaintively with a song entitled, "He's Just Behind the Times."

It was the story of an aging minister whose flock kept dwindling as the years crept upon him. The lantern slides showed him in the bloom of youth; in later years the pride of his fashionable congregation; then with an assistant and, finally, dispossessed of his charge, he sat on the steps of the church, a crushed and disappointed old man and died there of a broken heart while the music of the church organ peeled from within the cheery chapel.

I was gaunt and bronzed and my uniform was faded and had the room not been darkened, I would have felt that every eye was centered upon me as a loving reproduction of the picture on the screen. I felt uncomfortable and said to the doctor, "Come, let's get out of here, these fellows have evidently learned that I have just come in from the Front."

I spent many pleasant and instructive evenings with him. Night after night as we sat on the Luneta, he regaled me with eugenics. He told me of the fine two year old boy and the baby girl he had left with their mother when the call to duty came. I envied him when he outlined the ambitious plans he had in mind for the future of his boy and girl, although more than once I had to break up the meeting because of the salty ocean spray or the gleam of the southern Cross seemed to fill my eyes with a sort of mist.

When we got the cholera epidemic under control, I received the long delayed order home. The task awaiting me there was the care of several thousand insane and I made up my mind that if I could show the afflicted of the state the same kindly consideration that our Government exhibited toward the repatriated Filipino, I would meet the expectations of the friends who had vouched for me. I also resolved that I would pay a little attention to the study of eugenics myself.

The opportunity came soon enough. It was the time of great civic awakening and the state had just erected a magnificent asylum for the chronic insane that was designed for the purpose of relieving the almshouses of the burden of caring for the incurables who had been returned to county care after years of residence in the state hospitals for the insane.

I plunged into the work at once. Building operations, which had been in progress during my three years' absence, were just about completed and as each section became available we sent out for fifty or a hundred waiting inmates, selected from lists previously secured from almshouse superintendents. Never again will there come a time in my native state when so much human misery will be transported across its prairies in so short a period. The reader has only to refer to the press of that day to learn of the skeletons unearthed from the poor house closets.

They were brought in parties ranging from half a dozen to an entire coach load. An atmosphere of expectancy pervaded our institution and each batch of new arrivals drew a group of willing workers to the station, all eager to do their part in making the newcomers feel at home.

Many had to be carried to the wards on stretchers, some were blind, among them were dwarfs, idiots, half-wits and many so violently insane that they had been kept in seclusion for years. One coach with a load from another state hospital had every window protected by wooden slats fastened to the sash. Many were in mechanical restraint and a wholly unnecessary number of attendants or guards accompanied them. One woman in particular, whose case subsequently attained nationwide publicity and who had been an inmate of a cell in a poor house forty-three years and who had torn out her own eyeballs, had her body so distorted that she was carried in an ordinary clothes basket.

But all this is ancient history of the very recent past and merely leads up to an occurrence which for a time shook the entire charitable service of the state, made fugitives of several county officials and brought into being the subject of this story.

A few days after a coach load of women had been received, one of my most trusted nurses came timidly to my desk and in the most embarrassed manner said: "Doctor, I think it would be well for you to go over to Cottage No. 7 to see a woman whose appearance is suspicious. I have intended speaking to the ward doctor about it but could not muster the courage to do so."

I did not need to be told what her suspicions were. The agitation for the creation of our institution had frequently alluded to the danger which the female insane of the almshouse were exposed. I grabbed my hat and immediately proceeded to the cottage calling the chief nurse and any physician I met en route. We all reached there about the same time and the attendants promptly brought the patient into the reception room. The diagnosis was instantaneously and unanimously concurred in. Within an hour she was in the maternity ward of our hospital and dispatches were flying to the governor, the board of charities and to the judge and state's attorney of the woman's home county.

Institutional occurrences are often grossly distorted and pitiless publicity was our surest safeguard. Just one week from the date of her admission, she gave birth to a healthy girl baby.

Of the subsequent legal developments it is needless to speak. The woman was thirty-six years old, and so wholly demented that she knew neither time, place nor person. She had for seven years occupied a cell in a poorhouse, hence it was easy to trace responsibility to that institution. A degenerate deputy, who carried keys to all rooms, admitted his guilt by hastily quitting the state.

However, these matters concerned the prosecuting authorities. Our responsibilities had to do with the care of the mother and the newborn child. The former made an uneventful recovery and was soon back in the custodial ward among one hundred others who were classified according to the mistaken nomenclature of that day as Terminal Dements.

But the baby! She instantly became the pet of the institution. Nurses, the moment they were relieved from duty, rushed over to the hospital to overwhelm the innocent little creature with attention. Finally, we had to arrange a schedule by which three girls took charge of her in relays of eight hours each, off time. They, in turn, found a trustworthy patient who assumed its care and who remained its foster-mother during the four years it remained with us.

And those were four years of attention that few children have been privileged to enjoy. Willing hands provided the most exquisite embroideries, others purchased a handsome baby buggy, a perambulator was available before it could even stand and its little nursery was strewn with dolls and toys. Later, when she could run about the porches out on the lawns, she wore dresses that the children of the rich might envy -- all gifts of the attendants.

Old Lena, who became her foster-mother, guarded her jealously and when she began to talk, saw to it that she never heard an improper word. While presents were being showered upon the little one, she was enriching us, for her very presence was a benediction. Her home was in one of our cottages accommodating sixty of our least insane women. They were mostly mild mannered seniles whose memories were of the distant past. The advent of the baby seemed to bring them down to the present though, and it was a charming sight to enter the big day room and see a circle of elderly ladies eagerly interested in the antics of the baby as it played among its toys on the floor. The first thought of the average visitor was that the child was in danger, but the fear was quickly dispelled when he saw the expression of interest and affection on the faces of the patients.

We often brought the mother into its presence but never a sign of recognition was observed. For this we were really grateful, as otherwise we would have felt constrained to permit her to have a share in its bringing up, an association that would probably have been of no benefit to her and might have been prejudicial to the child. Occasionally, the authorities at the capital would send an agent of the children's bureau to report upon its progress and he would intimate to that the time was approaching when it must be "placed."

It was the day we dreaded, yet we knew that the child could not permanently continue in that atmosphere. We had begun to think of the time it would go off with other children to the adjacent school but when we thought of the humiliation it would feel when its playmates would finally acquaint it with the gruesome facts of its heredity, as school children invariably and tantalizingly will, we concluded that the supervising authorities were correct in their stand. We could not allow our affection for the child to interfere with its future.

Through the medium of the juvenile court, the placing of dependent children in our state is surrounded by every safeguard. The prospective home is carefully inspected and the character of the foster parents thoroughly inquired into. Before proceedings were instituted, I asked the court for a special concession and that was to permit the child to be taken from the state.

I knew an eastern banker who had been blessed with everything but children. His wife was a cultured woman and both were descendants of some of America's best and oldest families. Their home reflected their splendid intellectual endowments as well as their great wealth. They had been seeking the adoption of a little girl whose identity, after being legally placed in their custody, could not be traced. Even the child was never to know the couple other than as natural parents. This they found difficult as there was always a state agent, a parent or a probation officer who must have cognizance of the child's new environment. Fortunately, the banker was on intimate terms with the chief justice of his state and he prevailed upon that official to visit the judge of the juvenile court and assure him that the people with whom it was proposed to place the child were of such high quality and the home surroundings so perfect that he could ledge his word as a jurist that its future would in every way be safeguarded.

The judge, himself an indulgent father, knowing the tragedy of its birth and the shadows which might be thrown across its path through life, wisely concluded that it would be best to wholly obliterate the past and therefore out of a sense of judicial courtesy entered upon his docket "that case Number 141, female child, age four, be adopted by John Doe, with permission to take it beyond the borders of the state," observing only the precaution of having me sign the nominal bond required in such cases.

About the hardest part of the procedure was when I saw the entire party leave the courtroom without a look in my direction. This was prearranged, as the banker was particularly anxious that every avenue of future identification be closed.

I returned to the institution in no cheerful mood and the gloom on the faces of the attendants had a further depressing effect. It was previous to the time that the Geneva Cross had been copyrighted and we flew from our staff a red cross flag that could be seen for miles. The fact that it stood at half mast as I came up the hill was quite in keeping with my feelings and when I inquired about it the chief nurse said that Old Lena had gone out on the brow and lowered in a fit of despondency over her loss. We had never given the little girl any other name than Josephine, feeling that some day a surname would be attached through adoption.

An hour later, I received a telephone call from the lady in charge of the children's counter of the leading downtown department store. She said that a governess came in and bought half a dozen complete outfits for a little four year old girl, selecting the finest and most expensive in the house, then took the child into the dressing room, removed every stitch of clothing and clad her from head to foot with the new garments and asked that the bundle of discarded clothes be sent to the state hospital for the benefit of any needy chid. She said she wondered about the woman's credit but when she paid the entire amount in crisp greenbacks and added fifty dollars to be distributed among the needy, she realized that she was dealing with people of wealth. I could have told her that the private car of a railroad director was waiting on a side track to take the governess, the child and its foster parents to the new home in a western city to which they had decided to move in order to avoid any possibility of revealing the identity of the child. I could also have told her something of the former wearer of the discarded clothes, but I didn't.

Year after year rolled by, each filled with its quota of official burdens and strange occurrences. I did not correspond with the doctor nor with the banker. It was not necessary. Their names were sufficiently often in the public print, always in connection with some laudable undertaking, to keep me informed of their movements. Dr. Vender dropped in on me occasionally en route to Boston where his son, as certain as the Moslem to Mecca, had been attracted to Harvard.

When returning from his graduation the young man, at his father's request, spent six months as an interne with us in order to acquaint himself with institutional life. He was indeed a superb fellow -- all that his father could have desired. He had not yet become an eugenist but he exhibited every movement and expression of his high linage. He confided to me that his future was particularly rosy, as he was about to succeed to his father's practice and was engaged to the most charming girl west of the Mississippi. She was the daughter of a leading western financier of revolutionary ancestry and a mother of equal heritage who spent half her time near the fashionable boarding school in which her daughter was being educated, later accompanying her on a tour of Europe, ending with a finishing course in an exclusive French seminary.

Of course, I could excuse the young man's ardor but sometimes on my rounds with him I would stop and point out some particularly deteriorated patient and disabuse him of his set belief that these people had never been possessed of an intellect. I will confess that my knees trembled as I stopped in front of one particular woman, prematurely aged and wholly demented, and said:

180

"Now there is a woman who is wholly disoriented yet the tragedy of her life may be far-reaching and might extend to persons of distinction. Fortunately or unfortunately for them, her identity is totally obscured. She will pass out of our jurisdiction as case No. 4141 and even the name she bears may be fictitious."

My object was to impress upon him with the thought that a public charge should never be considered as a mere case but that each should be studied as an individual and every effort made to restore the latent intellect.

I was particular to impress upon him that acquired insanity was not transmissible and that only born defectives conveyed their abnormality to the next generation and that there were many striking exceptions even to this rule.

He said: "That may all be true, but I would hesitate to marry into a family of the heredity of the woman we just saw."

Again I felt shaky as I went with him to the maternity ward and called the attention of the nurse to the fact that the little girls were not dressed well enough. She told me that the supply of clothing was running low and when I pointed to a large box on a shelf she said:

"Why, doctor, don't you know about that box? It is filled with baby clothes and has been standing on that shelf unopened for fifteen years. It was there when I came and the girls told me that there is a tradition or a sentiment that says it must remain there until its former owner marries and has a baby, when it is to be sent as an anonymous gift."

I told her that institutions should foster sentiment in every way but that tradition is one of the things that stands in the way of progress. We ordered the box opened and the pretty garments distributed. The group of little tots scrambled over each other in trying to get a part of the richly embroidered stuff.

As we came away, the doctor said it must have been an unusual child that had worn such finery.

"Yes, it was an unusual child and she is wearing even finer clothes today."

At the conclusion of his internship he proceeded to his home and in due time we received cards to a wedding, "which marked the union of two of the most promising young people of the state, at which the elite of the country were present, including many guests from New England where the families of both contracting parties are highly connected."

About five years later I received a telegram from Dr. Vender asking me to come to his home on a professional errand. I went at once, knowing that he would only send for me on a matter of importance. Upon arrival, he told me that the call concerned one of his grandchildren. My voice quavered as I asked: "What, is one of your son's children afflicted?"

"On, no, it is my daughter's little three year old boy. You see she married a splendid young man who worked his way through college and who has risen to the head of his profession and is frequently mentioned as gubernatorial timber. He is a self-made man, the son of sturdy settlers, but I haven't been able to trace their genealogy back to the parent stock, so the slow development of this, their second child has given me much concern.

We went over to the young attorney's home and entered a domestic circle as charming as the fondest parent could wish. The little fellow that was causing so much anxiety was playing with building blocks and screaming with delight when his castles and structures collapsed.

Although not a psycho-analyst, I had seen my assistants apply it so often that I was familiar with at least the Binet-Simon test and it did not take long to determine that the little chap was not only normal mentally but exceedingly bright. He simply showed a slight retardation of speech. Everything he saw he called "Ooh" or "gooh." In this he did not differ from his parents or grandfather who persisted in using childish prattle instead of straight English when talking to him. I told him that I could plainly see that he had allowed his feelings to prevent him from calling in a specialist who could have removed his fears as quickly as I did.

"And now," he said, "we will go over to our house. My son will be more than anxious to see you. He treasures his internship in your institution as one of the milestones in his life. He never tires of telling of some of the characters he saw there and often recites the incident when you distributed a lot of baby clothes to a group of half orphans."

No need to describe the doctor's home. Enough has been said to indicate that it was all that his wealth and position and ancestry would insist that it be. It was a charming family dinner. The young doctor was present with his wife and two beautiful children. One was a girl four years old! She sat opposite me in a highchair and as I listened to the elder physician's discussion of eugenics, breeding and heredity, I kept observing the actions and manner of the little girl until at times I must have seemed inattentive to my host. In retrospection, I was back on the asylum hill or once more in the juvenile court. The intervening twenty years were swept away by every attitude of the little grandchild.

And what a magnificent woman her mother was! Radiant maternity shone from her eyes and her speech reflected the splendid educational advantages that had been hers. With pardonable pride her young husband told me how she had headed every patriotic move through the war, yet had found time to make daily visits to the orphan asylum of which she was a trustee and had never failed to attend the meetings of the board of visitors of the insane asylum, a position that the governor of the state had prevailed upon her to take in recognition of her great interest in the mentally afflicted.

During a lull in the elder physician's dissertation on eugenics I leaned across the table and said to the little girl:

"Tell me your name."

She promptly replied, "Josephine."

I then complimented the father upon his choice saying it had been a family name in our home for several generations and that the most interesting child I ever knew bore that name. He said, "I didn't name her. I wanted her named Abigail for my great grandmother and her grandparents each had a favorite name, but her mother said the name Josephine kept ringing in her ears long before the child was born and we were glad to let her have her way, although the name differed from those of the colonial ancestors on both sides."

I again impressed upon the mother the appropriateness of her choice and told the father that the great west had become great by reason of the sterling qualities of the constitutional fathers but that it had been necessary to discard a thousand and one traditions in meeting the problems that arose on every hand in its rapid upbuilding. What's in a name!

I would also have liked to say to the elder physician that not a small part of the success of our wonderful democracy was due to the law of natural selection in choosing helpmates and that eugenics, that is, applied eugenics, had been left to the pendant, the blue-stocking, the highbrow and stockman, but I couldn't afford to give him an opening for the resumption of his hobby. The crust upon which we stood was altogether too thin.

I did not call on the banker, although I stepped into a telephone booth at the depot and conversed with him. He was as anxious to see me as I to see him but we were both thinking of the incident of twenty years ago and the sacred bond of silence that had never been broken and which, in view of its happy outcome, must forever be maintained inviolate.

Dr. Vender, just before my train was due, thanked me profusely for the reassuring news that I had brought him, but even at this final parting he could not refrain from delivering a lecture on eugenics.

"You know, Doctor, I was greatly puzzled about my daughter's child. I knew her husband was faultless but I could not feel sure of his offspring. You see., he has no family tree and, of course, *knowing him as a young man of excellent habits whose parents were of the vigorous stock that reclaimed these western plains, I could not be so indelicate as to inquire beyond them. When the little boy was slow in developing speech, I became alarmed and sent for you. I did not feel like calling in even the most trusted local physician. I am greatly relieved to know that the child is normal. It was my one great dread.*

"Now, in the case of my son's wife, I had nothing to fear. Her parents are the very leaders of this section. Her father is of revolutionary stock, a banker and a railroad director, and her mother of even superior ancestry. I would have taken you up to their palatial home, as I am sure they would have deemed it a pleasure to entertain you, but I knew your time was limited and my son's wife insisted that you spend the evening with us. Ah, but she is a fine young woman. No fear of a blemish in the offspring of mothers like her. You can realize what a satisfaction it is to a student of eugenics like myself to see his only son married to a girl whose ancestors can not only be traced but who measure up in every particular to his own. In the case of my daughter's husband there might have been a shade of doubt, but the heredity of my son's wife is clearly established."

"Yes," I said as the train pulled up, "one look at her little Josephine reminded me of that."

* * *

Arguably, one of the most well-known or talked about patients to have lived at the Peoria State Hospital is "Old Book" or "Manual Bookbinder." Almost anyone who has a modicum of knowledge regarding the history of the Peoria State Hospital is familiar with the story of "Old Book" and the legend of the "Graveyard Elm." This story has been told so many times that it has become an urban legend.

"Old Book," it is said, received his name when he was committed to the Peoria State Hospital. Apparently, at the time of his admission, he had lost his ability to speak and, since it was known that his profession was that of a bookbinder, he was admitted under the name of "A Bookbinder." Over the years he would come to be known simply as "Old Book."

His story has been reported by the local media numerous times. One such story appeared on Sunday, June 30, 1974, in the **Peoria Journal Star**. It is not clear as to what records were utilized by the **Peoria Journal Star** for this article. According to this article:

> One of the stones in cemetery two contains the number 713 and records indicate that this is the grave of one Manual bookbinder, a native of Austria. A psychotic, he was admitted to the hospital sometime in 1904 at the age of 26. The records also say that he died there of pellagra in 1910.
>
> What the records do not say is if this patient could also be "Old Book," an inmate whose real name was never known.
>
> Nor do the records give any hint of the mystery that surrounds "Old Book's" death, or the drama that was played out at his burial, of the legend that grew around the magnificent elm that once stood near his grave. "Old Book" was a mystery even to those who knew him including Dr. George A. Zeller.[4]

There are no direct references to "Old Book" to be found in the Biennial Reports. However, if one looks in the statistical tables in the "Sixth Biennial Report of the Commissioner, Superintendent, and Treasurer of the Illinois Asylum for the Incurable Insane at Peoria" on page 32 listed under the "Nativity of All Patients Present June 30, 1906, there are six male patients from Austria. The "Eighth Biennial Report" contains, on page 8, a report dealing with an outbreak of pellagra. This same report claims that there were thirty-eight male deaths attributed to the pellagra outbreak. One could claim that this does in some ways substantiate the claims that there were thirty-eight male deaths attributed to the pellagra outbreak. One could claim that this does in some ways substantiate the claims made by the **Peoria Journal Star**.

The most reliable evidence that "Old Book" did actually exist was found in a 1905, Supervisors Journal A-1. This ledger contained the clothing accounts of the patients at the Peoria State Hospital. On pages two and twenty-four there are entries indicating that Bookbinder M. received a total of six handkerchiefs with a total value of twelve cents.

The picture on the left is the journal in which the name of Bookbinder, M. was found on page 2 and page 24. The picture below clearly shows the name of Bookbinder, M.

Zeller Library

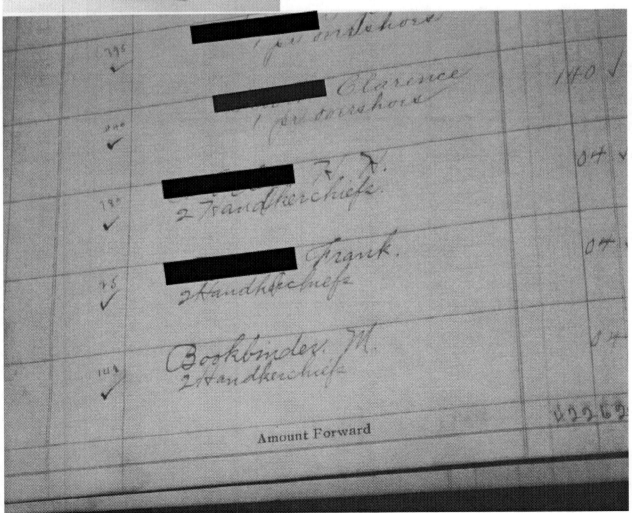

Amount Forward

There is no doubt that there was a patient at the Peoria State Hospital named M. Bookbinder. It is up to the individual to decide if the following story is actually based upon his tenure at the Peoria State Hospital. It will never be known with any certainty if Dr. Zeller embellished the story of this particular patient and took him from relative ambiguity to fame. One thing is certain, the mystery surrounding this patient has gained, for "Old Book" and the hospital, a certain notoriety.

This picture is of the cemetery in which "Old Book" is thought to be interred. Grave 713 is located behind the tree, but the stone marking this particular grave is missing.

The Graveyard Elm

When the governor placed me in charge of the big new asylum for the insane that the state had just erected, I recognized that along with the problem of the living, the disposal of the deal was one that must also have its share of attention.

We buried only the bodies of the friendless and unclaimed, as the remains of the well-to-do were shipped at the expense of the friends and relatives to such points as they designated.

As the rows of headstones multiplied and extended, our cemetery became an object of interest and the impressive service that marked each funeral were largely attended.

The burial corps consisted of a reliable employee and a half dozen insane men who were handy with the spade and who went mechanically through the process of digging a grave and just as mechanically refilled it after the coffin had been lowered.

As our inmates exceeded 2,000 in number, composed largely of patients of advanced years who were in indigent circumstances, our death rate was not only very high, but the percentage left with us for burial was unusually large.

The grave diggers were, for this reason, pretty constantly engaged and, between burials, setting up markers and keeping the weeds down were relieved of all other duties.

The institutional population was most cosmopolitan in its makeup and contained many interesting characters, with every conceivable vagary but the most unique of them all was A. Bookbinder.

He was sent to us from one of the larger poorhouses and bore mute evidence of the carelessness that is so often shown in the commitment of the insane, especially in the large cities.

When his malady seized him he was working in a printing house and as his mental aberration manifested itself in the loss of coherent speech the officer who took him into custody merely reported to the court that he was a bookbinder.

As he could not express himself in writing the clerk gave as his name that of his calling and he was committed to us A. Bookbinder.

The perversion of his name extended even farther for the terminal syllables were soon dropped and except upon the official records he became known to us as "Old Book."

He was strong and healthy, considerably demented but harmless, and the attendants were not long in finding in him a desirable worker and in time he became a member of the burial corps.

He developed a very interesting trait at the first funeral in which he participated. Ordinarily when the coffin was being lowered the shovelers stood back, silently awaiting the end of the ceremony, when they would lay to with vigor and complete the interment.

The dead were all strangers to us and our ceremony was simply a mark of respect rather than an indication of personal attachment to the deceased. Therefore, it may be imagined how surprised we were when, at the critical moment, Old Book removed his cap, began to wipe his eyes and finally give vent to loud lamentations. The first few times he did this his emotion became contagious and there were many moist eyes at the graveside, but when at each succeeding burial his feeling overcame him it was realized that Book was possessed of a mania that manifested itself in an uncontrollable grief.

Those of us who had studied association tests could see in this symptom the revival of some great crisis through which he had passed, some mighty sorrow he had experienced and which in itself might have been the cause of the dethronement of his reason.

On this account no one made light of his grief and everyone felt that if this poor friendless mortal could find relief for his great sorrow in tears it was better than he do so than suppress them.

"Book" had no favorites among the dead and he never varied the routine of his mourning. At the psychological moment he would step back, spade in hand, in an attitude of waiting. First his left and then his right sleeve would be raised to wipe away a furtive tear but as the coffin began to descend into the grave he would walk over and lean against the big elm that stood in the center of the lot and give vent to sobs that convulsed his frame and which could be heard by the entire assemblage.

The tree was of magnificent proportions and was of the variety known as the Ulmus Americana, or spreading elm. It had so long cast its shadow over the surrounding area that all other trees were dwarfed and its generous branches afforded shelter to hundreds of patients who sought this means of escape from the sun's rays during the hot summer months.

It was one of the finest of its species in the state and as "The Graveyard Elm" had been photographed many times and its picture had even found its way into our annual reports.

Birds built their nests in it and rabbits burrowed beneath its roots, for our premises being state property, were closed to hunters and it did not take long for the denizens of the forest to discover that the right of asylum extended to them as well as to the 2,000 unfortunate humans who were consigned to our care. This peaceful security extending to bird and beast, tree and shrub, flower and man blended them all into a gentle harmony that gave an atmosphere to the place that all visitors recognized and the institution became widely and favorably known for its motto, "Sane Surroundings for the Insane."

The infirmities of age and intercurrent disease continued to deplete our population about as fast as it was recruited. We were singularly free from epidemics and even from fatal accidents, but the average age of our inmates was fifty-eight years and we could not stay the hands of Father Time.

The only exercise that "Old Book" took consisted of attending funerals.

His long association with these functions had made him a fixture and a funeral would not have been considered complete without his presence.

The nurse in charge of his ward had a profound respect for his mania and always kept him posted as to the next funeral. If the weather was inclement they dressed him accordingly and not infrequently accompanied him, for our nurses flocked to the cemetery in large numbers on these occasions. Age did not lessen his outburst of grief but rather accentuated them, but on the other hand he suffered ten times more when deprived of the privilege of giving vent to his feelings, as was shown on one occasion when the hearse passed his cottage while taking a corpse uptown for shipment. It was with utmost difficulty that they were able to convince him that the body was not to be interred in our cemetery.

In the natural order of events it came Book's turn to be carried to his last resting place and, as might be inferred, this was an event that exited more than usual interest. The news spread rapidly that "Book" had shed his last tear and through that quick process by which word passes among the employees of an institution, it was agreed that they attend his funeral in a body.

It was an impressive sight. The hour was set for noon of a beautiful June day, a time that permitted the greatest attendance, and everyone came. Over against the hillside more than a hundred uniformed nurses were grouped like a great bank of white lilies while around the grave stood the staff and a large force of men, together with several hundred privileged patients. As was not infrequently the case, I officiated in person. The coffin rested upon two crossbeams over the open grave and four sturdy men stood by ready to man the ropes by which it was to be lowered. Just as the choir finished the last line of "Rock of Ages" the men grasped the ropes, stooped forward, and with a powerful muscular effort prepared to lift the coffin in order to permit the removal of the crossbeams and allow it to gently descend into the grave.

At a given signal they heaved away at the ropes and the next instant all four lay prone on their backs; for the coffin, instead of offering resistance, bounded into the air like an eggshell as if it were empty.

Any untoward occurrence at a burial is regrettable and always creates consternation and in this instance the effect was no less pronounced. The nurses shrieked and half of them ran away while the other half came over to the grave to see what the excitement was about.

In the midst of all this commotion a wailing voice was heard and every eye turned toward the big elm whence it emanated. Every man and woman stood transfixed, for there, just as had always been the case, stood "Old Book" weeping and moaning with an earnestness that outrivaled anything he had every shown before.

We could not be mistaken. It was the same, "Old Book" and there was the same old cloth cap and the same handkerchief around the neck, and the attitude with which we were all familiar.

I am not superstitious, and continuous association with the insane had long ago taught me to avoid psychic contamination, therefore I, in common with the other bystanders, stood transfixed at the sight of this apparition. There stood the nurses who were at his bedside when he died, there was the undertaker who had embalmed his body and the six men who as pallbearers had carried the heavy coffin from the hearse and placed it over the grave, yet there in plain sight and in the attitude so familiar to all of us stood "Book."

Even though he had been invisible his lamentations would have been sufficient to identify him. It was broad daylight and there could be no deception.

No one moved or spoke and a paralytic fear came over us.

Finally I took the initiative and summoned the helpers to remove the coffin lid.

Their hands trembled as they loosened the screws. Most of the bystanders turned their faces away. I nerved myself to step forward in order to peer into the empty coffin but just as they lifted the lid the wailing sound ceased and at the identical moment we gazed upon the calm features of our old mourner.

There he lay, cold in death dressed in his somber shroud with his hands folded across his breast. Everybody was invited to file by and identify the remains but it was noticed that after casting a glance at the corpse every eye wandered over to the old elm. The tree stood there in all its stateliness -- the apparition had vanished -- and the funeral was completed as if it had not suffered this uncanny interruption except that many were weeping throughout the delayed ceremony.

It was awful but it was real. I saw it, a hundred nurses saw it -- three hundred spectators saw and heard it.

I am not over credulous. Long residence among the primitive peoples of our Island possessions has schooled me against the acceptance of many popular beliefs, but this vision I can never dismiss from my mind.

It has this compensating feature that when those who participated in the drama tried to recite the incident to their friends they were promptly disbelieved and I was entirely willing to have the occurrence pass as a fantasy of institutional life.

I was doomed to have it revived a few weeks later, however, when the keeper of the cemetery came over to the office and said, "Doctor, there is something the matter with the Graveyard Elm, it seems to be withering and, although I have had the men pour hundreds of buckets of water about its roots every leaf has shriveled and I am afraid that it can not be saved."

There was nothing to do and in a few weeks it was bare of leaves and by late fall many of its lesser twigs had fallen.

In the course of time other braces dropped until finally only the main stem and large forks remained. There it stood plainly outlined against the sky, a monarch of the forest still, in spite of the absence of life. On a moonlight night its giant arms resembled those of a human skeleton and it came to be looked upon with a feeling of awe and dread, yet no one was willing to undertake the task of cutting it down.

One of our men tried it but at the first stroke he threw down his axe and ran to his quarters declaring that in the clouds of smoke that curled upward he could plainly outline the features of our departed mourner.

There is one unmarked grave in the cemetery and when visitors comment on the missing monument the guide hastily changes the subject and points with a shudder to the Graveyard Elm.

* * *

The last story is "Fainting Fanny." On Sunday, June 14, 1908, the <u>Peoria Journal</u> ran the following story:

Fainting Bertha Skips the Tra-La-Lu

Bertha Liebbecke, otherwise and more generally known to fame and the police, penitentiary wardens and asylum attendants of half the cities of the country as "Fainting Bertha," made her escape from the general asylum for the insane at South Bartonville last night and up to 2 o'clock this morning had not been found, though a large force of attendants are searching and the police and sheriff's forces in every town and county adjacent is on the lookout for her.

Bertha was in the Joliet penitentiary when she developed insanity and was brought to South Bartonville. There she still further complicated matters by a consumptive tendency. She was placed in the tuberculosis tent colony and within the last few months has shown a vast improvement and gained 17 pounds. Her blond good looks came back to her and she evidently made up her mind to move on.

She played a pretty trick in getting away. She has been allowed a little freedom of the ground adjacent to the colony under the eyes of the attendants and early last evening managed to transfer an old lady from another tent to her own and tucked her up snugly in bed. The old lady was missed early in the evening and a search instituted. Its culmination came at 9 o'clock when she was found peacefully snoring in Bertha's bed.

Bertha is still going. Just where she will turn up next is a matter that time only can tell. Her mother lives in Council Bluffs, Iowa.[5]

Two weeks later, on Monday, June 29, 1908, the <u>Peoria Journal</u> would report on Fainting Bertha and her propensity for escape once again.

Fainting Bertha, Will-O-Wisp
ONCE MORE ELUDES VIGILANCE OF ASYLUM ATTENDANTS
Captured Near Iowa Junction
Midnight Escapade Causes Epidemic Of Nervous Prostration South Bartonville Institution

Non-restraint is the case of Bertha Liebbecke -- more widely known to fame as "Fainting Bertha" -- is rapidly resulting in the General Asylum for the Insane South Bartonville. Bertha is "Will-O-The-Wisp" if the attendants' eye is off her for a minute and there is a crack big enough for a draft to come through; it is over the hills far away for Bertha. Her numerous getaways and recaptures are becoming an old tale.

It's A Habit

Among Bertha's more recent escapades is putting a well-nigh bedridden old woman from another ward in her bed and while the attendants were looking for the old woman, secure in the knowledge that she wouldn't get far away, Bertha was heading for Bridge Street, Peoria, where she was found a day or two later by the police. Last Friday night she vanished again and the woods were full of white aproned nurses until she was rounded up near Hollis and remained captive until male attendants arrived.

Midnight Getaway

This time it was about 11:30 when the nurse in C-5 Cottage had her back in bed for a moment. She had left Bertha slumbering sweetly and with her musical snores sounding in rhythm. She came back to find the cot empty and a window open which showed the way the flaxen-haired adventurer had gone, clad in sweet dishabille and such garments as she could catch up in transit.

Soon Brought Back

The general alarm was sounded and scores of attendants ranged the adjacent landscape, gradually widening their field of observation until shortly after midnight when Bertha was sighted near the Iowa Junction, two miles away and once more returned to the bosom of the paternal State Institution. It is evident something will have to be done with Bertha. She got out of the penitentiary and into the asylum by acting if she were insane -- perhaps she is. Then she got out of the asylum and into the tent colony by giving every appearance of tuberculosis in its worst form.

What's To Be Done

She has recovered, evidently, from tuberculosis but if the wander lust continues she will bring down Dr. Zeller's whitening locks in sorrow to the grave, while Head Physician Michell and the rank and file of attendants will be nervous wrecks.[6]

The following is Dr. Zeller's short story which may be attributed to Fainting Bertha.

Fainting Fanny

It would be idle to give Fanny's real name and, for that matter, it would be next to an impossibility. She was known to the police of twenty cities under twice that number of aliases but out of all this maze of names that of "Fainting Fanny" survived.

She was a thief, adventuress, pickpocket, shoplifter and fence, all in one. She had been under arrest hundreds of times for petty offenses and had been convicted of felony and had served in the penitentiaries of three states, always securing release through feigning insanity.

Her favorite method of procedure when "on the road" was to fall in a faint in a crowd and have kindly disposed bystanders carry her to some nearby shelter. These philanthropic individuals would discover later that, somehow, in the process of transporting the woman they had been relieved of a watch, a stickpin, or a purse, and in the course of time, she became known to the authorities as the most adroit swindler and confidence woman in the Mississippi Valley.

An ordinary jail would not hold her. She was such an expert at picking locks and obtaining possession of keys that jailers had almost a superstitious fear of her prowess.

When every other resource failed her she would be seized with a fainting spell and this was sure to cause her removal to the parlor or the hospital of the jail and while convalescing she would plan escape and invariably accomplish it. Her feigning was so artistically done that even the most hard-hearted sheriff would relax the rigid rules of the prison in order to make suitable provision for a sick woman. No officer cared to assume the risk of having a female prisoner die in a cell, unattended, and Fanny was careful not to offend in this particular. She not only survived these attacks but just as her condition seemed most critical and the jail attendant most fearful of the outcome, they would find her cot empty and the prisoner missing.

She found it impossible to escape from the penitentiaries; hence she would feign insanity and the warden would recommend her transfer to an insane asylum. In this manner she became known to many state institutions and her escapades gained wide publicity

In one of these asylums she donned a suit of men's clothing which she had, in some manner, surreptitiously smuggled into the ward. As she was an expert at embroidery she had possession of a pair of scissors and with these she cropped her hair close. Then she begrimed her face and hands with ink and floor polish and suddenly appeared before the nurses in the dayroom of the ward. They were horrified to discover a man invading a ward for female patients and promptly ordered "him" out, at the

191

same time telephoning headquarters to go after an escaped male patient who had wandered into their cottage and whom they had just sent adrift.

The nurses, when questioned, knew nothing of the man except that they had promptly ordered him out when he so unexpectedly entered the sitting room of the ward. It was then decided to interrogate the patients, who although insane, had among their number many of surprising intelligence. Among these was Fainting Fanny and it was decided to question her first of all. The nurses called her name up and down the halls and in the various bed rooms without response. A systematic search of the premises failed to discover her, yet it did not occur to anyone to associate her with the man that the nurses had driven from the ward.

The attendants in all of the male wards were directed to count their patients to determine where the man belonged, but no one was missing, all being present and accounted for.

The affair began to grown on my nerves. I had been the head of the institution for fifteen years and had seen it win recognition all over the world for its liberality toward the patients and for the unconscious discipline and unrelaxing vigilance with which it was conducted. Particularly did it excel in its leniency toward women inmates. The women patients roamed about the grounds quite as freely as the men. Apparently they were unattended but somewhere the watchful eye of a nurse was always upon them and what appeared to be a very careless and indifferent supervision was in reality the closest kind of human espionage.

Fanny was kept in this manner. She had made her escape from numerous institutions but when transferred to ours, it was decided that, since locks, bolts and screens would not hold her it might be well to give her a trial of our open door policy.

Before the search of the cottages had proceeded very far the nurses discovered Fanny's dress and outer garments tucked under the mattress of her bed and it soon dawned upon them that the "man" whom they had so unceremoniously driven out into the night was none other than Fanny herself.

It did not take long to act and in a few minutes the police of half a dozen towns were on the lookout for a man of small stature, with hair of light shade and close cropped, and wearing a grey suit and cloth cap.

She had been classed as a paranoiac, her particular psychosis being that of kleptomania. She was exceedingly shrewd in shoplifting but at the same time would give away valuable articles thus obtained to newsboys on the street or to maids of the hotels. She had been known to register in three hotels under three assumed names in one city in a single day and to fill a room in each with valuable loot before nightfall.

We depended upon this reckless disregard of the usual safeguards observed by the fugitive and were not mistaken.

Within two hours the police notified us that the patient was in the detention room at the city hall and two exceptionally reliable nurses were detailed to proceed there at once. This they did and the patient was back in her cottage before daylight.

Her detention had been simple enough. In her flight she had gone down a nearby ravine to the wagon road along which she proceeded leisurely to town. By the time she reached the city her shoes were thoroughly covered with mud and her vanity led her straight into the nearest shoe shining parlor. The Greek who proceeded to apply the polish may or may not have been surprised to have a man take his place on the bench and put forth a tiny foot encased in a woman's shoe, but he certainly was astonished when on the completion of the job the customer started to leave the shop without tendering the usual nickel, which, considering the amount of mud on the shoes might well in this instance, have been a dime. When he expostulated with her, she simply informed him that she had left her purse at home and would return later and pay the bill with interest. Had the Greek been as wily as his ancestors he *would have waited, for thirty minutes among a crowd of shoppers meant half a dozen pocketbooks for Fanny and it is likely that she would have well rewarded him.*

However, he was doing business on a cash basis and could not afford to be beaten out of the price of even one shine. So when she left, he quietly slipped out of the shop and pointed her out to the nearest policeman.

It happened that the officer had just received instructions to look out for an individual whose description tallied with that of the person designated by the Greek, and one look at the newly polished shoes convinced him that this was the escaped patient from the asylum. He escorted her to the police matron. That worthy individual was almost as much shocked at having the department for women invaded by a man as the nurses at the asylum had been in the earlier part of the evening, when the male apparition so suddenly and unexpectedly intruded, but upon the assurance of the police officer that the prisoner was really a woman masquerading in male attire, she consented to hold her until arrival of the nurses from the institution.

Of course, when Fanny realized that she was again in custody she threw the regulation fit, fainted once or twice, demanded fresh air and in every way tried to divert the attention of the authorities but it was all in vain, as they were thoroughly posted as to all of her subterfuges.

With the approach of spring, Fanny, never robust, began to show unmistakable signs of tuberculosis. She lost weight and had a persistent cough and her cheeks showed a hectic flush. I told the doctors to be particularly on their guard against deception, and the nurses were instructed to observe whether she was eating soap or resorting to any of the devices so common among those who had been inmates of prison. They reported that her symptoms were genuine, that she did not eat her meals and that she coughed much during the night. The thermometer showed the usual slight rise of temperature and above all, the microscope showed in the sputum the presence of tubercle bacilli in large numbers.

Even the craftiest malingerer could not simulate these symptoms, so we ordered the patient transferred to the tent colony, our open door and open air hospital for consumptives.

Fanny exhibited a commendable gratitude at thus having placed at her disposal curative agencies which only the wealthy members of the community at large could demand. The colony afforded her an excellent opportunity for demonstrating her culinary accomplishments and both patients and nurses lived high from the day of her transfer. Very often the entire ward dined out in the woods, under the trees and on these occasions Fanny assumed the role of hostess and contributed to an unusual degree to the palatableness of the lunch.

As might be expected this radical change in her diet and environment wrought a rapid and favorable change in her physical and mental condition. She gained weight at the rate of two pounds a week and the hectic flush disappeared from her cheeks.

Unconsciously, as her condition improved our vigilance relaxed and Fanny, instead of being a closely guarded patient, became a valuable aid to the nurses and assisted in the care of the sick.

On the first day of June we had a reassignment of the nursing staff and a new attendant who had reported for duty that day was detailed as night watch of the tent colony after having been specially instructed to keep an observing eye upon Fanny. About an hour before daylight the night physician was summoned to come to the colony in all haste, as Fanny's cot was empty and it was evident that she had made a successful escape. The night watch was nearly frantic and wrung her hands in despair, assuming all the blame and begging us to accept her resignation and permit her to return to her home and thus escape service in a field to which she was not suited.

There were half a dozen of us present, as it was customary to call the superintendent and staff officers whenever a great emergency arose, and the escape of an ex-convict was always considered an emergency.

We calmed the agitation of the nurse by assuring her that she was not to be held responsible, that the fault was ours for having assigned her to so difficult a task on the very first night of her service. We prevailed upon her to go to bed and rest and told her that the fugitive might be apprehended by the time she would resume duty on the ward the next night. She finally agreed to remain in the service but begged so hard to be allowed to continue in the colony that we decided not to change her, especially since she declared that she wished to demonstrate her ability to prevent further escapes. We all sympathized with her. She seemed to feel the loss of the patient keenly. She came on duty with absolute regularity and returned to her room as soon as relieved, seldom venturing out during the day and never leaving the premises. She formed no intimate friendships and only remained in the dining-room long enough to finish a hasty meal, after which she would retire to her room or seek a secluded place on the porch of the Nurses Home, where she would occupy herself with needle work or reading the papers.

Two weeks passed without a word from the fugitive and we began to feel that perhaps, after all, she was able to pass as a normal member of society, a situation that we would all heartily endorse and none would attempt to disturb.

About this time I received a letter from a lady in the southern part of the State asking about her daughter, saying that she had gone from home on the first day of the month to work in our institution, and had not written a line since nor answered any of the letters that she, as a solicitous mother, had written her. It was the identical girl who had allowed Fanny to escape!

I sent for her and showed her the letter from her mother and told her she was negligent in her filial duty and that she should not thus add to the distress of a mother who, for the first time perhaps, had a daughter away from home and among strangers.

In expostulating with this particular attendant for her unconcern toward her mother, I insisted that she write a letter on the spot.

While she scratched off the note I addressed a stamped envelope and had her place the letter inside, seal it, and drop it in the mail box in my presence. I wrote the mother that her daughter was well and that she had just written her a letter that must reach her in the mail with mine.

Having thus contributed to the comfort and peace of mind of the anxious mother, I considered the incident ended and we resumed the daily routine of institutional life, disturbed only by the thought of the next sensation Fanny might create while at large.

Several days later I received a telegram from the mother to whom I had written. It read: "Letter from my daughter was not written or signed by her. Am afraid she is ill and that news is being withheld from me."

I again sent for the girl and communicated the contents of the message to her.

From behind her heavy veil she exclaimed, "Oh, mother was always that way. Whenever one of us girls is away from home she worries if we don't write every day."

I reminded her that she had been with us nearly three weeks and had written her mother but once and then at my request, and that it was perfectly natural that a mother would worry at not hearing from her daughter for so long a time. I told her she would have to telegraph her mother at once, at our expense, and thus reassure her. I gave her a blank and she wrote, "Am well and doing well, Amie."

I had the message duly forwarded and excused the girl for the time being.

Within two hours I received a message from the mother saying: "Am coming at once, my daughter writes her name 'Amy' and the fact that the message was signed 'Amie' confirms my suspicion that she is not with you."

Now here was a mystery almost as deep as that of the disappearance of the patient and we eagerly awaited the arrival of the mother to help solve it.

She came on the first available train, a demure little widow whose face bore evidences of refinement mingled with lines of care that the hard struggle to bring up a family in southern Illinois had left there. She plainly exhibited symptoms of fatigue from travel and a look of anxiety that I knew would disappear the moment she was permitted to see her daughter. Not wishing to prolong her distress, I ordered the young lady to report at my office at once, without letting her know she was about to be ushered into the presence of her mother.

As I saw her approach the office door I stepped outside and into the staff room, not wishing to intrude upon what I regarded the sacred confidence of mother and daughter. While discussing the episode with the physicians and the chief nurse, a series of shrieks came from my office that caused us all to repair there at once. What we saw will never leave the memory of any of us. The mother was frantically screaming, "My daughter is dead. I knew it! Something told me they were deceiving me and now I have come two hundred miles only to find my misgivings true. Oh, Doctor, why did you do it? How could you misrepresent to a mother that her daughter was alive and well, when you knew that she had been murdered and her body secreted!"

I said, "Madam, calm yourself. "You are overcome by your long journey and by the anxiety you have felt. There is your daughter and we can all assure you that she has not suffered a day's illness since she has been with us."

"You lie," she screamed. "That is not my daughter! I never saw that woman in my life! She is an imposter whom you have hired to impersonate her. You forget the maternal instinct that was able to detect the fraud at a distance of two hundred miles, which could tell from the handwriting and from the telegram that something was wrong you could not be deceived by the most cunning actress in the world. You might have known that the love and devotion that a mother gives to her child could never be put aside by the substitution of a stranger. I want my child! Where is she? Speak, you men. I hold you equally responsible and will invoke the widow's curse upon your heads until she has been restored to me."

We had long since accustomed ourselves to startling situations. Life at the head of a large asylum for the insane prepares one for any strange development. This, however, was entirely new and unexpected. It had nothing to do with the insane. Both mother and daughter were presumed to be entirely rational, yet their actions bore a striking resemblance to the scenes we often witnessed on the wards where insane patients frequently spurned their own kin or claimed relationship to entire strangers. We turned to the daughter for a solution. She stood at the farther end of the room, neatly garbed in her nurse's uniform and apparently unmoved by the heartrending scene we had just witnessed and of which she was a part. I was about to question her when she uttered a maniacal shriek which sounded strangely familiar. Following this came hysterical laughter and in another moment she fell to the floor in a faint.

The chief nurse started to run for restoratives and the physicians came forward to assist me, but I waived them aside and told them to confine their attention to the mother. The prostrate girl had one convulsion after another, during which she tore off her nurses cap and disarranged her wig.

I had always made it a point to know my patients thoroughly and I suspected the moment I heard the story of the mother that the girl was none other than Fainting Fanny. The removal of the cap and wig instantly revealed the disguise that had so successfully deceived us during the past three weeks. I bent down and, shouting into her ear, said, "Fanny, come out of that fit and tell us where the attendant is that came on duty the night you were supposed to have escaped."

She opened her eyes and said, "Oh, it's all over with me. I just wanted to keep this up a week longer, until pay-day, and then I would never have troubled you again. I was going to buy a ticket for the west and after telling the governor of his hard-heartedness in refusing to pardon me, intended to open up a beauty parlor and lead an honest life. I would have restored your missing nurse to you and will do so now if you will promise to give me my freedom and stop the police from hounding me from one city to another."

Her statement that she could restore the nurse was the most hopeful feature of the entire mystery and I said to her calmly: "Fanny, is she alive?"

"Yes, but I will not produce her until assured of my liberty."

While all this was transpiring the mother had swooned and the doctors had a real case on hand. They carried her into an adjoining guest chamber and the moment she revived I assured her that her daughter was alive and that we would be able to explain the matter to her entire satisfaction. For this she seemed grateful, but she continued to sob and call for her child. The woman physician in charge of the female receiving service and who was an expert at writing up case histories was called in and we proceeded to extract from Fanny a statement as to the whereabouts of the missing attendant. It was a fine battle of mind against mind. Fanny was determined to purchase her freedom at the price of restoring the missing nurse and we were equally determined not to pay the price, much as we desired to shorten the agony of the mother.

I have never lied to my patients nor permitted my staff to do so. Many were brought to us under the most cunningly devised misrepresentations and we often experienced the greatest difficulty in gaining their confidence after such deceit. Members of the family or officers of the law in transporting patients not infrequently tell them they are starting out on an excursion or going to a hotel and when it develops later that they are in an insane asylum they rave for days and regard as a lie every statement subsequently made. I felt that we would be justified in promising Fanny her freedom in return for the information that would reunite the mother and daughter but resolved not to resort to this expedient until every other resource had been exhausted. Finally I said, "Fanny, tomorrow we surrender you to the penitentiary. You were only committed here pending your recovery and, that having been demonstrated, the law must take its course. Perhaps while meditating in the solitary there, you will conclude to tell us where the missing attendant has been all these weeks."

With a show of real feeling she said:

"Don't send me back to the penitentiary! I will die in the solitary! I can't live on bread and water. I have only now recovered from the tuberculosis I contracted while in the prisons and if you send me back you condemn me to death. Besides what will become of the poor girl if I am taken away? She will starve when there is no one to bring food to her." "If you want to add murder to your crimes, just keep on withholding the hiding place of the attendant, for tomorrow you go back to prison if she is not found within an hour. The moment she is restored to her mother you may return to the colony and resume the good living that has worked such wonderful improvement in your condition. If you go back to prison she will starve and, according to your own statement you will not be living off the fat of the land yourself."

Suddenly she recovered her composure and said, "There is no use of both of us starving; come, I will give you back your nurse." We followed her to the tent colony, hopeful, though skeptical. She led us to the rear, down the steps to the furnace room. It was summer time and no heat was required, hence there had been no occasion to enter the coal vault since late spring. She produced a key from her stocking and deftly unlocked the door. A faint voice from inside assured us that our search was about to end successfully.

I will not attempt to describe what followed. We simply found a girl, pale from long exclusion from sunlight but apparently otherwise unharmed. She wore the clothes of a patient and on the floor there was a mattress and plenty of good bedding while on a number of old packing boxes there was a set of dishes and all indications that the prisoner had not suffered for the comforts of life during her *imprisonment. I greeted her reassuringly, and told the nurses to give her every attention and to provide her with the best clothes to be had.*

Just as she was presentable she was taken to headquarters to meet her mother, a scene which we will not profane by an attempted description. After awhile we called them into the reception room and had the girl recite her experience.

She said that being new to the ways of an insane asylum, and having had only the preliminary instructions given by the chief nurse to novices, she went over to the colony in time to relieve the nurses of the evening shift. They showed her over the ward and explained to her that there was little to do until the rising hour in the morning and that if she needed assistance in the night she could call Fanny, who they said was an unusually bright patient but who needed watching. She said that, about midnight, Fanny came into the sitting room and said it was time to have the customary lunch of the night watch. The lunch proved to be a very hearty meal, for she had the free range of the diet kitchen. She then offered to show her over the place and took her down into the furnace room. When she reached the coal vault she pushed her into it and told her that she was a prisoner and must remain there a month. She ordered her to remove her uniform and exchange it for her own dress. During the first night Fanny brought down bedding, dishes and food and told her that henceforth she would visit her every night and that she would be liberally supplied with food. She was told to utter no sound on pain of instant death, and she obeyed hoping all the time that some one of the day nurses would have occasion to visit the vault and release her. Every night Fanny came, always bringing delicacies and enough food to last through the next day.

After hearing her story it was easy to understand the scheme. The new attendant was a stranger in the institution, having arrived on the afternoon preceding the night of her imprisonment, and Fanny, by dressing in a nurses garb could with the aid of the cap, quite successfully impersonate the new nurse, particularly since she was crafty enough to avoid the nurses society of any of the nurses in whose custody she had been in the past. Even the most vigilant and suspicious nurse would hesitate in believing that so notorious a patient could deliberately masquerade about the place in a nurses uniform and the very boldness of the act reduced to practically nothing her chance of detection. Her plan was to impersonate the nurse even on pay-day, draw her check and get beyond the borders of the state. It would have succeeded had it not been for the parental anxiety of the mother who would not be deceived.

Fanny was returned to the colony the next day and when the nurses who came to the ward in droves saw her in the garb of a patient they were disgusted with themselves for not having detected the disguise the first time she came into their dining room. In the afternoon they again dressed her in uniform just to see what change it would make in her appearance. Now that they were "wise" to it every one could detect the resemblance and all united in berating the stupidity that had so nearly caused the escape of a patient and the possible death by fright of one of their fellow nurses.

Of course, Fanny lost none of her popularity. Attendants upon the insane, like guards in a prison, admire just a little dash in their charges and this latest exploit of Fanny's added to all the others easily made her the institution celebrity.

She remained with us many years. Judges, Pardon Boards and Governors found it inexpedient to authorize her release and it was not accomplished until the Dispenser of the Greater Justice intervened and called her troubled spirit home.

Strangest of institution anomalies the girl whom she had so grievously wronged became her most devoted nurse during her final illness. It was a touching sight to see the lustrous eyes of the invalid looking up into the face of the gentle nurse. The features of the one reflected repentance, submission and gratitude and the other forgiveness, devotion and charity.

Attendants who tip-toed in and out of that sick room almost felt the halo that hovered over the death bed and none came away without a higher regard for the public service and a more tender feeling for those who either through mental aberration or moral obliquity required detention by the state.

As for the young attendant it can easily be understood that ample amends were made. She was placed under the special tutelage of the chief nurse and given double access to the laboratory and operating room. The time she spent in the coal cellar was deemed the equivalent of a year's service and this together with the extra instruction she received justified us in placing her in the second year of the training school, from which she graduated with flying colors a year later.

Who is that pleasant faced lady with the white wavy hair who met us at the door?" That is the matron of the institution. She was a widow in Southern Illinois who came to us ten years ago because she wanted to be near her daughter, who was one of our pupil nurses. A gentler soul was never vested with supervision over girls.

"And that splendid looking woman with the Red Cross brassard on her sleeve who just passed down the hall." That is our present chief nurse. She is a graduate of our school and is known throughout the state for her tender care of all new girls who enter the service and for the kindliness and thoroughness with which she gives them their initial instruction. She has had many advantageous offers to go elsewhere at higher pay but prefers to remain with us where she can be near her mother.

She has but one extravagance. Once a year she goes down to the nearby city and purchases a floral wreath and places it upon the grave of Fainting Fanny.

Memories of Peoria State Hospital

Contributed by Former Employees and Others --

Collected by Arlene Parr

Dr. Zeller's letter to his wife, Sophie *(The letter is typed as written to show Dr. Zeller's personality)*

Dear Sophie: If you ever have any of my letters published, don't have them headed "my dear or Sophie" or ended with "your darling husband." These things kill me when I see them preceding or closing a letter. I don't say you will have any published, but if you do you can have them, along with any heading they chose to make, just say "Of which the following is an extract" or "Written to his wife as follows" and its closing signature or at least the close needn't follow, for its heading usually discloses who the letter is from and to. Of course you are my darling Sophie and I your affectionate George, but the public knows that and takes it for granted. But I am perhaps wasting a lot of useless instruction. You can patch up the material for an article out of several different letters. I have taken to descriptive writing to you of late in order that it may serve me as a sort of diary in the future, hence advice like this and a few business matters I include in a separate sheet. That's what I should have done long ago, then you could have read them to whom you pleased. Today Capt. Santiago brought me down 16 yds. of very fine pina [cloth], the best I have seen. It looks for all the world like mosquito netting and I wish it were the finely woven kind, but I know it is the **primera** **classe** and I think you will appreciate it. The more it is washed the better it gets. I think this lot is equivalent to at least that many dollars. I am treating his wife for neuralgia of the eye of long standing. I think 16 yds. will make you a summer skirt, to be worn over other goods. I want to get at least 200 yds. of this stuff & I may send some to Christine or Clara, so as to divide my mail. In each case I will mark a piece for them and the others will be marked for you & they will gladly give them to you, as they will be so thoroughly tickled to receive one themselves. I sent Alice three pieces, so you needn't give her any unless you want to swap with her. I won't send this lot with this mail, for I just sent you the mat & other pina. I will also mail some to your father. I will bring lots of it home but don't want to keep you waiting until then, that's why I keep sending it now. If I ever get to Bano I will be able to secure many embroidered pieces, and they do say their embroidery is of a very high grade. None is done here.

Sunday, Apr. 22nd, just 60 days since we entered the Camarine, and took possession of the Capital. History is made very fast over here and when the Col. visited my quarters today & indulged in a little good natured grumbling about the slowness of things I overwhelmed him with a comparison of the province today compared to what it was 60 days ago and he was surprised at his own accomplishments. I think it remarkable and I use it as a basis in comparing what the next two months may bring about. We hear that Dewey has about decided to run for Pres. I think it more likely that he will take the vice pres. with Bryan at the head. Anyhow just watch the old goose relegated to the rear. An ambitious woman is playing house with him. Over here the soldier expresses universal contempt for him. The fleet he sunk consisted of mere skiffs compared to his own and it is generally accepted that he is responsible for our present dilemma on account of his coquetting with Aguinaldo, in fact he brought Aguinaldo over here from Hong Kong where he was a fugitive. He brought him in an American gunboat and no doubt gave him assurance which could only be given from Washington; so the country may inquire after a while why he cut the cable. Go it old man, who's afraid. Send me some photo films and a lot of stamps, if you haven't already done so. Save my letters and send me a print or two of all the pictures that turn out well. I can't label them for you. You will have to label them yourself for the time being. Our cook is a first class photographer and I may now get some good inside views. Don't try to develop prints from bad plates. I think they will average better henceforth. If we ever get where we have all our corps together I will have some developed here. I have a few films that turned out all right in the spoiled lot at Naic, but the steward who developed them is at another station and can't get at them. Someday I will send them along. Major Artand arrived today. He doesn't compare with Maj. Ireland, but he was the next in line and of course was promoted. A Maj. gets $208 a month. I read the Tribunes correspondence by R. H. Little. It is commonplace. Weather is ideal but rainy season is not far off. Many Insurrectos brought in last night. This is Apr. 23rd and I am in excellent health. Train leaves shortly so I close, with much love and the hope that you are bearing up courageously. Affectionately, your husband, Geo. A. Zeller

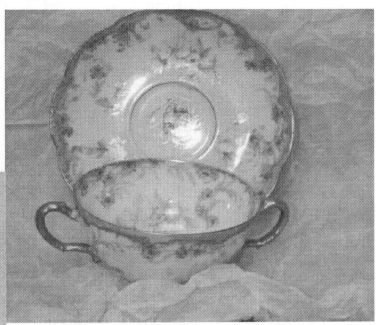

Gary Lisman

China used by Dr. and Mrs. Sophie Zeller, probably for visitng dignitaries, or perhaps for every day use. Contributed by Mildred Polson of Bartonville.

Dr. Zeller and wife, Sophie, during his military service in the Philippines.

Picture Credit: Zeller Family
Letter Credit: Alpha Park Library

Angel statue at a family cemetery in Spring Bay placed in memory of her by Dr. Zeller. It reads: "Erected by George A. Zeller in memory of his wife, Sophie. Buried in Springdale [Cemetery]."

Arlene Parr

Dr. Zeller's letter to his brother, Julius, while Dr. Z. was superintendent at PSH

Peoria State Hospital

November 26, 1913

Dear Julius,

Your views are mine exactly, only I have the absolutely unreasonable opposition of Sophie, who blindly believes that I could not be driven from this post and who consults only her personal convenience. For eleven years she has guarded the furniture of our headquarters against use and to pass it over to some one else seems preposterous. She has also a blind notion that the whole state should rise up and go to Springfield and demand my retention. It would be interesting to observe how much she would inconvenience herself in the interests of some one else similarly situated.

I am very clear in the matter. The alienist ranks any superintendent and if former incumbents have failed to bring the position up to its legal and moral standing it was because of their inability to grasp the field. I can bring it up to its full possibilities, just as I made the superintendency shine <u>out above</u> the swivel-chair administrators. As a matter of fact, I am as good as named as alienist. Gov. Dunne told me so and asked me to remain until he could find a good <u>Democratic</u> successor. Of course, it is possible that knockers will get their work in but everybody is boosting and the only adverse feeling is that I belong right where I am. As between staying, going out of the service entirely or going up to alienist, there is little choice.

To stay under a hostile administration is not easy. I will take what comes with equanimity and am making no great effort.

Public feeling seems to be so strong that added effort would be almost like casting doubt upon it. Then again, causes Sophie's awful dread and the thought of what I will have to witness when she has to pull away from a place that apparently was so distressing in its trivial matters. Of course, a place at large has possibilities of political rehabilitation that none can capitalize better than I while, to be let out entirely might also bring a wave of resentment or appreciation equally valuable politically. So you see there are many angles and I am floating along as always where my personal interests are involved, quite trusting to chance.

In my administrative work I plan and foresee and safeguard, but in personal matters I must depend somewhat upon public opinion, and it has always been kind to me. Even when most bitterly persecuted there was a support beyond belief.

You ought not save a letter like this. Sophie has not yet decided to go to Washington and I don't feel like in giving too much. We will be glad to have Alice with us indefinitely.

[Signed] Geo.

Letter written by Margaret Zeller to her mother, Alice Caroline Zeller, wife of Julius Christian Zeller, George Zeller's brother.

April 5, 1938

Dearest Mama,

I went to the picture show tonight to see Jeanette McDonald and Nelson Eddie in "Girl of the Gold West." Miss Peterson (not the laboratory technician but the O.T. lady) who has recently lost her sister came in after supper and asked me to go. I hated to refuse her as it is the first time she has asked me anyplace and she was nice about showing me how to recane the chair. Then too it seemed terrible to make a point of not going when she herself is grieved over her sister, so I went. To be perfectly honest I do not feel right with myself for having gone and I did not particularly enjoy the show although it is a splendid picture. We stopped by the club on the way home and picked up Uncle George. I had phoned him we would be by for him. . . .

Had some time on my hands this afternoon so went through the O.T. department. The patients are certainly doing some beautiful work. Some doing spool knitting and some very intricate cross stitch rugs and wall hangings. Others are piecing quilts, and still others quilting. Then there are a number weaving rugs and one girl is making woven table runners and pillow tops. I do want you to see the work they are doing if you come on a visit, and I do hope you do.

Its nearly one o'clock. So off to bed with you!

Love to all,
Margaret

Credits: Dr. Zeller's letter to Julius Zeller and Margaret Zeller's letter to her mother were contributed by Miriam Steffan of Columbia, Mo, descendant of Dr. Zeller.

Eleanor Lockhart of Oklahoma shares the following about her two great aunts, Eva and Esther Roberts, who both became nurses at the state hospital

(summarized from the Chuck Barnhart Show, WMBD, in 1951 - Eva Roberts, R.N.)

A young farm girl came to the state hospital in the year 1904, assigned to care for patients in the violent ward. Financially, the reward was not great. Twelve to fifteen hour-a-day shifts seven days a week for $18 a month (Dr. Zeller changed that to eight-hour days). But she had found her calling and stayed at the hospital for 46 years. It was reported that the patients thought of her a sacred symbol, and she was devoted to them. When she had worked 35 years, she could have retired then with a pension, but she worked on for 11 more because "I liked my job too much and I was strong and healthy enough to do it." It seems hard to believe that a young farm girl going to a place of this sort - being closed in with strange men and women whose minds are clouded - it seems incredible that she could find her happiness there. And yet, obviously she did. She is owed a vote of thanks for the work she has done in the service of mankind. There is no greater job that man can do.

* * *

Letter from Dr. Zeller upon Esther Roberts' retirement from Peoria State while he was at Alton State Hospital between his superintendency at PSH

ALTON STATE HOSPITAL
ALTON, ILLINOIS

Miss Esther Roberts   October
120 Terminal Station   9
Peoria, Illinois   1917

Dear Madam

It is with a feeling of genuine regret that I learn of your retirement from the service. No words at my command could express my appreciation of the long and faithful and loyal service you and your sister rendered. The "Roberts" cottages were always pointed out as models of neatness. The patients improved and their friends went away loud in their praise. We always gave you what others dubbed the filthy class, and they became tidy and in many instances were restored.

I am writing this as a personal tribute, but am also enclosing a copy which you may use as a testimonial in any way it may serve you.

Yours very truly,
GAZ:BAE
George A. Zeller
Enc.
Managing Officer

In front of Nurse's Residence (Bowen Building - Eva Roberts (arrow).   Eleanor Lockhart

Eleanor Lockhart

Eva Roberts, second from right, and her graduating class at Peoria State Hospital in 1915.

206

From Left - Eva Roberts, Mattie Deweese, and Esther Roberts.   Eleanor Lockhart

"Grandma's Walk to the Hospital" by Eliida Lakota

As a little girl my grandma, Beulah Lakota and Aunt Myrtle Engelgau told about their walk to the hospital on the long stairs from Highway 24 to the hilltop. Halfway up there was a bench to rest on - to catch their breath. The long walk was lit with street lights. At times they walked home late at night, pausing, I'm sure, to enjoy the view from the hill stairs.

Thinking the stairs were gone, imagine my pleasure two years ago while hiking I came to the old stairs - the old light poles and the remains of the old bench. I paused where my grandmother had paused; I felt her presence, it seemed, and we shared the view.

Stairs as it looks today.   **Gary Lisman**

208

Eliida Lakota

Left: Beulah Lakota, grandmother to Eliida Lakota. As a little girl, and later while working at the Peoria State Hospital, Beulah walked these stairs many times.

Right: This picture of the stairs was taken in 1946.

Mickey Epperson

Arrival at the Insane Asylum - *Grace Clark Brown, R.N.*

- excerpted from the Penny Press - September 28. 1972

It was a bitter cold day, with a gale blowing across the top of that hill where the Peoria State Hospital is located. We were carrying a suitcase and a silly hat.

It was a long walk between the old terminal station down by the old Acme [farm implement manufacturer] to the top of that hill, with a long flight of wooden steps. When we finally reached the top, we rested a spell and saw Peoria way off in the distance. By the time we reached what was then the institutional center the hand holding that silly hat box was frosted.

At the center, they told us to go to the C building, and pointed to the largest building in sight, much further on, and told us to find the housekeeper. The housekeeper took us to the third floor to a very clean, very bare dormitory for six girls, and we were left to our fate.

A friendly girl said that all-pervasive whistle we heard was the dinner call and took us to the dining room across the road in another building. There were long, long tables, enormous platters and big heavy bowls that sailed by once. You grabbed it as it sailed past you, good food but steam cooked with little seasoning. We soon learned that the employe's meal time was fun time.

When we asked how we found out about our work, the friendly girl took us to the hall, and there was a very large glass covered board with all the places by letter, and all the employes by name placed somewhere on that board to be shuffled by the chief nurse. Sure enough, there was Grace Clark under Infirmary A, on the afternoon shift, two to ten. (If your name ever came off that board, you no longer had a job.)

Our chief nurse was the beautiful, strict, idealistic Miss Mary Bird Talcott, who had served in the Spanish War. Miss Talcott watched that no skirts were more than three inches off the floor. The full skirts were a grey and white stripe with a full white sheeting apron, so if they were a little short they had a daring swing on the right girl. There were full sleeves, very much down to the hands, with stiff white cuffs tight around the wrists, A high white collar ruined your neck, and there was a stiff smooth white bib with wide straps over the shoulders.

Of course every woman's hair was long. The nurses thoroughly padded their hair with rolls of false hair, then they added many little rolled curls on top. The only frivolity permitted were gay silk scarfs pulled snugly over those nests of hair, crossed in the back and tied under the chins.

The first time we really saw Dr. Zeller, one of our friends had had a small fire start in a closet on her ward. Rags that had been used to refinish the ward floors had ignited, but she had put out the fire, which, it seemed, had been the wrong thing to do. When we gathered to go on duty, a number of people were there to give us a lesson on the proper conduct in case of fire. We seemed to remember a ward doctor and the chief nurses and maybe someone else telling us how to handle a chemical tank.

The person who we really remember is Dr. Zeller, tall and intense, with deep set eyes shaded with long bushy eyebrows. This is what we remember of his words, "The patients come first."

Memories of Harold D. Hayes

I grew up on McKinley Street in Bartonville. I am one of five children. Mother graduated from the Free Methodist College at Greenville, Illinois in 1906, but did not find work as a teacher. She worked at Peoria State Hospital from 1906 to 1911. She met my father there in 1910. Her older sister, who worked at the hospital, and my dad's sister were responsible for them both coming to the hospital. My dad was first to arrive.

The same railroad that served Keystone also served the hospital as an electric railroad between Bartonville and Pekin. At the foot of the old station on Illinois Avenue you can still read the letter at the top of the roof's gable of that electric railway system. Many people came from southern Illinois to work there. Mack Leiter was chief engineer for many years, and also the projectionist for the silent and sound movies shown in the old wooden structure recreation hall. My father was friends with him back in the early 1900s. He was responsible for my interest in the motion picture industry. The hospital generated their own direct current electricity. Huge railroad carloads of coal was taken up the valley just to the north of the hospital grounds.

A concrete staircase went from Illinois Avenue to the top of the bluff; at the top was the Receiving Unit. The staircase was dimly lighted and very steep for my three younger siblings. We had to rest several times while going up or down. I had a paper route there from 1932 through 1936. I bought a speedometer for my bike, installed it, and rode my bike clear to the top of the old road and as fast as I could back down. I think the speedometer read 30 M.P.H. A baseball diamond was to the east and south of the recreation hall and was used a great deal. I repaired a wheelchair for a WWI veteran who had lost both legs in France during the war. I remember the original old black-cindered road. It started up off Adams further south from the present Becker Drive entrance road, then it made a sharp right to the north and ran along about the center of the steep bluff, almost to the north border of the grounds.

For several years several large photos of the Peoria State Hospital hung on the west wall of the dining room at the restaurant across Roosevelt Street to the north from the old Bartonville Bank. As I recall, one of the larger photos was of the baseball diamond and recreation hall.

I knew Billie Barton, grandson of the man who originated Bartonville. I think they also started the original Bartonville Bank. The Barton residence mansion stood on the curved slope of Rt. 24 as you get into Bartonville from Peoria a little north of the current Kentucky Fried Chicken. Practically all of Bartonville is undermined with shafts and tunnels from the old mines. An air intake standpipe, from the mines, stood near the SE corner of my homestead property which was at 501 McKinley Ave. That entire block between Garfield and McClure is now a huge Shell gasoline station with 16 pumps.

The roof's gable of the old electric railway system.
Gary Lisman

Memories of Dr. Zeller -- told to Bertha Imes by her father, Charlie Garrison, who worked at PSH as an orderly on Ward C, caring for violent men, starting in 1912. She retold the story at the Peoria Women's Club in April, 2005.

On the tenth anniversary of Peoria State Hospital an Open House was being planned. My dad was one of the employees who was hanging a big anniversary banner at the bottom of the hill. Dr. Zeller went down to watch the workmen. At the time Adams Street was sparsely traveled, and he was standing in the middle of the road with his hands on his hips looking up at the banner when a fellow in a Model T Ford came along. He yelled at Dr. Zeller, "Get out of the road, you old S.O.B. before you get run over and killed.

Dr. Zeller, with his wry sense of humor, turned and looked after the guy, and with his hands still on his hips, stated, "H'm, it must of been somebody that know'd me."

Tuberculosis was so prevalent there. My dad was around 20 years old, 6' 3", and very thin. Dr. Zeller, being the caring person that he was, said to my father, "Garrison, didn't you tell me that you came from the farm?" to which my father answered yes. Dr. Zeller advised him to go back home to southern Illinois to the farm, which he did after working there approximately three years.

His brother had started a trucking company, Peoria Cartage Co., and in about 1927 he returned to Peoria with my mother to work for him. In time his five other brothers and two brothers-in-law also worked there. We all lived in the Averyville area, so I went to school with both siblings and cousins.

* * *

Thelma Cox (Thelma, who kept the Illinois State Employees Association Retirees Luncheon going for years, died in 2004)

I began working at Peoria State Hospital in 1941 as a stenographer in the office. Shortly afterward I was transferred to Z3, male receiving ward. One day a few years later I wanted to get weighed, so I went to the examining room. As I turned to leave, the door opened and in came a patient. He grabbed me and pushed me against the wall, put his arms and hands around my neck. I screamed and the patient in the clothing room heard me and got help. They took the patient out and I went back to my office saying, "This is the last time I'll ever go into that room again," as I was so scared, and I stayed away from this patient any time I saw him.

* * *

Ruth Evelyn Carson Reinhart (St. Francis Hospital School of Nursing - Class of 1947)

As student nurses we were assigned to Public Health or Bartonville State Hospital [PSH]. Since I was working the (Polio) Isolation Unit at St. Francis Hospital I was exempted from the state hospital.

We went on a tour of the state hospital. I remember a large open ward with at least 50 patients in chairs or wheelchairs with cloth vest and limb restraints and some had leather cuff restraints on their arms and legs. There was urine and feces on the floor, and only one aide was on duty. An RN supervisor had several units to be responsible for. Some patients were very loud, calling for help or for their relatives.

We walked through the tunnels, which connected the buildings. I remember the pipes overhead.

In my 40 years of working as an R.N. and supervisor (1947-1987), I preferred hospital nursing.

Clara Louise Zeller, *granddaughter of "Cap" Charles Alexander Zeller - steamboat owner and captain, and brother of Dr. Zeller*

When I was small we would visit Uncle George and Aunt Sophie at the Peoria State Hospital. He was very fond of my father, Arthur, who was his nephew. They lived in this really nice, big house on grounds [Michell Building, first administration building, pictured] with their living quarters in the up-stairs. His office was on the main floor. The huge dining room was also on the main floor. We some-times would have dinner with them.

He had inmates working for him. I remember this one large, but gentle, man who served the food. I was scared of him because sometimes he would be carrying a knife in his hand.

Uncle George and Aunt Sophie were very nice, but he seemed like such an austere gentleman. I was in awe of him. He had a chauffeur, but he usually wanted my dad to drive him around. When we were driving on the grounds he would have my dad pull over when he saw some inmates. He would get out and shake their hands, say a few words, and pat them on the back. He was so compassionate with them. They loved him and he loved them.

When he went to other state hospitals sometimes he would have my dad drive, and my mom and I would go with them. He was a charter member of the Creve Coeur Club. After retirement they lived in an apartment [in the Bowen Building].

Memories about mother, Leola Rabe, her Uncle John and Aunt Bernice, and Aunt Carrie, who worked at PSH between 1915 and 1926 - *furnished by daughter, Jean Howell*

My mother, Leola, would tell us stories about when she worked at Peoria State Hospital. Once in a while the patients would wander off and go down the hill to the river. For some that was okay, but others were not responsible and could not be allowed to go. She told of having to chase some of them down that hill all the way to the river trying to catch them before they hurt themselves. Then it was a long trek back up that hill with the patient struggling and they would have to call the orderlies to come and restrain them so they could get them back on hospital grounds. My mother said they would use straight jackets or towels wrapped around the patient.

One of the patients she told me about loved apples. Many mornings when my mother checked his room she would find apple cores under his bed where he hid them from the day before. He had apparently taken them from the dining room or kitchen during mealtime. This would happen frequently when apples were in season.

Mother told of how the hospital was associated with the Dr. Michell T.B.Sanitarium.* The state hospital was on the very west edge of Bartonville, and the sanitarium was on the very north edge of Peoria, past Averyville. It was her duty when the sanitarium ran out of milk to take two large pails of milk on the streetcar from the state hospital to the sanitarium. She had to carry them down the hill to the streetcar track, then back to the sanitarium once she got off the streetcar.

John Rabe was an orderly at the state hospital. He married a nurse from there, Bernice Robbins, at the Dr. Michell Sanitarium parlors November 20, 1916. Rev. Carpenter officiated. John served in France during WWI, where he was attacked with nerve gas. He returned in failing health, and although he was able to work for a time, he finally had to accept early retirement. His wife, Bernice, returned to work at the state hospital during the 1940s for awhile.

My Aunt Carrie also worked at the hospital.

My mother married in 1926, and as was the custom at that time, she became a housewife and mother. We loved to hear her talk of her "working days."

* Dr. Michell worked under Dr. Zeller at the Peoria State Hospital in 1905. In 1909 he went to Europe to take special training in mental disorders. Later he opened the Michell Sanitarium at 106 Glen Oak, with the help of his wife and one nurse. His humane treatment of the tuberculin patients and the mentally ill followed the pattern set by Dr. Zeller. He was a well-respected humanatarian in the community, and when he died in 1947, he left the sanitarium to the three local medical hospitals. After WWII it was used to house senior citizens, until 1971 when they were relocated to a new 60-bed facility called Galena Park Home. The original sanitarium was torn down. (Senior News, Nov. 2003, Steenrod)

Left to Right: Hazel Robbins, Carrie Rabe, Leola Rabe, and
Bernice Robbins Rabe. Credit for pictures: Jean Eyman Howell

John Rabe, right, worked at PSH after returning
from WWI. He married Bernice Robbins, in the
above picture, in 1916.

'Tony, The Epileptic,' A Story of Asylum Life Told By Dr. Zeller;

Sad Account of the Wrecked Life and Death of Patient - article from News-Democrat, Belleville, IL., Friday, August 4, 1916, Picture and story contributed by Dolly Catherine Barley's great-niece, Helen Sheldon, and great-great niece, Julie Matthews

"Epileptics are usually short lived. The recurring explosions of brain cells, the congestion and distortion of the features, the frightful tax on the rigid muscles together with the repeated injury of the soft parts and frequent fracture of the bones all tend to reduce the average length of their lives." Dr. George A. Zeller

While I was superintendent of the big asylum for the incurable insane and engaged in the task of removing a thousand patients from the county almshouses into the new institution where they were not only to come under the protecting wing of the State, but were to receive such care as an awakened and enlightened public conscience demanded and provided, I received a message that one hundred insane men were enroute from the asylum at Dunning, in two special coaches.

Dolly Barley, attendant

As usual on such occasions I summoned all the unengaged help and together with the party proceeded to the platform along the track of the railroad switch that entered our premises.

The experience was not a new one to us. It was merely a repetition of what we had been doing almost daily for months except that this was an unusual number and they were certain to be the most violent, troublesome and destructive patients that could be selected from among the two thousand that made up the population of the metropolitan poorhouse and madhouse.

Talk about getting your nerves steeled against such scenes. Why, every arrival simply awakened new chords of pity in our hearts and spurred us to greater endeavor in trying to make the lot of these unfortunates happier than it had been.

I see them now as they file out of the car. The big fellow wearing three overcoats on a hot day; another with two hats on his head and another in his hand. The next five with their arms folded and held across their chests in tightly laced straight jackets; a dozen with their hands or feet in leather wristlets or anklets and finally three "stretcher" cases--patients barely able to walk when the journey began, but now so utterly fatigued and helpless that they must be carried from the coach to the ambulance which we always had in readiness at such times.

Some were shrieking, some singing, some laughing and others with an air of calm submission. One with an attendant on either side holding arm and shoulder but the large number merely stoically falling in line in that institutionalized gait so characteristic of those who constituted the "chronic" population of the insane asylum of ten years ago.

The attendants who accompanied them seemed to think that the all important thing was to count, identify and check off the patients and to acquaint us with the undesirable qualities of each.

During the process we had an opportunity of studying the features and manners of the motley assortment and to estimate the number of extra attendants we might require to care for these people who, the moment they passed into our hands, were to be cared for without the employment of any form of mechanical restraint or seclusion and whose home with us was to be in cottages, the doors of which were never locked.

As they filed by interest suddenly centered in a young boy in knee breeches, carrying his personal belongings under his arm and we resolved to visit the ward later and see why this boy of tender years was so improperly classified as to be associated with grown men of every form of insanity.

We looked up his papers and they showed that he was committed to Dunning at the age of eleven and had spent five years there. He was an epileptic, subject to severe seizures and at such times became exceedingly violent, biting and scratching all who came in conflict with him. "Conflict" was the word and we determined that under a policy the cardinal points of which were non-restraint, non-imprisonment and non-resistance, there would be no conflict.

No one believed that this altruistic doctrine could apply to Tony's case.

We found him in every way an untamed colt. To our questions he simply replied with grimaces and if he uttered a sound it was merely a derisive grunt. He had picked up a generous vocabulary of profanity from his fellow patients, chewed much of their tobacco and rolled a cigarette every time he could get the "makings."

Tony seemed a problem, but we determined that since he was an epileptic his proper place was in the cottage for epileptics, and he was promptly transferred there. With this move he came into a new atmosphere.

Instead of the vigorous male attendants with whom he formerly came in contact he suddenly found himself in the custody of women only. The charge attendant was Dolly, known throughout the service for caring for a hundred insane and violent epileptics without male help and with never a hand of violence raised against her.

No one can now interpret what Tony's thoughts were, but Dolly received him as a member of her family and an hour later when a patient had a fit she directed Tony to bring her a pillow, and he promptly met her request with a grin and a flat refusal.

She had other trained patients at her disposal, however, who promptly responded and Tony looked on in amazement as they tenderly placed pillows under his head and elbows and stood by watching the fury of the attack expend itself in violent convulsions, twitching of the features and striking the floor with arms and legs. When the lethargy that invariably follows their seizures came she asked Tony to help carry him to bed. He obeyed like a little man and at supper asked why the men did not sit on the patient while he was writhing and why they put him to bed without handcuffs or anklets or why they put him in bed at all, why the bedroom door was not locked and why the windows were without bars or grating.

Dolly told him that it was unnecessary to resort to these measures, that epileptics had a kindred malady and that each must hold himself in readiness to assist his fellow in distress.

Next day Tony, to his astonishment, was permitted to go outside and he soon took an interest in the large flock of chickens the cottage maintained. At the end of the next meal he gathered the unconsumed bread and potatoes and anything else that would make chicken feed and he nearly killed the young chicks by overfeeding. Back to the farm--back to nature--was working a change in Tony's heart.

He saw the mother hen gather her helpless flock under her protecting wing at night, and it reminded him of Dolly's efforts in caring for the helpless victim of an epileptic seizure. He began to take an interest in things. The cottage had a little library and Dolly showed him picture books and taught him to read and write. Many letters came from the heartbroken parents in Chicago and we kept them informed of Tony's progress. The girls in the office allowed him the use of one of the typewriters and he quickly acquired the art of clicking off the letters.

His people were always grateful and appreciative, but when they finally received a typewritten letter from Tony himself, telling of the trees and the birds and the little herd of deer we kept in the park and of Dolly herself, they decided to pay him a visit.

And what a reunion it was! I saw him from day to day showing his mother the points of interest about the place. She had spent all her life in the crowded city and what she saw was as novel to her as to him. We made her the guest of the institution, and Dolly saw that she received every courtesy and consideration. When he brought his mother to my office, she apologized for intruding, but I told her that every part of the institution belonged to the inmates and their friends and that she was free to consider herself entirely at home anywhere.

When Sunday arrived she came in with her boy and asked if it was true that he was allowed to attend Chapel. She said that they could not take him to church or send him to school in Chicago because he was liable to have a fit at any time.

She said that was the reason he was sent to Dunning at the age of eleven. He was so frequently found on the sidewalk or in the street writhing in convulsions that the police had him sent to the detention hospital and later to the only place provided for such cases, the insane asylum.

We told her Tony had been attending Chapel for a year and was on the best terms with the priest, who believed that "He who watcheth the sparrow fall" would not feel His house desecrated if one of His children fell to the floor during services.

The years rolled by. The policies of the institution were only strengthened as it became evident that they were feasible and beneficial and were based upon human kindness. Tardily one after another of its principles were introduced into the other institutions until one day the President of the Board down at the Capitol issued an order declaring their universal adoption.

Tony unconsciously had grown into a man, but just as unconsciously the conviction came over him that his world was limited to the institutional premises and that his associates would always be those who shared his affliction. He resigned himself to the situation splendidly but when, after seven years' absence he finally accompanied his sister home on a visit he begged to return to his work, as he called it. He said:

"I must hurry back and take care of Dan. You know, Dan is my partner. We never go away from the cottage alone but always with a companion so that when one has a spell the other can stand by and help him. Dan has hard fits, but always goes to sleep when they are over and then I go back to the cottage and get some of the other boys to help me lead or carry him home. I guess he does the same for me, because, when I wake up in my room and find my tongue bitten and my lips bleeding I know that I must have had a spell, for the last thing I remember was that we started down the hill to get Dolly's evening paper. I must go back because Dan will be lonesome. He has no parents or brothers and sisters to write him. He will be waiting to hear me tell about Chicago and I want to see how many chickens the old hen hatched. She went on the nest the day I left, and Dolly said she would come off in three weeks with a new brood. I wish Dan could have come with me to Chicago, but I sent him a postal card of the lake front and I'll bet he is wondering at the sky scrapers and the big boats and the automobiles. The

boys in the parks in Chicago are not like the patients in our cottage. They don't have spells, so they don't have to look out for each other. I have been away for so long that I don't know any of them; while down at the cottage we are all friends."

And so they brought him back to resume his newer life, happy for the visit home and happier at the thought at being once more with his associates.

Dolly did not fail to make his return a notable event and she went down to the general kitchen and had one of the cooks fry one of the spring chickens, to which Tony and Dan did ample justice.

I watched all this development with the keenest interest, but the mutations of public life called higher and placed me upon the Board which has supervision over all the wards of the State. When I relinquished my position at the head of the institution with which I had been associated from the day it started to building I received many congratulations upon my promotion, but for each of these there arose a pang of regret at leaving the large family of unfortunates with whom I had been so closely identified. Not the least of these was Tony.

Occasionally I would receive a letter from him or Dolly and I always wrote a cheery reply. I did not visit them as often as I should have for the reason that the parting always seemed distressing to them and I know it was to me.

But the remainder of the story was soon told. Tony's convulsions reoccurred with unabated severity, despite the administration of every known remedy. Bromides even under the graded drop dose system had long since lost their efficacy. We tried the non-salt diet and the excessive salt seasoning, the non-meat diet and the excessive protein diet. The seizure chart was carefully kept and consulted but in the end we simply found that, like the rest of the scientific world, we stood helpless in the presence of this malady, which has baffled the skill of the medical world throughout the ages.

Epileptics are usually short lived. The recurring explosions of brain cells, the congestion and distortion of the features, the frightful tax on the rigid muscles together with the repeated injury of the soft parts and frequent fracture of the bones all tend to reduce the average length of their lives.

So I was not surprised when, on opening my official mail one morning I found the following letter:

Our beloved little boy Tony passed away in death, yesterday at 2:25 p.m., in a series of convulsions and it was the most easy death I ever witnessed. He never forgot you and last Tuesday was the last time I heard him speak of you. The Superintendent and the whole staff were so good to him also. This is four of my boys who have died in the short time of this year. I miss them all every day, but will miss Tony more as I have been with him every day for six years and ten months excepting my vacations, and the three weeks that he was home that time. Doctor, if you will write his mother it will do her so much good, as she thinks you are one of the best men in the world. I remain,

DOLLY.

This was the closing chapter then of the life of the little boy who came to us under such unpromising conditions ten years before.

Even though I had not been solicited by the faithful attendant I would have been prompted to do so by my sympathy for the family, so I wrote this letter to Dolly:

My dear Miss _____:

Your letter is a touching reminder of your deep devotion to your patients. What a glorious service it would be if all attendants had the interest of their patients as much at heart as you. I hope for your transfer to the new institution at Dixon and that you will have the opportunity of applying your rare tact in caring for the great army of epileptics that will gather there. Although I seldom see you, please rest assured that I hold you and your associates and all of my old patients in fond remembrance.

Very respectfully,

_____ "

And this to the bereaved mother:

Dear Madam:

Miss_____ has just informed me that your little Tony passed away. It must be a consolation for you to know that she was with him to the end. She is the dearest attendant in the world and she made life sweet for Tony and all the afflicted whom she serves. Tony was one of those who could not have all there was in life, but you may rest assured that he received all that a good and great state could give.

Very respectfully,

_____ "

In due time the answering letter came and with it a little black bordered card with the crucifix on one side and on the other a picture of the boy with the appropriate words:

"In Loving Memory of Anthony Edward _____.
Born October 28, 1891, at Chicago, Ill.
Died May 13, 1916, at Peoria, Ill."

The letter is filed with the records in the office in the capitol and will always serve as a model of simplicity and sincerity in expressing the grateful appreciation of a stricken family, a family which even in its bereavement sees the working of the wondrous plan of the Master. It reads:

Dear Doctor:

In the belief that gratitude felt but not expressed is meager return for the kindness rendered, we ask you to accept this brief note as a token of our sincere and grateful appreciation of your labor in behalf of our son and brother, Anthony.

What you did for Anthony you did for us and we assure you that every kindness shown to him found response in our hearts. His sickness was a sorrow to us, but a sorrow softened by the realization of your devoted and consistent care. Our hope is that the Master who guides our destinies may in the future grant you length of life, health, vigor and the same full measure of success, which has marked your work in the past.

So here you have the story of Tony's newer life. Not the life in the great beyond, where a forgiving Providence will give to each his own nor the first sixteen years which held out so little of hope or possibilities for this poor, afflicted little fellow. It is rather the story of his last ten years from the time he boarded the train at Dunning to go down into the interior of the state to what his people believed to be a hopeless existence in the wards of an institution, the very name of which, the Asylum for the Incurable Insane, precluded hope.

It is just a little human interest story in which institutional life abounds for those who care to seek them out.

Just the plain story of one short generation but one which had its influence even in the restricted sphere in which the drama was enacted. It is a story of a devoted girl, of a stricken boy who reacted and responded to kindly influences, of a family with many children whose parents came to realize that their blighted child became their greatest asset and that his entire career had a gentle and elevating influence over his brothers and sisters, over the nurses and attendants who cared for him, over his fellow sufferers and upon those holding high official station.

Even the name of the institution passed during his residence there. It is now designated "State Hospital" like others of its kind and if incurability must be the fate of some who enter it, that fact is at least not proclaimed in the name.

He saw and participated in the awakening of a great state which for two generations had failed to discharge its obligations to its most helpless subjects.

Even as he lay dying the new State Colony for Epileptics was nearing completion and for him a larger field of usefulness and enjoyment was opening.

This is not a fantasy. It is not a made-up story with imaginary characters, but in the imperfect chronicle of a real occurrence, the actors of which, with the exception of the poor Tony are still in the flesh, the institution still in being and the correspondence here quoted is a part of the official records of the State.

May I ask in what relation in life could Tony have left a greater impression upon his generation and where is there a public employe high or humble who is rendering a greater service to the State than the devoted and unassuming attendant, Dolly, who, down in the obscurity of a detached cottage of a state institution continues to hold the affections of her unfortunate charges and the gratitude of their friends at home.

* * *

The following article is from the <u>Peoria Star</u> , date unknown, about the Epileptic colony:

State Asylum Stands Alone In Its Class

Epileptics and others who are liable at any time to do themselves bodily harm are unceasingly watched and guarded and all precautions are taken in warding them from harm, both day and night, nurses and doctors being at their side in case of accident. And in the treatment of these patients the genius of the man at the head of the farm is displayed in the most favorable light. His deduction of their destructive traits as unemployed energy and the remedy for the same relieved both the attendants and the patients from violence and made possible the turning of this undesirable trait of character into a benefit to the hospital. In order that violent means might be unnecessary and that the patients might be relieved of their excess energy, which was desired from both viewpoints, he allowed them to work on the farms under the direct supervision of the head of the farm department and of attendants, and in this way turned the liability into an asset. The produce raised in this manner aids materially to maintain the farm, and the curbing of the spirits of the patients is a great benefit to all concerned, but in order that no harm will come to the patients because of their occupation in the fields, medical examinations are conducted daily and the attendants are eternally on the watch for signs of fatigue. When the patient is tired he is removed to the farm house and made to rest for the remainder of the day.

Ninety-three year old Pauline (Cox) Fales recalls her days as a nursing student (1930-1932) (Pauline passed away in July, 2004)

We lived on grounds while taking nurses' training. Our quarters were in the Nurses' Residence. We worked hard. We had to work and have class both. On day shift we started at 7 a.m. and worked until 3 p.m. We had one class from 10 to 11 a.m. There were separate wards for male and female patients, with both male and female attendants on each ward. On the men's wards we would do everything. There was a bath man, an attendant who bathed the patients. We took temperatures and fed the ones that needed to be fed.

I will never forget Riley. I remember being so tired from working so hard. He would yell, "nurrse, nurrse," wanting attention right now. He had arthritis so bad, his poor legs were pitiful, and he was bedfast. He would want the pillow moved just a little bit, and usually when I finished moving it like he wanted, the pillow was back where it was at the beginning, but he had gotten the attention he wanted. Riley was very demanding. He was there for years.

Another patient would eat for me and nobody else. One day the phone rang. It was my supervisor. She said, "Pauline, will you come feed him. He won't eat." I did, and he ate for me. We always tried to please the patients. The nurses gave the medicine and we marked everything on the chart at the end of the bed that we did. The R.N.s wore white uniforms. We wore striped blouses under white pinafore aprons with long skirts. They were terrible. My mother made mine.

When I worked in the women's receiving wards I helped with therapy. We did baths, (hydrotherapy) wrapping the patients in sheets. The baths were cold or warm, according to what we were told. The patients didn't like the cold baths. We worked in a lot of different wards for the experience.

Another patient I remember was Mary. She worked as a cook in the dining room in the women's hospital. She was a lovely person, and loved every minute of her working. She was in the dining room all the time. The women's and men's hospitals were across the street from each other. I worked at both of them. The main hospital was the Zeller hospital. I had my tonsils removed there.

I feel the patients were taken good care of. Dr. Zeller saw to that. We took patients to the dances and danced with them. There was a sunken garden over by the nurses' home where we played miniature golf with the patients. We helped them have a good time.

It was against the rules to be in nurses' training and be married. I had met my husband at the time, and we secretly married, so I didn't get to finish out my last year of nurses' training, but I still have very warm memories of my time at Peoria State Hospital.

Gary Lisman

Pauline (Cox) Fales in front of Nurses' Residence in 1931.   Pauline Fales

Opposite Page: Pauline Fales 73 years later. Even though Pauline married and didn't finish nurses' training, she has always had very warm memories of her two years spent at Peoria State Hospital. Not only did her time there impact her life with a better understanding of the mentally ill and compassion for them, but she made friends that have lasted a lifetime.

Farm Colony Number Two

Colony Number Two, consisting of two frame buildings joined, is two stories and accommodates thirty-two patients. There are many aged people among this group and an observer would be inclined to believe they are persons who have been assigned where they might absorb sunshine and inhale good, fresh air; in other words, enjoy an outing. Their duties are of an easy nature - caring for the garden and vineyard and light farm work.

E. B. Bentley, Welfare Bulletin, February & March 1930

Life On the Farm - *Jewel "Judy" Bradshaw Keil. (Her father was farm boss and later laundry manager.)*

Dad was Dr. Zeller's chauffeur before I was born in 1930. He worked as farm boss (turkey farm and grape arbor) starting in 1940, and laundry manager in the 50s. Dad thought Dr. Zeller was wonderful and did a lot for the patients. He started them working on the farms for occupational therapy. He also was trying to get rid of electric shock therapy.

Between 1932 and 1940, because of politics, Dad was out of a job there. We moved on a farm at Alton that belonged to Dr. Waters, then superintendent of PSH, and got work outside the state. We then moved back to Peoria in 1940.

My mom worked with the patients and she took care of the household and supervised the patients there. Earl, a patient who called her mom, helped her in the dining room and around the house. Another patient, Sam, was a chef of German heritage. He helped Mom in the kitchen. He was an excellent cook. He made Swedish pancakes and other delicacies. He was very intelligent. He had the Shakespeare works and also Homer's Iliad. I borrowed them while I was in high school.

As I recall, Dr. Waters, the superintendent at the time, had horses that he kept at our farm.

There were about thirty patients living in a dormitory. Most worked on our farm. Some worked on Farm Number One, a ways away, which was a hog farm. The hog farm later became Abbott Center, the children's unit. We went to dances and movies in the main part of PSH. Neighbors were welcome to come, too.

Dad also served as laundry manager in the 1950s. When I was 18 I had to move out as I was no longer a dependent. I went to college at Bradley University and lived in a dormitory.

Right: House where Judy and her family lived. Some patients that lived in a dormitory helped in the house; others helped on the farm.

Pictured is Judy, her sister, Velma, and "Mom" Donahue, the wife of an employee who helped on the farm, holding their dog, JoJo.

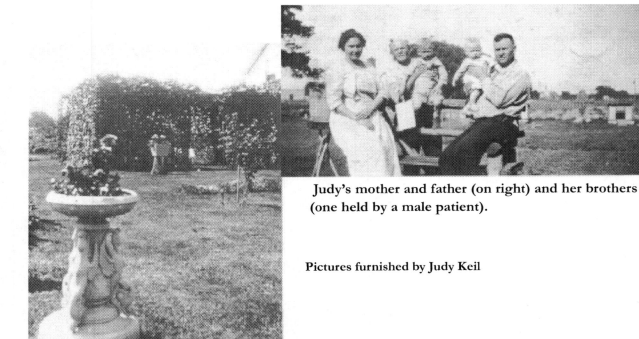

Judy's mother and father (on right) and her brothers (one held by a male patient).

Pictures furnished by Judy Keil

The grape arbor. This was part of the farm tended by the patients.

Farm Colony Number Three

Colony Number Three is a rented proposition. The building is a frame structure, two stories, and cares for nineteen patients. The farm consists of 235 acres and has been rented for the ensuing year on a fifty-fifty basis. B. R. Berings, the landlord, says that he has received more than $1,500 rental during the past year. If that is true, the institution received more, because it had the use of the garden, the orchard and the dwelling for caring for this number of patients. The farm detail makes its home in Farm Colony Number Three. Generally, they are husky chaps, who manage the heavy machinery, including the tractor, and teams which perform the more arduous work.

Each colony has its garden and garden detail. This can best be attested by visiting the basement in any of these Farm Colonies.

My Grandfather and Dr. Zeller - Betty Jones -1930s

I lived on a farm next to Farm Colony Number Three, which was across from Allied Mills. They raised hogs and cows in that farm colony. My grandfather owned the farm where I lived, which was between two railroad tracks. My family and I lived in a house next door to my grandparents' house. When I was four I was helping work the farm. I would sit on a horse and guide it while my brother, who was three years older than I, would guide the hand plow behind me. We all had our jobs. My father worked in the mines.

Dr. Zeller was a friend of my grandfather and had a lot of respect for him. My grandfather was so good with animals, so sometimes he would go to the farm colony and treat the animals, and sometimes give Dr. Zeller advice about the animals. Dr. Zeller was a very busy man, but when he drove by in his buggy and would see my grandfather or my dad, he would stop for awhile to visit. My grandfather died of yellow jaundice when I was around seven years old.

Butchering was done on the farm for meat for the hospital patients. Also patients picked vegetables from the gardens for canning. For instance, green beans would be taken to the wards and the patients would break them, then they would be taken back to the main kitchen for canning. Even patients from the violent wards helped to get the vegetables ready for canning. There were ice houses to keep meat and vegetables fresh and also fruit cellars. Some of the reliable patients lived on the farm.

I remember there was a mattress factory on the grounds of Peoria State. A shoe factory was in a little building next to the Bowen Building.

Dr. Zeller seemed quiet and a very nice person. Sometime when he went to the wards he would get in line, get an aluminum tray and a spoon (no forks or knifes were used at that time) and would eat with the patients. They would usually have homemade bread and homemade butter along with the meal. Patients would also hang around the Administration Building. Dr. Zeller would shake their hand and talk with them.

Starting in 1943, I worked at PSH as an attendant and later as an LPN until Peoria State closed. I remember D row had 150 beds, and C row had 96 beds. A-row patients were the most reliable. 5C were the violent men and 9C was occupied by the violent women. Hospitals A and B were at the top of the hill.

Farm Colony Number One was at the Old Abbott Center. Dairy cows were milked in the quonset hut. Patients that lived there worked on the farms. Farm Colony Number Two was where the Alpha Park Library is now, across the street from Farm One. There was a house there and a lovely big farmhouse back further down the road.

Horse Barn   **Alpha Park Library**

LeRoy H. Kocher - *Business Manager at PSH, by son, Ken Kocher*

My dad worked at Peoria State Hospital for 34 years, starting in 1932. When he was promoted to business manager in the early 1940s we moved to a three-bedroom cottage on grounds, which was designated as Cottage 3. All items needed to live comfortably were furnished and owned by the state, including linens and dishes. I was in the 3rd grade.

The superintendent and his assistant, doctors, business manager, personnel director, chief engineer, and head farmer all had to live on grounds. Dr. Alexander lived in Cottage 1, Dr. Goldschmidt in Cottage 2, and Ben Burdick in Cottage 5.

Marshall and Michael Lipkin lived next door to us in Cottage 4. Their mother was Dr. Tankel. Michael and I were about the same age, with Marshall a little older. We loved to play "werewolf." Mike and I would hide, and Marshall would be the werewolf. Perhaps that was the start of his love for acting, as he is now a well-known actor in the tri-county area. One of our hideouts would be at the top of the water tower. It was the old one that is no longer there.

Dr. Ellingsworth was the superintendent when we first moved there. He had a pony and ponycart, riding around the grounds in it. We got to feed the pony.

We liked the patients and would trade comic books with some of them. Mike and I would ride all over the grounds on our bikes. The wards were set up with six or seven steps up to the front porch, which went into the main floor where the patients had their activities during the day. They slept on the second floor. They had walkout basements, which was the patients' dining room. There were ramps under the building, where trucks came in to deliver food. Mike and I couldn't resist riding the ramps, and one day a patient came out, perhaps to dump some garbage, and was startled by us and dropped what he was carrying. I don't think it hurt him, but we didn't wait to find out, riding away scared.

Softball was an important activity for the patients and employees. There was a nice ball diamond with lights. My brother and I played on the employees' team. One of the pitchers on the patient team was Johnny. He was crazy, but such a good pitcher. He was so good that when the employee team played at Pekin Mineral Springs Park, they took Johnny along to pitch. We would trade comic books with Johnny, and one day he told us about the time he walked across the Mississippi River under water. We were fascinated with how he said he did it. He said he used a perfume bottle atomizer filled with air, and kept breathing that air to keep his oxygen. Johnny lived on one of the unlocked C-wards.

George was known to have been a black semi-pro baseball player. He was first baseman, and was also a great hitter, never missing a ball. He was out of touch with reality most of the time, talking to himself and making weird motions. But when that ball made contact it brought him back to reality.

Maury, another patient, was left fielder. He was epileptic, and there had to be time-outs during the game when he had a seizure.

Roscoe was my favorite. He delivered groceries to the houses. He seemed very normal, but we assumed he had a stroke as a young person and one side was paralyzed, so he dragged his leg as he walked. Dad's salary was low because his living quarters and food reduced his salary. Roscoe liked dad and always took care of "Mr. Roy."

Dad was well liked by all the patients and fellow employees and would take time to talk with the patients and would sometimes give them money to spend in the commissary. Dad had lost an arm in a factory accident when he was younger, so he went back to school to qualify to get a better job. He never let this keep him from making a good life for his family, starting out as a clerk at PSH and working his way up.

Movies were shown every Wednesday night at the main amusement hall. Nick Frasco ran the movie projector. At times outsiders were banned from coming to see the movies, probably because on the way home some boys would cut through by the powerhouse, where there was a whistle. They would tie bricks on the whistle and then take off running. There were dances two nights a week. The orchestra that played for the dances was made up of patients and employees. Shuffleboard, ping pong, and basketball were also popular activities.

Some patients mowed our yard but didn't do a good job. They would argue about which portion of the yard they were to do and sometimes would ram their mowers together.

I worked two summers while in high school for Swords, McDougal and Hartman. They had the contract to place underground telephone cables. I helped dig trenches for the cables with a pick and shovel. Once we were in front of 9C, a women's locked ward. A patient, that apparently had privileges to clean, came out on the porch with a mop and bucket. She didn't like the fact that I was there, so she slid a mop across the porch and knocked off my ball cap with the mop handle and yelled at me to "get out of here." I "got out of there" before she could throw her bucket of water on me. I bought my first car with the money I made those two summers.

My dad retired from Peoria State Hospital in 1966. Unfortunately, he died in 1968 and didn't get to do all the things he and my mother had planned together.

Ken Kocher

Business Manager LeRoy Kocher and his staff in his office at Peoria State Hospital.

Farm Colony Number One

Forty-seven males are provided for in Farm Colony Number One. The building is of brick with concrete floors and included a full basement and steam heating plant in the basement. Someone has had the foresight to select a real fireman, who is on duty at three o'clock in the morning and faithfully attends his duties throughout the day. During the severest of these January days neither those in authority nor inmates have made complaint of the cold.

The first floor is used as a kitchen, dining room, lounging and reading room. On this floor the farm superintendent, Mr. C. H. Upp and his wife, who is employed as a housekeeper, have their quarters. The second floor is used entirely as a dormitory. Inmates care for the cleanliness of the rooms and the preparing of the cots. No one could justly complain of the cleanliness or the care that is being taken of these household duties in any of the Farm Colonies. Ten inmates are quartered in what is known as the Annex, just across the public highway from Colony Number One, making a total of fifty-seven cared for at Farm Colony Number One.

Here are located the cattle and hog barns one and seven-tenths miles from the administration building. The institution has a total of 130 cattle and 384 hogs. The dairyman has his rooms at the Annex. He and a detail of nine men in this colony milk the forty-five cows and perform some sort of duty for the state. If not detailed in the cattle or hog barns, caring for the homes, preparing the meals or shoveling snow, they were hauling manure, repairing the system of roads or hauling and unloading coal. They seem to perform those duties without complaint and with no further direction than many that have been given them in the morning.

When the dining hour arrives, a farm bell makes the announcement, and inmates, like so many farm hands, respond from all parts of the 737-acre farm, going to their respective homes. When the meal is finished, they as quietly depart, resume their respective duties, or enter upon some new work.

E. B. Bentley, Welfare Bulletin, February & March 1930

Jean Merriman's memories about his parents - Guy and Freeda Merriman

My mother and father both worked at Farm Colony #1, starting in 1934, as I remember. They were supposed to live in the farm residence, which later became Abbott Center, because they supervised the patients; Mother in the kitchen, and Dad the dairy and hog farm. We lived in a house across the gully from Mr. Wolschlag, farm boss, right north of what is now Alpha Park Library. Since my three older brothers and three sisters and I were at the house, my mother usually managed to come home to stay with us when she wasn't working.

The patients that worked on the farm lived there, sleeping in the dormitory on the top floor. The main floor was the dining area, with the kitchen on the south and a large room for patients to sit in. The north end of the building had rooms for employees.

Dad took a young mentally handicapped patient, Gene, under his wing. Gene worked on the farm, but he was always there with Dad. I remember an African American gentleman. Dad told me he was born a slave. He was a quiet old man who liked kids. I was only six, and I would crawl up on his lap and he would talk to me.

Dad had a close call with another patient. He was helping the patients cut corn for silage. They were using corn knives, and for some reason the patient lost it and came at my dad with the knife. Dad talked him into giving him the knife, and said he would talk to him when they got back to the residence. He was later transferred back to the main hospital.

We moved to Peoria around 1936 from Bartonville. Dad started hauling milk from the dairy farm to Schwab's Dairy on Western Avenue in Peoria. Mom stopped working shortly after moving to Peoria to take care of the family. Dad then went into barbering - shaving and cutting hair in the basement of the residence and the main hospital. He didn't have to have a barbering license, but eventually got one. My brothers, brother-in-law, and I built a house on Pfeiffer Road for our parents. I was 27 when my dad died in 1954. Mother died in 1981.

Clayton and the hog farm - Dick Lawless memories

I was a pipefitter at PSH from 1953-1964. Clayton, a patient and ex-railroader, wore his bib overalls with pants tucked into his socks. He always looked neat and had a good watch on a chain. He would take care of about 300 hogs every day on the farm, then stop at my building. He loved caring for the hogs. We became friends, and I delighted in getting him presents on special occasions. Once in awhile my wife would make cookies and tell me to take them to Clayton. When he was asked by the staff for them he would say, "You're not getting any of these." His watch was just perfect, so a guy I worked with and I would sometimes go to see Clayton, and Bill would say to me, "What time is it?" And I would see Clayton getting his watch out, and I would say, "It's a quarter after three" and Clayton would say, "Wait a minute, wait a minute, it's five after three. He would be right, but I would tease him, saying, "You had better get the oil changed in that watch."

Cattle on Farm Colony One.   **Alpha Park Library**

231

Guy Merriman hauling milk from the dairy farm to Schwab's Dairy in Peoria.   Jean Merriman

Hogs on Farm Colony One.   Alpha Park Library

Memories of a Long-standing Peoria State Hospital Supervising Nurse - Beulah Bell

When I went to work at Peoria State Hospital in 1937, Dr. Zeller was already retired. He still kept his residence there. He spent many hours in the Sunken Garden, enjoying the sunshine.

I went from high school in 1930 to nurses' training at Jacksonville State Hospital. I graduated from nurses' training at Jacksonville. I transferred from there to Peoria State Hospital because my husband worked for Caterpillar.

One day several nurses, myself included, went to the Bowen building on our lunch hour for something to do. The student nurses had their residence there. We knew we had no business being there. While there we looked out the window and saw the chief nurse coming in the front door. We didn't dare go out that way so we crawled out a window - those white uniformed prissy nurses crawling out the window where we had no business being in the first place.

I think the most disturbing period I had at PSH was when the employees went on strike. If anyone would have asked me I would have sworn they would never do that, but they did. Mr. Lagerbloom was chief nurse at that time. He told me to put all the employees who did come to work on twelve-hour shifts. Bill Becker brought help from his Alcoholic Unit to help us bath and feed our old men on the Infirmary. Maybe I didn't try hard enough to understand the employees and their union feelings, but my concern was getting all these people bathed, fed and medicated. We had some wonderful employees at PSH over the years. They were faithful and devoted. They deserve a lot of credit.

We had a male patient called Homer, who took care of the supervisors. When it snowed he always saw to it that our cars were cleaned off by the end of our shift. We had a patient by the name of Mary. She worked faithfully with the nurses in the operating room. There were many such people throughout the hospital who helped so much.

We had a young doctor by the name of Dr. Tarjan. He taught me so many things. When he left Peoria State he went to California and became very high in the psychiatric world. He was only at Peoria State a short time. He was a very brilliant and pleasant person, and great to work with.

Mary Danner - *hydrotherapist for some 30 years at PSH*
(Mary turned 95 in 2004)

I loved my job at Peoria State Hospital as a hydrotherapist. I had to have six months training first. A nurse, Minnie Hill, did some of the training and I also worked under a registered hydrotherapist, named Gertrude Haughey. I continued working under Gertrude after I finished my training, and when she retired, I was promoted to the head hydrotherapist for the women.

Each procedure was done only with a doctor's order. Even though it sounded harsh, many patients, such as manic-depressives that came in needed to be stabilized. When they came in depressed they would be wrapped in cold sheets, and when manic they would usually be given a warm, continuous bath. The sheet wrap was done by having the patient strip, and we would wrap them in a sheet dampened with cold tap water. They would stand with arms out. The sheet was wrapped around their shoulders from back to front - then with their arms by their sides it was pulled around their arms to the back with the bottom of the sheet coming up between their legs. They were then laid on another cold sheet, wrapped again, and a wool blanket was wrapped around them. They would have a cold towel on their heads. Gradually the body temperature would rise as the sheets warmed up, and this would form a sedative reaction. I had help from nursing students and an attendant. When the patient needed to be calmed down, they would be given a warm continuous bath. They would be put in a bathtub with a canvas cover, and warm water would continuously run to keep an even temperature. This would relax the patient. Each procedure would take 1 to 1 1/2 hours.

Pulse would be taken before the procedure, then every half hour. With new patients, I would explain the whole procedure to them before it was done. This would reduce their anxiety. But there were still violent patients. At the beginning, we were not to wear uniforms because of the patients tearing them, so we had to wrap ourselves in sheets (see photo; Mary is on the left.) There were times when I would give treatments to seven patients twice a day.

Alcoholics were also treated with "elimination" baths. When the bath was over the water was discolored. We had to watch them very closely as they could go into convulsions.

When patients were sluggish we would have them stand in the shower and spray a spurt of warm water on them, then a spurt of cold water, and continue with this routine for five to seven minutes. This would stimulate a depressed person. I remember one woman in particular that this procedure helped. If someone would take her for a walk, she would lie down, so she was given this treatment.

Another, a manic-depressive, had gone to a church while a funeral service was on. The priest was in the middle of the service when she walked up to him and said, "Why don't you just shut up and let this man go to heaven in peace?" Of course, she ended up at PSH. She had a beautiful voice. She would stand and sing, but wouldn't eat. She would usually get continuous sedative baths. Her husband would visit her. They had five children. She got better, but when she had a relapse she would always come to my hydro door and let me know she was back.

Another patient was a young girl, a chronic runaway, about 16, that I got permission from the doctor to have her help me in hydro with cleaning and such. I told her I had to trust her, and she promised me that I could trust her. I took her home with me (with the doctor's permission). My daughter was about her age. We went to Pekin to a carnival. They rode on the rides and she stayed all night, then went back with me the next morning. She continued to help me and was very gentle with the patients. Dr. Emil Levitin would send patients to me telling them, "Go to the little white-haired lady in hydro - she will take care of you." Other doctors that referred patients to me were Dr. Molly Robertson, whom I loved, and Dr. Esther Stone of the receiving ward.

One patient cried all the time. She had group sessions with a psychologist. She was treated in hydro, and when she went back to the ward a psychiatrist from Peoria asked her, "Well, how are you?" She said, "I'm not very good. Mrs. Danner told me I was going to have to have surgery. She told me that I had a dislocated bladder. She said it was behind my eyeballs." I was then told, "Mary Danner, you upset our meeting today."

[With a giggle, this little lady finished with another memory.] When I first worked at the hospital, around 1942, I was an attendant and lived in one of the cottages, since the Nurses' Residence was already full. The small room had two single beds and a wardrobe in it. I roomed with a young girl who was supposed to be 18 to work there, but she revealed to me that she had lied and she was only 16. She was working on Z-1, the men's hospital ward. She had a ribbon in her hair which was a safety issue, and the head nurse made her remove it. That night a man died, and she had to get him ready to be "laid out." When he arrived at the morgue, the workers couldn't stop laughing. She had tied her ribbon around his private part. She told me what happened, stating that he would be the only one to go to heaven in a package. I asked her why she did it.   She said about the nurse, "She made me mad." This story went all over the hill.

Mary, center, wrapping a female patient.   **Mary Danner**

Forever Friends - *Four nursing students did their two-month psychiatric training at PSH in 1946. Memories given at the 56th nurses reunion - Class of 1948 Mennonite School of Nursing, Bloomington. They are as follows: Jane (Davis) Rieger, R.N., Betty (Rosendahl) Wagner, R.N., Mickey (Dunlap) Epperson, R.N., and Mary (Twist) Freese, R.N.*

All: We all remember Artie. The day we arrived at Peoria State Hospital, a patient met us at our car, grabbed our luggage before we could blink an eye, and carried it into the Nurse's Residence, which would be our home for two months. He was mentally challenged, but very polite. He had ground privileges, so he would always be around. **Mickey and Mary:** We had a wiener roast the last day we were there. Artie started the fire for us.

Jane: My first day on the hospital ward we had an orientation. I will never forget the feeling when we walked into the ward and we heard the sound of the key turning in the lock. It was scary. One of our assignments was to give medication, under the supervision of the charge nurse. We were transferred to different wards. A patient, Ivan, on one ward was very intimidating. We were told never to turn our back on him because he had a sexual problem. Some people were there for dementia. I remember rows and rows of metal cots for bedfast patients. We had to change the linens. We would just get done and would have to start over again. We also did case studies. One was of the most beautiful girl I have ever seen in my life. She had postpartum psychosis. She had killed her six-month-old baby. She had thrown it down the stairs and then stabbed it with a butcher knife. Her husband was in the service. He was very handsome. He came to visit her and she didn't even know him. This made a lasting impression .We were assigned to help with recreation in the big day rooms. I was taught by the patients how to play pinochle. There were dances every Monday and Thursday night, and we danced with the patients. We ate in the hospital cafeteria. We had plenty to eat. They had really good food, the huge dishes of ice cream with fresh strawberries comes to mind. We were there over Christmas, and News Years Eve we were allowed to stay out all night as long as we were at work at 7 a.m. Some of us and our boyfriends went into Peoria and got back between 3 and 4 in the morning, but we were at work on time. We remember the tavern at the bottom of the steps, called the "Blue Gardens." We were too young to drink, and of course, that was against the rules, but we would sometimes go there to eat hamburgers. They would play the song, "Open the Door, Richard" frequently.

Betty: My Dad took Jane and me to Bartonville to begin our psychiatric training. Dad thought Artie was a staff member when he came out to help get us settled into our new quarters. My first assignment was 9C, the women's violent ward. One day a nineteen-year-old girl had me backed up against one of the exam tables. If she liked you she wouldn't hurt you, so I was safe but still scared. We helped wrap patients in cold sheets for therapy - then they were put in a tub with warm water running continuously, which would soothe them. When I was working at the Zeller Hospital in admitting, I was preparing to give medications. I came out of the drug room with the pills and started down the hall to the day room. Here comes Ivan, the patient Betty referred to with the sex problem. Fortunately, "Rags" one of the attendants, came out of another room and accompanied me to the day room. Sometimes I would sit under the stairway with a patient, Hazel, putting together jigsaw puzzles when I was supposed to be doing other duties. I remember one little guy we danced with who, while dancing (shuffling) would be constantly whistling along with the music. Some of the nurses felt uncomfortable going and dancing with the patients, but we thoroughly enjoyed it. Some of the men were very good dancers. They would always pick a nurse first, and when all the nurses were taken, they would ask the women patients.

Mickey: At our orientation we were told never to mistreat a patient, and during the two months I was there I never saw any patient mistreated. Even in the violent ward the patients seemed to respect us, because of our uniforms, so I became unafraid of them. Some of us had roommates from other nursing schools. There was a patient who called herself the "bath lady." This was her job and she loved it. We would help put the patients into the bathtub and she would bathe them. Another patient passed out linens (towels, etc.) in the dormitory ward. She would get upset if anyone of us would take them before she passed them out. We were never wallflowers at the dances. We did a lot of square dancing. Our psychiatric classes were very good. We had an especially good professor - a doctor who graduated from medical school in Austria. He was an Austrian Jew and he told us stories of how he had escaped the Nazis. Once when my boyfriend, who later became my husband, came to see me, he didn't get out of the car because a patient was beating on a motorcycle beside his car. I came out and told the patient to stop, and he left. Also, my husband recalls that a patient was pushing a wheelbarrow upside down. He asked him why, and he said, "If I would turn it over, they would fill it up." Also mentally retarded patients were among those who mowed grass with push lawn mowers. Some pushed them upside down, but this was accepted by the staff - the patient still gained the satisfaction of working. For the most part, the patients were happy. They had a nice bed, three meals a day, and medical care.

Mary: Mickey and I were at PSH in April and May. If we had class on our day off, we still had to go. We had to work either day or evening shift, and our days off were rotated. I remember a heavy African American man that scrubbed the floor in the utility room. He always had suds all over the floor. We would hand him bed pans through a door in the wall - there were bedpan flushers, he flipped the lid shut and it was flushed and given back to us clean. There were a lot of alcoholics. Some needed to dry out. They were mixed in with all the rest of the patients. If any confused patient attacked us, the alcoholics would come to our defense. They were more normal as they got dried out. They were our protection. We had to be in the room when some patients got shock therapy - we were to take care of them immediately after, and it scared us to death. They were rigid and not responsive right away, with some having delayed reactions and going into convulsions. It was not pleasant. On our days off, we would walk down the many steps to the bottom of the hill and take a bus to downtown Peoria. We would mostly window shop, as money was not plentiful. Sometimes we would have ice cream before going back to the hospital. We didn't get home very much, because of the long bus trips.

All: We worked very hard, but oh, we had such good times, too!

Left: Betty and roommate

Jane, Mickey, Mary, and Betty in 2004 at their 56th reunion, Gary Lisman at Mary's home in Seymour, Illinois.

Left: Jane and roommate

237

PSH Powerhouse and More - *by Marion "Bub" Veaughn*

I started working at PSH on March 7, 1947, as an attendant on the wards. My career was interrupted by the Korean War, in which I served from November of 1950 to 1952, then returned to PSH. I worked in the laundry for a short while, then became a stationary engineer, working in the powerhouse, making steam and generating electricity with coal. I usually stayed in the powerhouse during working hours, bringing a box lunch. Another duty was maintaining the tunnels by fixing leaks in water pipes, etc. My co-workers and I also dug graves at the cemeteries. We would dig six or eight at a time. When there was a funeral we would be on hand to cover the grave if needed. Many times the patients would shovel the dirt over the wooden box or caskets (in later years).

I remember living in the Employee Residence, the existing Bowen Building. Single people had a small room and married ones a larger room. The bathrooms were located in the hallways. When I married in 1954 I moved off grounds.

A patient, Jimmy, was assigned to the powerhouse, cleaning and sweeping. He would run errands for the engineers, and would make money going to the commissary for cigarettes by charging an extra dime for each pack.

I fondly remember an old patient, Walter, a WWI veteran, who bused tables in the commissary. I'm not sure why he was there. He seemed as normal as I, and he talked to everyone who came in. Many of the employees came from Southern Illinois, so when Walter was asked who a new employee was, he would say, "just another big butter and egg man from down home."

A humorous incident happened when Peoria State Hospital closed in 1973. Dick Hurst, chief engineer at Galesburg Mental Health Center, was there looking at equipment in the Bowen Building. He had formerly been an engineer at PSH. He was in the elevator when the generator was turned off for the last time. He might have been there to this day if someone hadn't heard him knocking on the elevator door.

The generator was turned on again to rescue him.

Powerhouse as it looks today.   Melody Bridges

Original Powerhouse - razed in early1950s   **Biennial Reports**

Pump Room in Old Powerhouse   **Biennial Reports**

The Power House supplies heat and light to the institution. A carload of coal is burned each day. The Maintenance Department includes truck drivers, steamfitters, plumbers, carpenters, painters, automotive mechanic, machinists, laborers, grounds personnel and power plant engineers, fireman and maintenance workers.

From an Open House Brochure

Fond memories of PSH - *Todd W. Garrison, son of Lucile Garrison-Lane-Clevenger*

I have many fond memories of Peoria State Hospital. After my father's death in 1953, my mother started her job as a secretary there, and retired from Zeller Zone Center in 1984.

My first memory of the hospital was before my mother started working there. I was about six years old. My parents rented a house in front of Keystone Steel and Wire on Adams Street (my father worked at Keystone). During the summers, patients would come down and sit on the hill of the hospital grounds across the street. As a young kid it seemed like hundreds of people. I was never afraid, for my parents never spoke of the mentally ill in a negative way. I never remember hearing the word "crazy" but only that these people were sick and needed help.

A story that I heard from my parents was that one day a patient escaped and knocked on the door of our home. My dad went to answer the door and found this man, bloody from breaking out of the hospital, asking for help. My father called the police and the patient was returned to the hospital.

After my mother started working at the hospital, I would go to patient activities with her in the evenings. I went to patient dances and movies. I remember watching a John Payne movie there, but can't remember the title. I always remember the beautiful flower gardens on campus; it was a very busy, bustling hospital back then.

One of my best friends at Limestone High School was Paul Springer. His father, Harold Springer, was the administrator there in the early 1960s; my mother was his secretary. The Springers lived in one of the houses on campus, as did other personnel.

The summer of 1963 after my third year of college I worked in the pharmacy there. The head pharmacist, as I remember, was Mr. Kessinger. I think before he came to Peoria State he owned a pharmacy in Peoria. The pharmacy was very busy dispensing medication for patients and supplies for the surgery department.

When I come home, I will drive around the old hospital grounds. I have very fond memories of that place in my past history. I suppose it was from my involvement there that I eventually started working in mental health in 1979. I received my master's degree in counseling from Bradley University in 1984 and am a Licensed Clinical Professional Counselor currently working in the mental health department at Provena St. Joseph Medical Center in Joliet, Illinois.

Our Billie Boy - *by Barbara Runyan, former Executive Director of Mental Health Association of Illinois Valley*

Billie was abandoned as an infant on a doorstep in Chicago. After numerous placements over several years, he was transferred to Peoria State Hospital. PSH staff brought him to the attention of one of Mental Health Association's volunteers, Betty Belfer. She and her husband, Sam, took Billie under their wing and provided many wonderful opportunities for him. Billie was blind and also hyperactive. My husband, myself, and our four children started to include him in some of our family activities. Billie would rock back and forth constantly, something my children found annoying. They were successful in helping him reduce this behavior by making it a stipulation when taking him to any of their activities. He loved music and could play the guitar.

Later, Billie was placed in a local nursing home. He roomed with an elderly black man who wanted quiet. He became very frustrated when he could not listen to TV or play his radio. My husband took a TV set apart and utilized the audio portion through earphones. This gave Billie the entertainment he wanted without disturbing his roommate.

Later, Billie was given the opportunity to learn how to develop x-ray film and eventually was employed by a hospital out East. Gainful employment opened up a new world to him. He traveled to Jerusalem with a tour group and couldn't contain his excitement as he explained all the things he had "seen" through the tour guide's eyes.

He has since married and still calls us occasionally just to catch up on things.

Billie's 75 cents for St. Jude kids raised millions of dollars - *excerpted from story in 1959 Jim Maloof told to the Journal Star*

Jim Maloof, local realtor and advocate of St. Jude, brought his friend, Danny Thomas, to Peoria State Hospital in 1959. He said, "I'm introducing Danny to Dr. Klein, and I literally had to yell at the top of my voice to be heard. Believe this or not, above all this noise. . .above everything else that was happening came a youngster's voice.

"That youngster's voice said, 'Danny, Danny Thomas, if you're here, if you're really here I've got to see you.'

"It was such a pathetic cry. About 75 feet away a nurse pointed down to a youngster in a wheelchair. Danny said, 'Take me to that kid.' Immediately Danny saw that the youngster was blind and he was trembling so hard. He had some kind of palsy. And in his hand was a white envelope pinched in his fists, and he couldn't hold it still. Danny knelt down in front of this youngster and reached over and touched him. . . .the youngster reached over and touched his face and said, 'Are you really Danny Thomas?' Yes, yes.

The youngster said when he found out Danny Thomas was coming, he started saving candy and gum money. He had something for Danny. He said, 'I want to give you this for those kids that you're trying to save.'

"Danny Thomas wept as hard as any adult I have ever seen in my life. He finally pulled himself together and asked what was in the envelope. He said, '75 cents, and it's all yours Danny.'

"The kid was 11 years old, blind, palsy, named Billy Johnson. Danny picked the youngster up and took him over to a little recreational area. He told me to get up and sing a song while he pulled himself together.

"Danny vowed then and there that 75 cents of Billy Johnson's would be in the cornerstone of the

St. Jude statue which would someday go in front of the St. Jude hospital in Memphis. Danny took that 75 cents and told that story in such a way he raised millions of dollars.

"But what you have to hear is how that   youngster's voice sounded like a bell over and above all that noise. It was just meant to be."

Peoria Journal Star
Danny Thomas standing on right, and Jim Maloof, second from right, meeting Billy Johnson.

Peoria Journal Star
Danny Thomas, Dr. Klein, and George Shadid standing, with Billy Johnson standing on left.

Journal Star
From left, Danny Thomas, Billy Johnson, Jim Maloof and George Shadid. Billy is presenting his 75 cents to Danny Thomas.

Journal Star
Pictured: Dr. Klein, Danny Thomas, Jim Maloof, and George Shadid, while Danny is speaking to Billy Johnson. (Man in hat - unknown)

Grown-up Bill Johnson

In an interview with Bill Johnson, I discovered what had happened to him over the years.

Bill was at Peoria State Hospital from 1956 to 1962, transferring to Jacksonville School for the Blind in 1966. He said he would be sent back to PSH during summer and spring breaks, so he kept in touch with those that meant the most to him. In 1966 he was sent to Bellwood Nursing Home. He then moved to Chicago, staying at the YMCA, and working at a workshop there. In 1970 he was at a real low in his life, having broken up with a girlfriend, and was planning to commit suicide by jumping out of a window. Fortunately, a friend, Rita, called him to say she was getting married, and also a resident of the "Y" invited him to church, which was a turning point for him. He became a born-again Christian.

His friend, Rita, was an airline stewardess who had befriended him on some trips. They would go out for a hamburger when she came to Chicago. Eventually he went to live with Rita and her husband until he got established at the Mountainside Hospital, Mt. Clair, New Jersey, where he became an x-ray darkroom technician. He was employed there from 1973 to 1994, when he was laid off because of automation. He had met his two birth sisters in 1974, and finally met his birth mother in 1994. She is now deceased.

Bill met his wife, Nancy, in 1984, and they married in 1991. He plays guitar and keyboard, and Nancy sings and plays the accordion. They sometimes perform at churches and at nursing homes.

Bill has some unpleasant memories of Peoria State, noting that some of the staff were very harsh, but some were nice. He remembered the hydrotherapy baths, stating that Ernie Dare was the hydrotherapist at the time. Although Ernie was nice to him, he didn't appreciate the baths but said they were relaxing. He recalls Stan Musial and Curt Flood coming to speak about baseball. The most pleasant memories were of the volunteers. Two of the volunteers were previously mentioned, and a third was Elsie Schelm. Elsie befriended Bill while volunteering at PSH. Over the years he would continue to stay with her and her husband some. They even continued to help him out while he was in Chicago, visiting him and buying him clothes and giving him money. Her attorney husband was instrumental in finding his biological mother. He composed poems, which he set to music, for these favorite volunteers (on page 4)

He continued a relationship with Danny Thomas and Jim Maloof. Bill stated he went to several St. Jude conventions, and was recognized by Danny Thomas at some of them. Danny would tell the story of the 75 cents, and in 1988 in Washington, D.C., Bill gave him another 75 cents to start a research wing in Memphis. He said on two different occasions Danny gave him first $50, then $100. Danny also paid for his flight and hotel to bring him to one of the conventions. Bill said he would have private conversations with Danny after the telethons.

Poems written by Bill Johnson and set to music, in memory of his experiences at Peoria State Hospital

The Institution

One day I was put away,
In a bad place I did stay.
All the windows they were barred,
Life in there was also hard.

There were children just like me,
In this place we were not free.
People then they took me out,
When I left I raised a shout!

Thank you, Christ, for what they've done.
Show them that the victory's won!
I rejoice and give you praise,
You were with me through those days!

The Volunteers

In the institution there,
Volunteers their love did share!
Elsie took me to the fair,
As a child what fun was there!

Then the Runyans took me out,
To their home and all about!
With them, Christ, I had such fun,
Please bless them, God's only Son!

Come to them, Eternal Lord,
Come and be their Great Reward!
For them you were sacrificed,
O Dear Christ, You've paid the Price!

Betty Belfer, Christ Please Bless

Betty Belfer, Christ please bless,
Come to her take her distress!
You're the God of Abraham,
And You are the Great I Am!

Betty's daughter, Mary, bless,
Come to her Christ, give her rest!
They for me have done so much,
Give them both your tender touch!

May I hear, "My Son, well, done?"
When my victory is won!
I'll walk the Golden Strand,
In Your Holy Promised Land!

Note: Betty died of ill health in 2003

Danny Thomas and Bill Johnson, ALSAC*   Jerry Luther
Mardi Gras, New Orleans. October 21, 1989

*American Lebanese Syrian Associated Charities

244

Milford won the hearts of everyone in the building *by Jackson Myers, Director of Activity Therapy, Peoria State Hospital*

It was February 14, 1962, my first day at Peoria State Hospital. I became a mentor to Bill Turner, who worked his way up through the ranks from janitor, finally getting his bachelor's degree at Bradley, and working with me throughout the years in the Activity Therapy Department.

Our first activity building was Lohmann Hall. I became the first director of the new activity building. We moved into it on January 1, 1967. It was what is now The Courtyard, Stone Country, and The Phoenix Club with hallways to connect the buildings.

At Lohmann Hall we had a patient who was the janitor. He was prone to seizures and once was walking up the walk and had a seizure. I held him down until it was over. When he died one of the other patients, Milford, who usually just sat in a chair, came in the very next day and asked for his job.

Milford did get the job and became a favorite. He won the hearts of everyone in the building. We had six staff members, and there were three people from Volunteer Services. The patient library and home living were in what is now The Courtyard, plus another room in the middle, with the back half being used for storage and the front half for dances, parties, and the workshop. The building which is now the Phoenix Club was used for the woodshop and creative arts programs. Stone Country was the gymnasium.

Milford would dust mop the hallways and the gym and help set up programs. He took his job seriously and would hang around looking for things to do. He always kept the place looking good. He would do anything he was asked to do. You couldn't ask for a better person. Every morning after taking his meds, he would come over and stay until 11 a.m., then came back at 1 p.m. and stayed until 4:30 p.m. when we all went home. He had seizures and the nursing staff worked around his schedule.

Milford was short and stocky. He would talk staccato. He was funny. He always liked a good joke, but although he wouldn't tell them himself, we sometimes would help him pull a prank on another or tell a joke. He would laugh his deep laugh and his pot belly would shake like a bowlful of jelly. But he had such sad eyes. He chewed snuff and usually had it down the corners of his mouth.

I didn't know of any family that he had.

He even asked Bill, who was only 30, to adopt him. At that time he was around 60 years old. He looked forward to Christmas and his birthday and we saw that he got a present or two. When he got cards he would shake the envelopes to see if any money was in them, and usually found a dollar bill in them. He would always get so excited and went around saying, "Merry, Merry, Happy, Happy." (for Merry Christmas and Happy New Year).

Milford was with us for about 10 years, but when PSH closed, he went to a nursing home. He was a real joy to have around.

The Chaplain's Comments - *Rev. Eimo Hinrichs*

When I first came to Peoria State Hospital in 1962, we had services in the old gymnasium, a big barn-like structure. We averaged 140 people per Sunday at our Protestant service. There was a certain amount of movement - patients coming and going - but hospital attendants were there to keep control. The worship service was a little over half an hour, as the patients didn't have a long attention span. The patient population was about 2,450 at the time.

After the gymnasium was torn down, the worship services were held for awhile in the basement of the C-Row building. Later the new auditorium was constructed and services were held there. A new Catholic parish was started in Bartonville in the late 60s, and the parishioners worshiped along with the patients in the auditorium for several years.

Dr. Zeller had been concerned about the patients' religious well-being as well as their mental and physical health. But there was no continuity because we had different ministers each week and they came in cold as to the needs of the patients. There were no full-time chaplains until the 1950s.

I think B-Hall is the building used for the services mentioned in the biennial report, but it burned several years after I started. It was just an oblong-shaped building and it didn't have a stage. It was next to the 5B Alcohol Treatment Ward. It was used by Activity Therapy for their program. I used the hall every year for seminars for area clergy, and as many as 75 would attend. I would invite a speaker related to mental health and pay an honorarium.

Patients I remember include Karl, who was in his 60s. He used to stop and see me almost every morning in my office. He was afraid that he had committed the unpardonable sin. Every day he would go over details of why he thought he had committed that sin. He would appear to be somewhat relieved after talking with me and our praying together. But the next day, he would be in as deep despair as before. Larry was a gentleman in his 50s who was admitted several times to the alcoholism unit. He made a good living going to gun shows and engraving the names of people on their gun stocks. At the hospital, he offered to use his small tool to engrave your name on a watch, ring or piece of jewelry. It would take him only a matter of seconds to skillfully engrave one's name or initials. He claimed he once engraved the entire Lord's prayer on a penny.

Another gentleman, in his 60s, was transferred from Chicago State Hospital to the maximum security ward after one violent incident related to his mental illness. He soon became known as an expert checker player. Since I considered myself a fairly good player, I took him on one day. Within a matter of minutes, he had defeated me and still remained the undisputed champion.

James, in his 50s, was skillful in greeting people who were coming into the administration building from the outside. He asked questions to see if he could discover some connection between them and people he knew, especially if they were African-American, and then he would solicit some financial help for himself. He seemed to be quite comfortable and institutionalized at the hospital. So I was rather surprised when he left on an unauthorized absence. About six months later, I was in Minneapolis for a convention. In the basement of the hotel was a shoe shine shop. To my amazement, James was working in that shop shining shoes. He pretended not to know who I was. Since he appeared to be surviving quite well and making it on the outside, I felt there was no point in notifying anyone I had seen him. He had succeeded in deinstitutionalizing himself, even before this concept was fully in practice.

Another gentleman was always well-dressed, with a suit coat and tie. I was not aware he had inherited considerable family wealth until one day I was told that he was taking a chauffeured vacation trip down south.

The mid-60s were the beginning of de-institutionalization in the state hospitals. The use of the new medications made it possible to place a great number of people in the community, either living on their own or in sheltered care or nursing care facilities. By the early 70s the population had dropped to about 650. The less severely disturbed people were being admitted to Zeller, and gradually all the admissions were shifted to Zeller. The decision was made in 1972 to phase out the hospital completely. There were about 450 people who were transferred to Galesburg State Hospital, and some to Zeller. The hospital was officially closed in December of 1973. I was serving Zeller Mental Health Center when it opened in 1967, so I served at both places until Peoria State Hospital was completely closed.

Elliott! - by Margaret E. Vogelsang, RN, MS, PA-C (did her psychiatric nurses training at PSH in 1962)

Oh heavens, my first day on the men's locked ward, what can I expect?" The thought was not even completed before Elliott rolled up in his wheelchair, with a *"Hi kid, you're sure a skinny little uptight priss, aren't you?"*

What a pair we made, a skinny little 19-year-old student nurse, and Elliott, a fifty something. . .well, Elliott was Elliott. Clinically, I learned that he was diagnosed with what was then called manic-depressive disorder. This hospitalization, one of many, was a result of manic behavior. Elliott was hopping down the steps of the county courthouse on his head.

In his depressive phase he was near catatonic, never moving, never speaking, just sitting and staring at the floor. He was led to his next "assignment" whether it be to eat, to wash, to brush, or to go to the bathroom. He would slowly phase into "normal" only to suddenly burst without warning into his manic phase, shouting, singing, jumping from bed to bed, urinating on pillows, beds, linens and anyone who tried to subdue him. Personally, I learned that the best way to control him during these times was to take his artificial legs from him. This confined him to a wheelchair and limited his movements to areas where the large chair would fit. Additionally, it prevented him from hiding and jumping out unexpectedly, shouting Tarzan-like at startled staff and patients. His usual response to the irate victim was *"it was only a joke. Relax, have a little fun."*

Elliott had been diagnosed with manic-depressive disorder many years prior to our meeting and had been hospitalized all over the country. One winter "up North," he ran away in the middle of the night in his pajamas and slippers. He froze both his feet and required amputations below the knees. He was fitted with bilateral feet and legs and was very mobile and agile. . .thus the necessity for *"stealing his feet"* when he misbehaved.

I spent a six-week rotation on the men's locked ward and chose Elliott as my case study, or Elliott selected me and elected to be my case study. He monopolized my time, waited at the door when I arrived, and escorted me to the door when I left. I saw him phase through depression, normalcy and mania, but in truth, he spent most of the time in his wheelchair because *"they stole my feet again, kid."*

He regaled me with wonderful stories of his life and escapades.

> *I was born into the circus; my mother was a trapeze artist, and performed almost to the day I was born. I was a wire-walker and was the star with Barnam and Bailey. I had command performances before all the kings and queens in Europe. They loved me, center ring, star of the show. I was in the "Road Shows" with Crosby and Hope, you know.*

He described his grand finale as "The Slide of Death" in which he slid on his head from the high wire down the guide wire to the ground with no safety harness. "Sure, Elliott" I would say, and smile condescendingly as I listened to the delusions of this uninhibited wild man. There was no therapeutic time that I had envisioned. We played chess, pinochle, and sang together as we played duets on the piano. I enjoyed our time together, and he loved shocking me with some wild and frequently lewd tale. But no matter how much he nagged, cajoled and pleaded, I refused to sit on his lap so he could wheel me through the ward. *"You're such a little uptight priss. Why don't you loosen up, kid?"*

Eventually the fun had to end, and I had to get to the business of writing my case study. Off to "the stacks" I went to look into Elliott's past history. What a sight! When the charts were stacked one upon the other they were higher than my head. It took days to find the beginning of his mental health history. One day, in the midst of all those dusty and musty reams of paper, I found a very large manila envelope. There it was, folded, creased and yellowed with age - a large poster (although the size was closer to a billboard) proclaiming the center ring attraction of Barnum and Bailey Circus: "FEATUR-ING THE HEADLINE STAR OF EUROPEAN HEADS OF STATE. ELLIOTT AND THE SLIDE OF DEATH!" There he was: his picture, sliding on his head from the high wire to the ground on a guide-wire with no safety harness. There was a letter from Bob Hope and Bing Crosby sending get well greetings and regrets that he would not be with them when they started filming their next Road Show with Dorothy Lamour. Oh, my gosh, it was all true; he was the star of Barnum and Bailey. He did perform the Slide of Death, and he was in the movies with Bing Crosby and Bob Hope. Amazingly, they thought enough of him to send a personal note in a get-well card. He wasn't a crazy, delusional old man. He was Elliott with an exclamation point!

The last day he wheeled with me to the door, he chastised me because I had learned nothing; *"you're still the same skinny little uptight priss you were the day I got you."* But, he said softly with a wistful smile, *"you're walking out and they're locking the door with me still inside."* I looked back once; the orderly waited with him so he could watch me go through the open door. I smiled, waved and blew him a kiss. Then I walked away with no regrets. I was 19, my psychiatry rotation was over, and I had my whole life ahead of me. I was surprised, however, how often, as time passed, that I thought of him and wondered what had become of him.

About fifteen years later I read his obituary, and I wept.

NOTE: Patient's name changed to protect his privacy and history.

Memories of PSH - *Anonymous, Licensed Practical Nurse, 1963-1969*

When I first started to work at Peoria State Hospital I worked in the Zeller Hospital building. The hospital was really two separate buildings joined by a long hallway separating the men and the women. I worked on the men's ward. We had lots of surgical patients, some with ulcers on their legs. One man had only one leg, and others needed to be in wheelchairs. The old wooden wheelchairs were so cumbersome that it was hard for patients to get through the doors; they wouldn't fold up and were hard to handle. Some of these patients hadn't been out of the unit for 14-15 years because the wheelchairs were so bad.

I had graduated as an LPN from the Peoria School of Nursing which was affiliated with ICC and located at the Allied Agencies building. My psychiatric nurses training was done at PSH and I applied to work there, but after graduation I took a job at Pekin Hospital on Pediatrics. After a month I quit there and fortunately when I got home a letter was waiting for me about a job at PSH. I took it and also worked at St. Francis two days a week for several years.

When I complained about the wheelchairs, the other nurses laughed at me. I decided to take action but they told me it wouldn't do any good. I wrote to the governor anyway, stating that the patients were being restrained in their mobility because they couldn't navigate those old chairs. I told them we needed twelve new wheelchairs for our unit and twelve for the women's unit. Two or three doctors signed it too. My fellow nurses said, "Lady, don't hold your breath, you will turn purple." I did receive a letter back that they had received my request, and that it was under advisement.

One day two or three months later, a big truck arrived and unloaded twelve wheelchairs for the men's unit, and twelve for the women's unit. I hadn't received any correspondence back so this was a surprise. It wasn't until after this that I received a letter of congratulations for my thoughtfulness in looking out for the patients' interests.

With the new-found freedom for the wheelchair patients, I would bring two sandwiches for two of the patients and wheel them out under the shade trees. They would eat and we would talk about cars and other interests. So before I knew it I had lost 24 pounds.

250

PSH Memories - *Eunice Burgeson, R.N., PSH 1963-1970*

I began working as a registered nurse on the newly developed Physical Rehabilitation Unit at Peoria State Hospital in October, 1963. The unit was located on the second floor of the Talcott Building. Adeline Merdian, R.N., was the unit supervisor. Dr. H. Worley Kendell was our rehab physician consultant. Dr. Breton was the unit physician. She was funny. Each morning when she got to work she would take two aspirin, "Just in case I get a headache today." Mrs. Merdian trained us in all the techniques. There was one nurse's aide, Mrs. Deemy, and myself. Mrs. Merdian sent me to the Rehabilitation Training Program at St. Francis Hospital for additional training. Most of the patients had been hospitalized for many years and had limited movement of their joints due to sitting all the time. Some patients had paralysis from strokes, deformities from arthritis, or from catatonic states. With Dr. Kendell's guidance we developed exercise routines to loosen and strengthen joints. Our patient load grew, and before long we outgrew the space at Talcott.

We moved across the campus to the Pollak Building. It had been the tuberculosis unit for many years. We had more beds and a larger treatment area. The day we moved, March 25, there was a terrible ice storm. It took a long time to navigate the Garfield Hill to get to work. We put patients on buses and slipped and slid around the curves from Talcott to Pollak. Fortunately, there were no falls. The next day the ice was gone.

One of the most difficult patients that I remember was Marjorie C. She was young and had been in a terrible auto accident in the Chicago area. Her husband abandoned her because she had been with another man when the accident happened. She had no other family who cared, so she ended up at Chicago State Hospital. She was referred to our program. She had massive brain trauma and spastic limbs. She couldn't talk. She came to us with huge bedsores that took a year to heal. Eventually, she was able to sit in a wheelchair and could form a few words. Our social worker found out she had small children and arranged for a visit. That was a great day for her.

I remember the strike. I had to work on the D-Row. There were 50 to 60 patients and me. I had to give medication. I didn't know any of the patients and there were no such things as identification bracelets. Most of the patients were non-communicative. I found one patient who seemed to be alert and could tell me who was who. What a relief when the strike was over.

When Dr. Cameron was superintendent, he developed a federal grant to fund rehab training for the nurses' aids. I had the opportunity to develop that training and held classes for it. It was a challenge and an experience to remember. When that grant ended, I learned that there was a PSH unit at Zeller Mental Health Center. Jerry Yalowitz called it the Comprehensive Geriatric Treatment Service. It was also funded by a federal grant. I interviewed and was chosen as supervisor for the PSH unit on Unit 4 at Zeller. A second unit was on 3B in the PSH grounds.

I was sad when PSH closed. The care and treatment of the patients was good and the staff were dedicated and well trained. They were wonderful and caring people. The memories are good!

Accomplished Artist from England - contributed by Georgie Camper, former PSH Librarian - 1964-72

My office window overlooked the sunken garden in front of the Administration Building at PSH. It was a beautiful sight to see the carefully groomed garden, the wildlife playing there and the American flag whipping in the breeze. The hospital was situated under one of the direct flight patterns to the Greater Peoria Regional Airport and many aircraft flew over the hospital grounds every day.

I have many fond memories of the patients and the staff at PSH. Life there was good to me and for me. I loved my work and felt that I was privileged to be a part of helping people regain their mental health. I will always be grateful for the happy years I spent there and for the people with whom I shared those years. I learned that anyone can be a victim of mental illness. Our patients were of many nationalities, economic incomes, ages, religions and educational levels of achievement. My interaction with these people was a fascinating and rewarding experience and I was blessed to have been a part of the history of this fine institution.

One patient who impressed me very much was a large, very attractive woman, probably in her late 30s, who had been born in England. This beautiful lady had a college degree in art, she liked to talk, was very interesting, and was a severe schizophrenic.

The collection of paintings she had with her displayed talent, she specialized in nature art. Her main interest was painting wildflowers. She had traveled extensively and had pictures of wildflowers from almost every country she had visited. She was one of the most talented wildflower artists whose work I had seen, her work was very delicate and ethereal.

Old Patient Library - Christmas Party

New Patient Library - Activity Bldg.

Even though she was talkative and friendly she was reluctant to give information about her past. Her interests were varied. She read a lot and could converse in a wide range of subjects. Mood swings are common in patients with schizophrenia and so it was with this resident. One day she checked herself out of Peoria State Hospital and was never heard from again - she didn't say good-bye

NOTE: The patient had checked herself into the hospital, therefore, she was eligible to check herself out.

Georgie Camper

Patient Library Arts Group. Georgie Camper, head librarian, presenting a book review as part of an adult education program. This picture was used for a mental health display at the Heart of Illinois Fair on July 7, 1966.

Fun Times at Abbott Center - Betty Noack, Activity Therapy

During my years at Abbott Center, I worked with children ages 6-12. These children were institutionalized and hardly saw their parents. I talked to my supervisor and asked if I could plan a weekend with the children, inviting their parents to participate. I was told to plan it and get back to her. The food would be prepared by our kitchen, the office would send invitations, and I planned games and activities involving both the children and the parent.

Parents arrived on Saturday and the activities continued through Sunday. We had sack races, a softball game, and a scavenger hunt. The picnic included hamburgers, hot dogs, and salads. Out of twelve sets of parents, all but two sets were able to attend. It was a fun weekend for all. The parents were pleased with the outing and felt better about their child being there.

Abbott Center   Milner Library

Recollections of PSH - *By Linda Kersh, LCSW*

One of my first assignments was working on 4-C, the women's violent ward. While introducing myself to a lady I knew to be in her late 50s, she was adamant that she was much younger than I (20 at the time). Part of our community reintegration for these individuals who had been institutionalized for upwards of 20 years were trips to department stores. They did not know what an escalator was and were quite fearful. Nor did they know about many of the modern household appliances.

One time when I took a group of ladies to my home for tea, they were absolutely shy and charming. At the hospital they were violent and aggressive. But they responded in a kind, loving way to our family puppy. They became loving, positive, kind and gentle around the puppy. As well, they were very loving when interacting with another staff member's cats.

My recollections of my work experience at PSH include the type of treatment (therapies) which were provided. Didactic classes about very practical skills were taught. These include such fundamentals as grooming, cooking, sewing, bed making, household tasks, exercise, community reintegrations, budgeting, and manners.

Seemingly, the more meaningful therapeutic approaches were in the vocational area. There was one Swedish immigrant lady who kept the sunken gardens in impeccable condition year round. Although she did not speak a word of English and had been hospitalized since she was 17 (then approximately 60) she communicated through her nurturing loving care of nature's bounty.

One very large, awkward-appearing gentleman, dressed in bib overalls, would get up to work on the food truck at 4 a.m. every day of the week. Another very large, formidable woman worked in the paring room from 4 a.m. to 1 p.m. helping to prepare the food for the 3,000-some patients "on the hill." Some worked in the clothing room. One perky, bubbly, obese little woman helped clean office

One of the outstanding flower gardens at PSH.   Julie Matthews

space. Others worked assisting with clerical work and still others tended to the farm crops and animals in the earlier days.

Doctors, staff, and nursing students lived on the grounds of PSH. PSH was a self-contained community unto itself with its own firehouse and hook and ladder, fire truck, hospital, security staff, boiler house and town square.

Seemingly everyone pitched in and played a role in the entire operation. Freud said, "love and work," and these approaches were expressed and personified through the nurturing care exchanged and the labors of love expressed through care and love.

The cemetery was full of rows and rows of numbered gravestones, some for individuals unknown for decades within the gates of PSH. However, to each other and those of us who worked there they were each unique individuals with their own personality and skills, gifts and feelings which found expression in a myriad of nurturing, giving, loving ways. They were not anonymous by the nature of the gravestone which marked their existence but rather independent individuals with each their own needs and gifts. They are not forgotten.

Waving Good-bye to the last patients at PSH - By Linda Kersh

It was a mild, overcast, midwinter morn in December, 1973. Eighteen ladies bathed, coiffed and dressed in their Sunday best jersey print dresses with black patent leather pumps, all toting a large black plastic garbage bag which held all their worldly possessions, boarded the steps of an orange school bus.

This was the only home any of them could remember during their adults years. On average they had resided at PSH 16.1 years. The majority of them had been admitted to the maximum security ward. These ladies were the last patients from PSH who were not ready for family homes or community living facilities because of other intractable, persistent symptoms of major mental illness. As they compliantly boarded the bus the mood matched the somber gray December day. Their faces were expressionless, unfazed by anxiety or fear that an entirely new chapter was unfolding in their lives. After decades of institutionalization at PSH (many had transferred from Kankakee, Manteno, Madden, Elgin and other northern state psychiatric facilities), they were ending their hospitalization at PSH to be transferred to Galesburg State Research Hospital. For those saying good-bye, feelings were mixed, anxious for them yet anticipating that when they finished their treatment they, too, would one day get to return to the lesser restrictive environment of the community.

Mental Health Pills - *by Dan Shinn, Activity Therapist at Peoria State Hospital and later at Zeller Mental Health Center*

On my first day on the job, January 11, 1964, I immediately fell in love with the Boys' Unit at Abbott Center, the boys, and most especially Peoria State Hospital. The most cherished memories I had there centered around our Boy Scouts of America Troop that my colleague, Bill, and I supervised. We camped out on grounds; we went for overnight trips to Rice Lake; we went to Camp Wokanda west of Mossville, and we went for week-long campouts at Wilderness Camp in London Mills. Our emotionally disturbed boys always cooperated with us and with camp counselors, and several boys were inducted over the years into the Order of the Arrow, an honor society restricted to only the most dedicated, hard-working scouts. The boys also demonstrated excellent behavioral skills, and on many occasions we saw little need to medicate them for behavioral control purposes, since they didn't exhibit any inappropriate behaviors.

Scouting trips did, however, create some problems for us. I will always recall the day that we were going on a weekend campout with many other Peoria area troops. As we left the unit that day, Les, a technician on the unit, came running out the door and said, "You forgot the boys' medication." Bill told him to put it somewhere in the back of the Metro van we were driving, and little did we know that Les placed the packets in the air void (metal container) filled with ice, to keep the meat safe. We drove to the site south of Bartonville to a farmer's property that was hilly, forested and beautiful. We were assigned specific areas to camp, and when we arrived at the unloading site, we started carrying our gear back into the woods -- about one-half mile. We tried to make it all in one trip, but it was too much for the boys and they kept dropping their loads. This resulted in smashed food, such as bread and broken eggs, but most of all it caused the ice to melt in the air void, since it was very heavy and dropped many times. To make matters worse, there had been a storm the night before and the area was flooded. We had to go back to the road and portage all our gear to higher ground on the opposite side of the road -- this time about three-fourths of a mile. Needless to say, we were all extremely tired and hungry.

We had planned to have baked ham that evening, but we decided to do Sloppy Joes instead, since they were much quicker. We ate numerous sandwiches. Bill, being famous for the quantity of food he could eat, had seven. I had three. The boys had their fill, and as we were sitting around the campfire, Bill said, "I feel really funny, I can't move!" I said that I felt funny, also, and we both lay back on the ground and literally passed out. We must have been out for an hour or so. I came to first, and the boys were chasing one another around the area, having a great time with no supervision. Bill came to a little later, and we tried to determine what had happened. We looked in the air void, and in the bottom of the water were all the brown pill packages that Les had stowed when we left the unit. There wasn't a pill to be found. They had all melted, permeated the meat, and we all had been eating "mental health pill" laden meat. It didn't affect the boys at all. Bill and I were greatly affected, and we thank our lucky stars to this day that none of the boys decided to misbehave or do something stupid or dangerous.

Misty, The Ghost - *by Dan Shinn, Activity Therapist at Peoria State Hospital*

One evening in the 1960s I took the boys from 4B to the edge of the property where a farmer always built a big stack of straw bales. I am convinced he put them there every year because he knew we had a great time playing "King of the Hill." He never complained when we messed the stack up pretty badly.

At dusk I told the boys we had to get back to the unit. We walked along the cemetery road as a shortcut to come out behind the "C" row.

One of the boys cried, "Look!" In front of a large tree was a misty figure with a flowing gown. The boys asked me if I saw it and I asked them the same question in return.

It truly could have just been mist, but that spot was the only place where there was mist, and it most certainly looked like a human figure. I didn't say much about this over the years until stories of the haunting of Peoria State emerged. I am intrigued by that memory to this day.

Could there be a misty figure in front of the tree?   Gary Lisman

The Necklace Story - *Eliida Lakota*

"Good Morning, Cindy." I had just arrived for my morning exercise group on 8C and was greeted by Cindy, a young, slim, dark-haired woman, who, on a good day, was good company. This was a good day. 8C was maximum security for women. Here were housed some mentally retarded adults, schizophrenics, criminally insane, potentially violent women with a variety of diagnoses, new patients here for screening, and occasional runaway teens.

On this day the large day room was quiet. Some ladies were watching TV from large colorful bucket-style chairs. Others were milling around, reading, visiting or just waiting for me. I wore jeans and a casual shirt, as I would be sitting on the floor for exercises and later we were going for a picnic near the cemetery under the old maple tree.

After exercises, a number of women walked with me to the Sewing Room in the Activity Building, where Catherine worked with us on our current project. We were making long skirts and bonnets for the bicentennial celebration. Also, at the same time, many of the staff and patients were building an old western town in the parking lot behind the Activity Building. The town was only store fronts but was looking good. (We were planning a fake bank robbery on horseback to take place during the all-day celebration). The celebration would be open to the public. Everyone was excited and looking forward to the big day.

On the way back to 8C near lunchtime Cindy found a dead bird. She was a very sensitive young woman and felt sad about this beautiful creature's life ending. We speculated on how it might have died, as it seemed to be uninjured. We decided to have a funeral for the bird after our picnic.

We returned to the unit, gathered more ladies, met a group of men from 9C to accompany us with their activity director, Ed Dickenson, and walked to the old maple tree near the largest cemetery. The kitchen had sent sack lunches for us to carry, so off we went.

On this day Cindy was wearing a lovely charm necklace. I commented on it, and she told me she had won it at the Bingo night that week. It

Eliida wearing the necklace that "broke the curse."   Gary Lisman

259

was the custom to pull out boxes of jewelry and buttons, purses, etc., that had been donated and stored in the quonset hut for the past years and use them for Bingo prizes. It was not uncommon to see the ladies wearing old broaches or bracelets. But I mentioned to Catherine to look at this necklace, and what a shame for it to be lost, as Cindy would probably lay it in the grass somewhere and forget it.

A couple of days later on my arrival to 8C I found Cindy huddled in a corner near the nurse's station. It was a bad day for Cindy. She was cowering with fear in her eyes as I approached. One side of her head was bloody, she had pulled out her hair by the roots during the night. I tried to comfort her. She had a small lock of hair wrapped around her finger about to pull it out and I tried to stop her. "Keep away from me," she warned. I tried again to comfort her. "Keep away," she repeated. "I hope your boys burn to death in your home."

Of course I didn't take what she said personally, but the staff and I were concerned with bringing her back to reality and to see her smile and to feel safe. Soon she regained her composure, but now suffered from guilt for what she had said. She considered me a friendly support person and now feared the consequences of her curse on my family. No amount of reassurance by any of the staff gave her any relief from the guilt she felt.

She obsessed about her deed for days. One day, while she was confessing to Catherine the regret she felt for putting this curse on my family Catherine told her that together they could devise a way to break the curse. She could do a truly good deed for me, a ritual of forgiveness to see if it might break the curse. Cindy decided to give me the necklace that I had admired, with Catherine's encouragement. The next day at work Catherine approached me with her story and gave me the necklace from Cindy. At first I felt a little guilty about it, but when I saw Cindy later on 8C I was relieved to see her back to normal - no longer obsessing with her guilt - and we both were proud whenever I wore the necklace. We had a special closeness and understanding from then on.

"A Normal Day" - *Eliida Lakota*

On some Fridays I would take six to ten well-behaved women to the Veterans' Cottage to spend the day. It was an earned privilege and very sought after. The cottage was set up like a little house with a living room, dining room, and a brick outdoor grilling area. The lawn was wide and green, overlooking the valley. There was always a breeze there - we could spread blankets on the soft grass and relax and talk.

The day at the cottage consisted of doing the things that people do in their homes. They listened to the radio, planned and prepared lunch, embroidered, and some would play croquet on the lawn. I remember one day in the living room seeing a lady lying on the couch, her feet over the back, music playing and she was reading a modern romance magazine. It was like having a "normal" day in a "normal" life. We made fruitcakes once, to serve for the Thanksgiving dinner we shared here. I still go back to the Vets cottage and reminisce, weekly.

Gary Lisman

Items made by the patients in Activity Therapy at Peoria State Hospital - quilt, picture, and ash-trays. The table is made from the pillars on the porches of the Bowen Building.

Stann Richards - Training at PSH in 1968 and 1969

I did 18 weeks of training at Peoria State Hospital while working at Zeller Mental Health Center. I started at Zeller on Unit I as a ward clerk, then took six weeks of aid training at PSH in 1968 and six weeks in 1969. I transferred to Unit 6 in 1970, and again got six weeks of training at PSH, this time for activity therapy. We were then called Activity Program Aides.

When I started my training at PSH they had just finished the Activity Center and the gift and barber shops. This was really a big deal for the patients.

I remember a week-long carnival; also outdoor movies and skits. Each one of the rows would get to attend one night, i.e. A-Row the first night and B-Row the second night. There would be 200-300 folks each night It was a very special time for them.

I worked at Zeller full-time until 1976. I had started working part-time at the Peoria Area Mental Health Clinic in 1970, which was later renamed the Human Service Center. Peoria State Hospital was downsizing then and I was hired to do an activity program one night a week for discharged PSH clients who were now living in shelter care facilities, the YMCA, and the Julian Hotel. Ironically, none of them showed up (lack of transportation) but other folks who had been discharged from Zeller came.

Community-based programs are the focus now, and the treatment concept has also changed at the HSC. Instead of psychotherapists we now have case managers. On a typical day as a case manager, I will help my clients with budgets (our agency is payee), with setting up their medications, making sure they get to doctor appointments, check their jobs in the community, or take them shopping. Sometimes I go with a client to see his psychiatrist.

When the therapist title was replaced with case manager, we lost 15 to 20 people, but have refilled these positions plus hired 10 to15 more.

It seems some clients continue to feel paranoid, anxious, and abandoned since the closure of Zeller Mental Health Center. No community resources have been used to replace Zeller except outside of this community, and beds in this community have not been provided as promised.

Patients Given Hope with Workshop! - *Maxine Childress*

I came to work at Peoria State Hospital late in its life, 1969. The grounds were beautiful and spacious. As a whole, I thought patients had a good life, nourishing food and activities, in addition to their medical care.

Several male patients had assignments on the food trucks that brought the food to the ward dining rooms. They were proud to be assigned to these jobs and enjoyed their responsibilities. These were voluntary assignments.

A few of the experiences I had that gave me a sense of satisfaction were trying to communicate with patients that had other than English as their first language or only language. One lady (from Eastern Europe, I believe), who did very little except sit in the day room, I was able to convince to come to a sewing session. We made reversible rain scarves with plastic and fabric. I wasn't sure she was getting a great deal from it, but later I noticed she was wearing it pulled back tied under her hair in a fashion familiar to her.

There was a Chinese man who communicated with others very seldom and minimally. He worked in the workshop. He was able to do good work and in a quick manner. He was especially good at making ribbon bows. We had a ten-minute break mid-morning and mid-afternoon. There were coffee and cookies available. Even though he was encouraged to participate, he would not do more than sit with the group while I encouraged interaction from all present. After many weeks he finally accepted a cookie. Even such a small thing brought great satisfaction to me.

To see patients who were very anxious and not able to sit still long be able to channel that anxiety into productive work was great for both staff and patients. They were able to earn money on a piece-work basis and were paid weekly. At Christmas time we took them off grounds for dinner where they received bonus checks. The workshop's first supervisor, Howard Cain, did an outstanding job of organizing and procuring work that patients were able to do. It was real work that needed to be done correctly and in a timely manner. Besides providing meaningful work to fill the hours, the workshop tried to promote basic work skills such as punctuality, sticking with a task, engaging in appropriate social interaction and appropriate grooming. The workshop was begun in approximately 1970 by Jack Myers, activity department director, with the help of Howard Cain. I followed Vicki Lockhart as Howard's assistant. When Peoria State Hospital was closing, a grant was obtained and we continued the workshop at Zeller Mental Health Center in 1973. Later I became workshop supervisor. We worked in a storage area on the first floor until another larger storage area became available.

I was always impressed by the attitude of most of the staff at Peoria State Hospital in their desire to be of service to the patients. They were caring and almost like family members to the patients. These staff members gave unselfishly of themselves to another human being in need of care and love. At approximately $2 an hour it certainly wasn't for the money.

In the activity department, we each worked mostly day programs. We also worked four-hour evening programs each week. Patients were picked up on the wards and escorted to the central activity building and returned after the program was finished. There were Saturday programs also. A church service was available on Sunday.

I was very sad to see Peoria State Hospital close. Patients were wrenched from their safe haven to an uncertain future. Many resisted being moved. The man who looked after the sunken garden next to the administration building was very faithful about taking care of the flowers. I heard he resisted the move vigorously and did not live long after his forced move.

Durru Sumer, M.D. - worked at PSH from 1969-1973

My practice on the Alcoholic Unit is full of good memories. It was very satisfying to see patients who came in severely intoxicated and occasionally with delirium tremens, then to see their improvement after giving them medication such as B vitamins and Librium, among others. I also enjoyed the friendships and frequent breakfast picnics on the edge of the hospital grounds with unit staff listening to jokes from Howard Lauderbaugh and chats with JoAnn Gross, Dan Shambaugh, Marvin Turl, Rev. Hinrichs, and many other names I can't recall. At times, my enjoyable work became rather unpleasant.

One day when I was on duty I was urgently called to a unit where there was an injury. I rushed there and to my horror I saw a man's body on the floor. His head was lying in a pool of blood. I immediately took his pulse and listened to his heart. He was alive! I started an IV and transferred him to the hospital's emergency room, which was St. Francis Hospital, for further treatment. (He remained in St. Francis Hospital for a month, but unfortunately, he died.) Meanwhile, the nurses on the unit had cleaned the bloody area. I thought I had done a good job.

The next morning I was summoned by Dr. Staras, the administrator, who asked me why I did not first call the police. This never entered my mind at the time. Apparently one of the staff members had called the police department after the patient went to the hospital. So now it was implied as an incident that I was hiding a crime from the police. Hence, I was reprimanded. I had to appear in court in front of representatives from Springfield. I had to defend myself. Eventually, I was acquitted.

From that day on I did not enjoy my work there. Some other misfortunes occurred in other units and these eventually contributed to the hospital's closing. Also, the hospital resident population was reduced every year. All of these events caused the hospital's eventual closing.

Patients Full of Surprises - *Ron Cordes - Psychologist (Social Worker at Peoria State Hospital)*

Hank was in a catatonic state for over 30 years, never having uttered one word for the last 25 of those years. For some reason, Hank was always kept on the locked ward, 2-C, rather than one of the open cottages where people were free to come and go as they chose. Hank usually just sat in a chair, with legs up on the seat of it, or would smoke a state-issued cigarette. Hank had no relatives and to our knowledge no visitors for many years. One day, on a supervised field trip, Hank, along with other select patients from his unit, went out to a local pizza restaurant for lunch. As everyone awaited the pizza to arrive at the table, Hank suddenly stood up, walked over to a complete stranger's table, and helped himself to a piece of pizza. When I went over to apologize to the other customer, Hank blurted out his first words in many years, "Damn good pizza." Ironically several weeks later Hank was discovered missing after a return to the ward from lunch. An alert was put out and the next day Hank's body was discovered at the bottom of the "Big Hill" by a streambed. Medical findings revealed that he had a major head injury, and it was surmised that Hank had slipped on a rock during his venture away from his home.

One of the most amazing characters was an elderly gentleman who, although a patient, always insisted on wearing a suit or sport coat on the unit. This man was a salesman and a very good one at that, having sold magazines for many years. The problem was that he would fail to turn in the money he collected, which got him into repeated problems. This man was so impressive that he would return to the same person's home and could sell the person another subscription, sometimes to the same magazine, even though the original subscription had never been received . When you first met him on his unit, an outsider could not tell if he was a resident or a staff person. He was known to sell a subscription or two to the unsuspecting.

I remember one court hearing (held in the Administration Building) when Judge Sullivan, a very dignified man who always wore a top hat, was presiding. When it came time to swear in the witness, which happened to be a patient, he asked the clerk to do so. The clerk stated, "Do you promise to tell the truth, the whole truth. . ." to which the patient replied, "No I will not!" This was the only time that I ever saw this dignified judge appeared flustered and finally indicated after a long pause to have the court record show that patient would not take the oath.

Dance With Death - *Dr. Steven Hamon*

The men's ward on C Row at Peoria State Hospital where I worked as a psychiatric aide held an afternoon dance with the women's ward next door. This affair consisted of cookies and juice sent over by Dietary, eight to ten assorted records ranging from Elvis to Mitch Miller, and a Ronco record player.

These were the days long before American Gigolo, but my job was to help patients socialize and mix. I was to do this, in part, by modeling socializing and mixing behaviors myself. One of the veteran nurses aided me in my modeling pursuits by pointing out a neatly dressed woman, seated alone, for me to invite to dance. Frankly, I had thought this woman was a staff member because her normal appearance and behavior stood out in stark contrast to the oddities of the patients around her.

I danced with the lady and had an enjoyable conversation, the topic of which I've long since forgotten. Later, as I helped the nurses clean up after the event, I asked the veteran what in the world my normative dance partner was in the hospital <u>for</u> "Life," she answered, "Mrs. Doe hates men, and proved it by killing her husband and sons."

Circle Dance   Alpha Park Library

As the Juggernut Turns - Dr. Steven Hamon

The Peoria State Hospital had several long, low buildings that were home to persons we would now call mentally handicapped. During third shift, after everyone was quiet, women on one wing of the unit, men on the other, the bulk of the night was spent in the nurse's station. In between inspection walks the nurse and I (there were only two staff per unit) kept an eagle-eye on the darkened day room. We were watching for shadowy forms, most often creeping from the men's wing, with but one destination in mind.

One night a diminutive nurse whom I'll call Lyla caught a gentle giant, whom I'll call George, just before he managed to slip into the women's wing. George was plenty angry that his painstaking progress across the day room had ended so abruptly, and without the desired tryst, but he complied when Lyla ordered him back to bed.

The next morning I entered the day room from the laundry room where I'd been helping a patient do her morning chores. The scene that greeted me was chilling! Lyla, who had been standing in front of the nurse's station, was backed up to the wall. Twice her height and towering over her with a metal folding chair raised menacingly above his head, stood George.

As I came fully into the day room, I heard George growl, "I'm gonna have to kill you," to Lyla. Instinctively, I shouted, "George!!" George started momentarily, then face twisted with anger, chair still held high, cleared the length of the day room in what seemed to be three steps, so that now he towered over me!

An instinct for self-preservation prompted me to say firmly, "Put that chair down and go sit down!" For an instant George raised the chair even higher. Then, suddenly, the anger left his face and he said, "OK," lowered the chair, and sat down.

George was cooperative, but sulky, the rest of the morning, and the daybook entry noted that George had refused breakfast that day. For a vastly different reason, I did too.

Letters to the Editor - from the <u>*Peoria Journal Star*</u>*, Wednesday, October 4, 1972*

Winter At Peoria State

Recently, much has been written about Peoria State Hospital, all of it on the negative side. One would think that of the thousands of people, employees, patients, student nurses, resident physicians and interns who have walked those halls and strolled through these grounds, who received indescribable benefits from this institution, that someone would step forward and request to see the other side of the coin.

At age 70 the face of the institution is showing lines of age but there were brighter days when Peoria State Hospital was alive and bustling with activity.

During the Summer of its existence this institution was a center for Psychiatric research, training, and treatment. Area children played on the grounds, attended movies with the patients and yes, even had their tonsils removed here.

The great and near great cared for those that were born on our shores and also those that read the message at the base of the Statue of Liberty. Many devoted their lives to make the existence of the elite to the dregs of humanity a bit more comfortable. Cast into the granite of history are names such as the Dares, the Goldschmidts, the Watts, the Zellers, the Baers and many more.

The weeds are taking over not only our cemetery but also the sunken garden, the rose and petunia beds. Why? Because the patients, whose labor of love kept the beauty of this institution are no longer here. When there were 2500 patients here the lawns were trimmed, the flower gardens weedless and yes, the cemetery was an area of quiet peace and beauty.

The rows of numbered stones in the cemetery illustrate the fact that here at last is an area where everyone is equal. The last one, we will call him John, who cared for the rose beds and helped in the sunken garden, refused to leave when he was informed that he was going to a sheltered care home. He died two days later in the arms of a truck driver.

Here, we are now in the Winter of our existence. We have many scars and bruises from the years of hard use. But please do not ridicule our efforts, defame our accomplishments or whip us without reason. As we have felt for our elderly charges, if we must die, please allow us to die with dignity --

Arthur Lagerbloom, R.N.
Director of Nursing Services
Peoria State Hospital

We Didn't Goof - *Wanda Loucks' article (next page) in response to a __PJS__ editorial (below), and Emma Leman's response, (contributed by Phyllis Fritz, daughter of Wanda, and acknowledged by Lee Wilton, daughter of Emma).*

We All Goofed - *C.L.Dancey (from an Editorial in the __Journal Star__ dated April 30, 1976)*

When you look backwards, some of the things we have done look downright silly in retrospect, although in all honesty we didn't realize it at the time. The plain truth is that for many years the chief function of the Peoria State Hospital at Bartonville was to house elderly persons, in fact. There was a lot more of that than there was treatment of the mentally ill or even housing the mentally ill.

Then, along came a perfectly logical philosophy (together with chemical and drug discoveries that made treatment of many mentally ill a workable and successful thing on a scale previously unknown). That philosophy was that the state shouldn't "warehouse" such people, but should go in heavily for brief, in house treatment and out patient treatment which would take care of most of them more effectively at less cost.

In our age of specialization, however, nobody seemed to think about the major problem there that they were actually dealing with because by the new definitions it wasn't the "proper" problem of that particular department. So, the elderly were kicked out and eventually the whole institution at Bartonville shut down.

So, now we have a multi-million dollar facility in a beautiful setting that is going to pot, and we are having a devil of a time figuring out what to do with it. Meanwhile, we have already spent other billions building other facilities and subsidizing other places to "warehouse" all those elderly. It seems that somehow we missed the boat by the simple separation of specialist jurisdictions, finance and interest, and have really misused available resources at both ends as a result. We have spent money at both ends to, primarily, in fact, instead of in theory, move large numbers of the elderly out of ongoing facilities in a beautiful setting and into new facilities.

Certainly, the original theory was correct -- but nobody thought of the simple fact that if you removed the stigma and the mixing of the elderly with certain kinds of mentally ill, the facility already existed for one of what could have been the biggest and best "nursing home" around, perhaps. Government just can't shift gears from one tunnel vision "jurisdiction" to another that easily.

But it is hard to believe that the original facility was really hopeless from the start. It was made hopeless. It was placed in a purposeful position of declining maintenance and declining population on the road to the "new system." And we pay for it coming and going, both.

In all fairness, this was not evident to me, or apparently anybody else, at the time. We thought "one problem at a time." But it suggests that in future we ought to learn from our past oversights and "look around" early when "phasing out" something to pursue a new philosophy.

We waited too long. Whether a facility for the elderly would have been the best use or not, the time to have decided on the best disposition and arranging for it was when they decided to "phase it down" and eventually out. It's too late now to realize its value in either immediate use or sale.

Another big investment by *somebody* will have to be made there all over again to get whatever new thing is now to evolve.

And it didn't have to lay there burning money and rotting in value at the same time all these years. We all goofed.

We Didn't Goof By Trying to Save Peoria State

After reading your editorial of April 30, I would like to comment, "No, we did not all goof." There were many people who saw the future but our "big shots" didn't listen. Those of us who worked at Peoria State Hospital knew we were doing a good job and the people who lived there were happy and well cared for.

New nursing and shelter care homes that house 500 people are not better than Peoria State was. They are big institutions also, but do not give the care we did. They are in the business to make money. I saw people that lived at PSH for over 50 years cry when they were sent out from their home and I cried with them. We cared. In nursing homes they don't get the food, necessary clothing or prompt medical care that was there at PSH.

When many were sent to Galesburg, I went with them and couldn't really believe how far behind PSH their treatment programs for the retarded and mentally ill were. Of course the population at Peoria was down but that only gave us a chance to work with the people as individuals and make progress not dreamed of.

The thrill of hearing a person speak after remaining silent for over 30 years is wonderful. Only with programs like PSH had was this possible. To see people return to PSH unhappy, undernourished and in a poor mental state is heart breaking.

Five years before PSH closed I talked with Mr. Lauterbaugh about renovating the large dorms to give more privacy, but he was only one person that cared. I don't care what Gov. Kerner did with race tracks, when it came to the mentally ill, he cared.

As for saving money to close state institutions, that is ridiculous. The federal government pays the nursing homes a large per cent of the cost to keep patients and we the taxpayers pay federal taxes as well as state taxes.

Those of us who tried to save PSH, in all its beautiful setting, know we gave it everything we had but couldn't get the "right" people to listen. It wasn't to save our jobs -- it was the people who lived there.

You see, Mr. Dancey, we cared. We don't have to look back and say we goofed. We just say everyone around Peoria lost. -- **Wanda Loucks, Galesburg**

Mrs. Henry W. Leman
5809 Prospect Rd.
Peoria, Illinois 61614

June 8, 1976

Dear Wanda:

Some weeks ago I read your most impressive article in the Peoria Journal in regard to Peoria State Hospital. Although it is more than twenty years ago that I was a volunteer at P.S.H. your article brought back memories of an experience that I repeat at every opportunity I have. I was assigned to the Cottage where the senile residents lived. Here I was introduced to a young woman afflicted with epilepsy whose family did not want to cope with her illness and had her committed to State. She was so hurt that she refused to talk. I don't remember how long this condition existed nor do I remember how long we worked with her -- but what I do remember is that when she began to talk the nurse on the floor broke down and cried for joy. Now you see why your letter touched me so deeply. Thank God for people like you.

Another reason your letter interested me is because my grandson, Peter Wilton, 24 years old is a resident there. It gives me confidence to know there are compassionate people like you there to see to the welfare of those who need to be there.

I am not able to travel to Galesburg and I doubt if we will ever meet -- but I will certainly remember you in my prayers. God bless you and all others like you.

Sincerely
Emma Leman

Arvel Rowland - Employee Extraordinaire

"Arvel Rowland was one of the most caring and generous persons I have ever met. His concern, care and involvement with our patients by helping to meet their needs (from clothes, to money, to a friend to talk to) was well-known. He also was a friend to all his fellow employees and most generous in sharing his sense of humor, his ready smile and Trefzger's bakery goods with all. He was one of God's 'angels' here on earth." Marjorie Gudat, former Zeller Mental Health Center Employee

In a Mental Health Open House brochure from Peoria State Hospital, a section was devoted to Arvel Rowland. At the time his title was "Maintenance Equipment Operator." It stated that Arvel was selected as the outstanding employee of hospital services other than "Patient Care Services." It reads as follows:

Arvel, as he is called by co-workers and patients, started his hospital career in the butcher shop on June 14, 1952. Here he realized the therapeutic potential in interpersonal relationships with patients, and was able to assist those on Industrial Assignment to the shop to regain self-confidence and emotional health through his interest and guidance. A number of patients were able to leave the hospital and find employment in butcher shops or markets.

From 1953 to 1956, Mr. Rowland drove various types of trucks of the hospital services. He became known for his safe and courteous driving; he was instrumental in rearranging routings of daily deliveries, effecting a more efficient use of equipment.

His interest in patient care continued with those assigned to truck details. He was instrumental in reuniting one patient and his family, which culminated in the patient's return to the community. Dr. Otto L. Bettag, Director of the Department of Public Welfare, commended Arvel in March, 1956 . . .for his quick thinking in preventing a situation which could have had disastrous results."

In August, 1956, Arvel's driving assignment was changed to one in which he contacted a great number of people -- patients, employees, official visitors and members of the community. Driving the hospital station wagon he has greatly assisted in hospital sponsored excursions, and his fine relationships and skillful approach has helped allay patients' anxieties while being driven to medical facilities of the community.

A nominating statement of a fellow employee reflects the hospital feeling toward Arvel: *"Mr. Rowland, assigned to our department, belongs to all departments. The gracious way in which he serves us all -- employees and patients -- makes him one of those persons of whom we wonder: 'Could he ever be replaced by another single person?'"*

Mr. Rowland is thirty-five years of age, is married and the father of a four-year-old daughter. He is an enthusiastic bowler, with this interest developed while assisting in patient activities.

The Rowland family reside in Bellevue, where his enthusiasm for his work, and dedication to hospital service, find expression in his community efforts to interpret the program of the hospital, and to help eradicate any stigma attached to mental illness.

* * *

In 1978 Arvel received his 25-year service award, working at Peoria State Hospital, then transferring to Zeller Mental Health Center when Peoria State closed. The following note was received from Arvel In September, 1979, terminally ill with cancer. This note was in response to "thank you" sales given by co-workers *"to thank Arvel for being such a wonderful person to so many people for so many years."*

A SPECIAL THANK YOU
From
ARVEL ROWLAND

With much gratitude and many thanks, I would like to take this opportunity to thank each and everyone of you for giving me a Special Day.

When my wife came home and told me my friends at Zeller wanted to give me a special day my emotions overcame me. I didn't want your time given to me when perhaps someone else might need it, but after thinking about what an honor you were giving me, I realized you wanted to be part of my family and to show your love for me.

Anna Baker and Lena Lakota and each and everyone of you I understand worked so hard to make that day possible for me. All of you have been so kind already by sending cards, the phone calls and your visits to my home that this thing you done just got to my heart I can't say it in words. But it did give me the opportunity to sit down with myself and really think what friends and love are. With this in mind I would like to share my feelings with you.

I feel that we're not just employees working with each other day by day, but a family. We all have a lot of compassion to give others or we would not be in this field of work. We as human beings are all different in personalities, likes and dislikes. This is what makes us fit into each others lives, hearts and feelings Without each person who has touched my life I wouldn't be the person I am today.

I want to thank you all for your love, kindness and thoughts for me at this time. I have been told that my illness is taking my life, but my work is not done. I have more work to do, it will not be here on earth, it will be with God in heaven. I have been called so I must go. I am at peace with myself, my precious family and dear friends. You have made my life very rewarding. I can rest assured that my wife will have the love and family she will need because she will continue on with your love for her. For this, my friends, my dear friends, I say thank you from the bottom of my heart.

[His death occurred in April of 1980, after a long illness.]

A Ghostly Experience - By Melody Bridges

A few years ago my sister, her daughter, and I decided we were going to go inside the Bowen Building to look around. We entered in the basement very early in the morning, taking flashlights to make sure we could find our way up the stairs. It was a very cool morning and we had just gotten inside an old opening in the basement and were deciding which way to go. There are several very dark tunnels going different ways, but we headed for the old stairway.

My niece and my sister were ahead of me when I noticed, out of the corner of my eye, a shadowy figure coming up very quickly behind me. It was larger than me and seemed to be a man. He came up so close as if to lean over my shoulder. I could feel his cool, musty presence, and I kind of gasped and swung around.

My sister asked what was wrong. I said that nothing was wrong, but I thought someone had come up behind me. Needless to say my niece took off running for the opening, and my sister started to leave also. I stood there for a minute and tried to talk them into coming back, but it was the end of our trip.

My sister asked me if I had ever heard of the story of "Ed" and "Al." I hadn't, but apparently they are two ghosts that are rumored to haunt the old Bowen Building.

Maybe it was one of them. . . .

Melody Bridges

Hope First Step On Long Road To Recovery - By Nanette Larson

When I was 10 years old, I had a vision. It was my vision to grow up and become a nurse. Sometime in my teens I learned that girls could be doctors, and I had a new vision. By the time I was 14, I wanted to grow up and become a doctor. A missionary doctor, actually. I could see where I was going. I graduated from high school at the top of my class and left for college, vision intact.

"Where there is no vision," the proverb says, "the people perish." Persons with mental illnesses have been dying inside, and the mental health service delivery system has been dying because we have lacked vision. But it is a brand new day in the world of mental health. The Vision Statement which opens the Final Report of the President's New Freedom Commission on Mental Health, released in July, says, "We envision a future when everyone with a mental illness will recover, a future when mental illnesses can be prevented or cured, a future when mental illnesses are detected early, and a future when everyone with a mental illness at any stage of life has access to effective treatment and supports -- essentials for living, working, learning and participating fully in the community."

Such vision has not necessarily been well-received within the mental health system. Some simply do not believe that recovery is possible, clearly having never met a person with a chronic condition, be it mental illness or cancer, who has experienced recovery. Some are afraid of giving persons false hope, perhaps never having stopped to consider the fact that the very definition of hope defies any connection to true or false. Yet, according to the commissions's report, "Science has shown that having hope plays an integral role in an individual's recovery."

Remember that vision I had long ago, to become a doctor? Well, it changed. It died, actually. By the time I reached graduation, I had no vision whatsoever. I had lost hope for a life worth living.

For many years I loved my life that way, dead on the inside, working diligently most days just to stay alive. You may be thinking that I must have had a break when I was in college, suffered from depression or some form of mental illness. This is true, but more fundamentally what was broken was my vision. I lived in that condition for countless years, as do many, many persons with mental illnesses.

Then I met a person who had vision. And this individual lit what became the first sparks of new hope in my darkened world, the sparks of hope for recovery. Recovery, in the Commission's Final Report, refers to "the process in which people are able to live, work, learn and participate fully in their communities." My recovery is about regaining those things that have been lost to me. It is about total health. It is about taking responsibility for my mental and emotional health, which includes having friends and family who support me. All this, and more, began with the sparks of hope called recovery.

My story is not as unique as many think it is. There are countless stories of recovery to be told. Persons whose lives were once completely lost to mental illness now fully participate in work and marriage and community living. Individuals whose lives were once out of balance, through education and wellness planning, have found balance once again. Persons whose symptoms once kept them in institutions now live in the community and work as mentors and peer counselors at community mental health centers. For every diagnosis that has been stereotyped as a "lifelong, deteriorating condition," I could share stories of hope from persons whose resilience for life has defeated that prediction and enabled a life of recovery.

It is now my vision always to have a vision, never to be stagnant, not to maintain, as is often the language of traditional mental health systems, but to keep moving forward. For our mental health system to move forward, we must embrace a vision of recovery for all persons with mental illness. Many say accepting the illness is the first step to recovery. I would say the first step to recovery is the acknowledgment of hope.

Nanette Larson is the director of Consumer Services Development for the Illinois Division of Mental Health and associate network manager for the North Central Mental Health Network. She lives and works in Peoria.

Taken from VIEWPOINTS, <u>Peoria Journal Star</u>, October 5, 2003.

Progress in Mental Health Care; Still Much to be Done
By DeWayne Bartels, Senior Reporter, _Times Newspapers_, Peoria

Several years ago while I was a participant in the University of Illinois' Mini Medical School, a most interesting presenter spoke to the class. His name was Dr. Timothy Bruce.

Bruce made me think about mental illness in a different way. Since that talk with Bruce I have been fortunate to be introduced to many people who have shaped my perception of mental illness. It was an evolution on my part. Evolution is part of understanding. That is why the stories contained in the volumes recounting the history of Peoria's mental health institutions are so important.

We have made progress in Peoria in treatment. We are making progress in understanding mental illness. We are making progress in caring about mental illness. It is an evolutionary trail. Despite our forward advances we still have strides to make. One big one is in providing parity to patients with insurance. A psychologist, Bruce said public awareness and understanding of mental illness was only part of the problem surrounding mental illness.

Bruce, working for the University of Illinois College of Medicine at the-then Zeller Mental Health Center, said blame should not all be heaped on insurance companies. _"This is a complex issue, just like mental illness. Mental illness is not like other medical issues. It's harder to document progress in mental illness. It's hard, but not impossible. The field of mental health needs to adopt objective standards everyone can follow. The insurance companies have a perfect right to ask me or any other mental health professional, 'Can you show me improvement?' "_

Bruce said some movement in that direction is occurring, but a truly standardized measurement system could still be a decade away. That leaves a huge problem still looming - lack of parity for mental health coverage.

"There has to be a balance. Cost containment for the sake of cost containment is not fair," Bruce said, _"But we have to make some movement too. Historically there has been reason for districts. In the early days of this field scientific methods were not always used."_

Bruce added, _"Lack of parity forces people into limited options, forcing them into community mental health systems that are not adequately prepared to accommodate them. Others end up trying to treat themselves by reading books or taking herbs like St. Johns Wort to try to treat depression."_

Bruce said greater public understanding of this issue is at the heart of the cure. And, once again he put the burden on his own profession. _"The professional organizations in mental health have to be more aggressive. We need public service announcements to educate the public. Some people still want to look at this issue in a social Darwinism light -- survival of the fittest. Are we so calloused as a society we will allow that to happen? Or will we recognize it as a moral issue?"_

Only time will answer the questions posed by Bruce. This volume is a step in the right direction.

Appendix I

PEORIA, ILLINOIS 1893:

THE FIRST PETITION SENT OUT BY THE PHILANTHROPIC COMMITTEE OF THE PEORIA WOMEN'S CLUB TO ORGANIZATIONS OF REPRESENTATIVE MEN, ASKING THE ESTABLISHMENT OF AN ASYLUM FOR THE INCURABLE INSANE.

Realizing the sad condition of the incurable and pauper insane of our state, over two thousand of whom are confined in the county poor farms, we pray your honorable body during its present session to enact a law whereby these unfortunates may be placed in the care of the state.

It is only necessary to consider the past and present condition of this large class of helpless ones to be energetically alive to the fact that from a humanitarian standpoint it is the crying need of our times.

At present confined in our county poor farms they are without scientific treatment, or even proper care, since in these institutions no facilities exist for the care of the insane, and many recent exposures of abuses in county houses prove the pitiable condition of these unfortunates who should appeal more strongly than any other class to our sympathies and practical benevolence.

From careful computation based on reliable data we find that the cost of caring for the pauper insane in a suitable asylum will be less when so provided for than by the present system of scattering them around in poor farms. The financial question is of secondary consideration, but in dealing with all sides of an important subject that of cost has its place in the ethics of political economy.

Appendix II

Dedication speech by Governor John Altgeld on June 6, 1896.
"Corner Stone Laid," article from the <u>Peoria Daily Transcript.</u>

Mr. Chairman and Fellow Citizens of Illinois: The founding of a new institution is always an important event in the history of any state. It affects thousands of citizens not only for years but for centuries. It affects coming generations for a long time. Such an institution as we have assembled here today to lay the corner stone marks advancement. It shows the wonderful strides of civilization.

There was a time when the unfortunates of the world were left to die by the wayside. At times they were taken out and destroyed. They were considered a burden and a drawback. The insane at that time were supposed to be afflicted and possessed of the devil or an evil person. The idea that the insane were suffering from a different kind of disease was never thought of. They were chained to the floor or penned up; they were treated worse than animals.

Disease of the Brain:

Toward the beginning of the century it was discovered that insanity was a disease of the brain and that in many cases it could be cured. Where it could not be cured the subject was an object of pity and not possessed of an evil spirit. Man then looked about him for a mode of treatment.

Then came the charitable institutions. A number of states took up the matter, and if there is nothing to distinguish this county these institutions alone are sufficient to make it glorious and immortal. These institutions are purely charitable not educational. They are simply organized benevolences. Until this century the world knew little about charitable institutions.

In Illinois:

Our own state which had a history of only half a century had distinguished itself in these institutions. We have the feeble minded and the institution for the deaf and dumb, the blind. In order that these latter might not be turned out into the world to feel for jobs the state has established workshops for the blind. "We have the old soldier's home for the men who gave their vitality and their best years for their country. When they were old, broken down and poor, Illinois came forward and said: *"I'll take care of you."* The soldiers' orphans' home was established that the orphans of the old soldiers might not grow up on the streets in ignorance. The Illinois soldiers' orphans' home is one of the finest in the country.

We have four great insane asylums outside the hospital maintained by Cook County. At Elgin there are one thousand two hundred patients, Jacksonville one thousand two hundred, Aurora, one thousand, Kankakee more than two thousand two hundred. It is one of the largest and best in the civilized world.

New Asylums:

So rapid has been our growth and so great our increase in population that it was found necessary to do even more. Upwards of two thousand insane patients are in our poorhouses. In some of these their treatment is excellent; in many a disgrace. The legislature decided that two more insane asylums were necessary, one of which should be located in this section, and the other in the northwestern portion of the state. One has been located in Peoria and the other in Rock Island. This is the history of our state in regard to charities.

The people have given of their substance, have given liberally. All they ask is that it be expended with reasonable care. The institutions of our state are in excellent condition. They have been well managed for a number of years.

The Peoria Asylum:

I like the situation of the Peoria asylum. It is a beautiful place, a beautiful view. It looks like a healthy place and I think it will be one of the largest of the state institutions. Its conditions and management will largely depend upon you. See that it is not made a convenient place for the dependent relatives of prominent citizens. See that it is not a place of reward for politicians. See that it is managed on pure scientific principles. I regard the present trustees of the asylum as among the honest representative business men else I would not have appointed them. I trust the trustees throughout ages will continue so.

The best of trustees will succumb to pressure long continued. You should stand by them in their independence.

Waited Long:

Peoria has waited long and patiently. The second city of the state has contributed its share to every state institution. Finally it became a matter of justice that Peoria should have this institution, and I said to the citizens that if Peoria would furnish the site I would recommend that the asylum be located here. The people responded nobly and presented to the state this magnificent site which had not cost the state a cent. On behalf of the people of the state of Illinois I want to thank Peoria. I want to thank you for the interest shown and for this reception. It's a healthy sign and I hope the interest will continue.

No matter who may be governor he will always be ready to cooperate with you. I thank you.

(<u>Peoria Daily Transcript</u>, P. 2-3)

Appendix III

Contents of the Corner Stone:

1. Our National Flag.
2. Cabinet photo of Governor Altgeld
3. Coins of 1894-1896.
4. Printed report of Insane Asylum at Jacksonville for 1892.
5. Printed report of Insane Asylum at Elgin for 1892.
6. Printed report of Insane Asylum at Kankakee for 1890.
7. Printed report of auxiliary to state board of charities for 1896.
8. Printed report of trustees of Peoria Parks.
9. Printed report of board of supervisors of Peoria County for 1895.
10. List of names and commissioners of Peoria County for 1895.
11. Original petition from Women's Club for asylum for the pauper insane.
12. Calendar of Peoria Women's Club.
13. Report of Young Women's Christian Association for 1896.
14. Rules and regulations of Relief Corps.
15. Roster of Bryner Post.
16. Colonel Thrush Camp 25, Sons of Veterans
17. Memorial Day Association.
18. Relief Corps Badge.
19. Badges of Women's Societies.
20. Woman's Christian Home Mission. Union.
21. Ladies' Memorial Day Association.
22. Illinois Women's Christian Temperance
23. Women's Board of Cottage Hospital.
24. Women's Relief Corps of Bryner Post, G.A.R.
25. Peoria Women's Christian Temperance Union.
26. Bradley Home for Aged Women.
27. Old Settlers' Association of Peoria County.
28. Illinois Sunday School Association.
29. Annual reports of Guyer Memorial Home for Aged People.
30. Home for the Friendless.
31. Cottage Hospital and Training School for Nurses.
32. Industrial School for Girls.
33. Peoria Public Schools for 1895.
34. Order of King's Daughters' Day Nursery.
35. Order of King's Daughters' kindergarten.
36. List of members and committees for board of school inspectors for 1896-1897.
37. Design for Peoria County Soldiers' Monument.
38. Small national flag.
39. Silk flag.
40. The United Mine Workers' Journal.
41. The Peoria Transcript.
42. The Peoria Herald.
43. Peoria Sonne.
44. Taglicher Peroial Demokrat.
45. The Peoria Evening Times.
46. The People and Mirror.
47. The first annual report of the board of trustees of Pleasure Driveway and Park District of Peoria.
48. List of officers of the city of Peoria for 1896.
49. City comptroller's report for 1895.
50. Peoria Medical Journal for April, 1896.
51. Chicago & Alton Railroad time card.
52. Programme of the ceremonies.
53. Carriage, reception and committee badges.

Appendix IV

WHAT IS THE MEANING OF PSYCHIATRIC NURSING

By: Telma Robinson

Heretofore it was thought that psychiatric nursing was concerned solely with the nursing care of psychotic or frankly mental patients, but today it takes in a much broader field. Modern psychiatric nursing has a definite three fold program: (1) the nursing of the psychotic patient; (1) the mental as well as the general nursing of those patients suffering from physical illnesses or accident; and (3) prevention of mental illnesses in those who are neither mentally or physically sick.

The successful nurse is the one who recognizes the fact that every sick person is a mentally changed person irrespective of his illness – whether he be a medical, surgical or tubercular patient – and should not be approached with the same attitude as one would use toward the same individual if he were well. All physical illnesses have associated mental and emotional aspects. While but few patients in general hospitals are psychotic both nurses and doctor should realize the fact that many are mental patients in the sense that their handicap cannot be adequately studied or interpreted until their individual personalities and their individual personal situations are taken into account. Emotional needs and problems arise in connection with every physical as well as every mental disease; in fact, it is known that many physical symptoms are often not of an organic origin but are due to unsolved problems of the inner life. The physical and mental spheres of personality are so closely interwoven and inter dependent that almost all physical disturbances create some mental difficulties, so the nurse, then should realize that she cannot nurse the body alone; and that all nursing should be "psychiatric" to some degree. She must realize that the personality of the patient has needs as well as his organs, and that the personal factors in disease require consideration and attention no less than the impersonal organic ones. She will apply the same principles in trying to understand the behavior and attitude of all her patients whether they be frankly mental or suffer from definite physical disease.

In dealing with the psychotic patient, psychiatric nursing will include the general physical care of the patient, close accurate study of symptoms; use of psychotherapy; socialization of patient thru the medium of personal contacts, occupation and recreation therapy and habit training; use of procedure employed more often or only in the care of the mental patient as artificial and force feeding, sedative and stimulating hydrotherapy; etc; and constant vigilance against exhaustion in the excited patient and self destruction in the depressed.

Psychiatric nursing should not limit its activities to care of those who are considered truly psychotic and of those who have personality changes due to physical disease, but it should step outside the hospital walls and include in its scope the prevention of mental disease in those who are threatened and increasing the mental health of those who are neither already ill nor threatened with illness. This may be done by the nurse with the psychiatric view point who is employed in clinics, public health, industry, private duty, school nursing, etc. Where she comes in contact with not only the patient but also the family and friends who have been thrown into an abnormal, trying situation and who may have beginning personality defects, that show themselves under strain, that could be corrected if recognized and the laws of good mental health applied by a nurse who knew and understood the principles of this broader type of psychiatric nursing.

Appendix V

The following letter was subsequently filed with the members of the General Assembly in February of 1973. This letter summarizes the Commission's findings and their recommendations:

February, 1973

TO: Honorable Members of the General Assembly

Our investigation of the three tragic patient deaths at Peoria State Hospital this past summer established they were indirectly caused by a combination of medical neglect and inadequate staff supervision. At our public hearings, Dr. Henry D. Staras, the Superintendent of the Hospital, assumed full responsibility for the conditions that led to these deaths.

Jerome S. probably died from a vicious assault by one of two fellow patients, both of whom had previously and consistently inflicted assaults on S. and other patients. Patient Bernard R. died following an epileptic seizure which may have been induced by an assault from another violence-prone patient, and from medical neglect. The third victim, patient James L., died from spinal meningitis caused by an acute ear infection which, through medical neglect, had been ignored and not properly treated.

We strongly condemn the administration at Peoria State Hospital, and particularly the inexcusably deplorable management of its Superintendent, Dr. Staras. We recommend that Dr. Staras be replaced by a person with those professional and management capabilities necessary to ensure the best possible care to mentally retarded persons, and to otherwise discharge the important functions and duties of a large institution. Most importantly, all necessary precautions must be taken to avoid future tragedies.

House Joint Resolution 146 essentially instructed the Commission to investigate (1) the reported beating on May 21, 1972 of Jerome S., a patient at the Peoria State Hospital at Bartonville, and (2) all aspects of the relationship between the hospital administration and the Bartonville Police, and specifically the reporting of occurrences of criminal assault or other criminal activity.

After House Joint Resolution 146 was adopted by the House, and before it was adopted in the Senate, S. died. After we had initiated our investigation two other patients, Bernard R. and James L., died.

The Commission decided to expand the mandate of the resolution to include the investigation of the three deaths with the encouragement and concurrence of Representative Gerald A. Bradley, the sponsor of the resolution.

During our investigation a total of 57 persons were interviewed, many of them employees of Peoria State Hospital. During the course of these interviews our staff members made visual inspections of the physical facilities and conditions at the hospital and found them to be deplorable. Public hearings were conducted in Peoria at which 25 witnesses testified.

A separate chapter of this report is devoted to our findings in connection with each of the three deaths, and also with regard to the relationship between the hospital management and the Bartonville Police Department from the standpoint of reporting criminal assaults and serious incidents. Following is a summary of Chapter 2, 3, 4 and 5.

Death of Jerome S. *Jerome S. was found on May 21 1972 by hospital employees, critically wounded from a brutal assault apparently by another patient. We could not establish with certainty who had committed the assault. However, the most logical suspect was subsequently transferred from Peoria State Hospital to the state institution at Menard pursuant to the directions of Dr. Staras. S. died on June 23, 1972, at St. Francis Hospital in Peoria.*

Jerome S. had been repeatedly beaten on several occasions during the preceding months. At the time of his assault on May 21, 1972, five ward aides were on duty. Three of them were engaged in therapeutic activities and field trips elsewhere on the hospital grounds and in the City of Peoria. The two aides on the ward did not witness the assault which was committed in an area which was beyond their immediate surveillance.

Death of Bernard R. *R. was struck on the head with a chair by another patient, Robert L., on July 19, 1972 at 4:25 p.m., and shortly thereafter suffered an epileptic seizure. Dr. Jose Ante, the Medical Officer of the Day and a limited-license physician educated in the Philippines, failed to promptly and properly attend to S's injuries. It was not until 2:30 a.m. the following day that S. was admitted to St. Francis Hospital where he died at 11:55 a.m.*

Dr. Ante, who was invited to testify at our public hearings, invoked the Fifth Amendment. He said he feared the possibility of another agency bringing criminal negligence charges against him.

Death of James L. *James L. died on August 30, 1972, from a chronic infection which remained unattended through medical neglect. He had a history of ear infections for several months prior to his death. As time passed his behavior became more erratic, with frequent entries made in the incident book maintained on each ward that L. should be examined by a physician. Finally, a hospital aide requested that L. be immediately examined by a doctor because pus and an extremely putrid odor exuded from L's left ear. On August 24, 1972, Dr. Simplicio Legaspi, a limited-license physician, performed a cursory and inadequate examination, and prescribed ear washes and hydrogen peroxide swabbing. Dr. Legaspi was also educated in the Philippines.*

The following day a hospital aide noticed foreign matter of a metallic nature lodged in L's ear, probably gum wrapper tinfoil, self-inserted and decomposing. L. was admitted to the institution's hospital at 7:00 p.m. on August 29, 1972, and by 9:00 a.m. the following morning he died from spinal meningitis induced by the highly advanced ear infection. It is believed that L's death could possibly have been averted had antibiotics been administered several days before when he first displayed symptoms of acute infection. When questioned at our public hearings Dr. Legaspi could not satisfactorily explain his improper diagnosis and treatment of L.

Relationship Between Hospital and Bartonville Police. *It had been alleged that the Peoria State Hospital administration had resisted and obstructed efforts to improve the relationship between the hospital and the adjacent Bartonville Police Department. Our investigation confirmed this to be essentially true.*

We established that here was a strong hospital policy against reporting serious instances of assault to the Bartonville Police Department. Only in dire emergencies and then only at the belated request of high ranking supervisory personnel at the hospital was this done.

In the case of the Jerome S's beating we find that the hospital was remiss in not promptly notifying the Bartonville Police Department and allowing the physical evidence relating to the crime to be "cleaned up" by staff personnel.

During the public hearings the commission received a promise from the hospital administration to promptly establish and implement a policy to report all serious incidents to the police department without delay, and otherwise cooperate with that department.

Other Findings. *Although our investigation was conducted within the parameters of House Joint Resolution 146 many witnesses whom we interviewed, some of whom testified at our public hearings, made many other observations. Some of them could be construed as directly relevant to the mandate of that resolution. Some, however, were not totally material but of sufficient importance to the matter of mental retardation treatment as to warrant official notice in this report. They are discussed in Chapter VI.* (A report to the Illinois General Assembly, February 1973)

These matters are listed as follows:

1. *The segregation of violent and aggressive patients from docile patients;*
2. *The disorganized system of management;*
3. *Staff inadequacies;*
4. *The demise of therapy;*
5. *Use of drugs;*
6. *Mental retardation treatment concepts;*
7. *The physical condition and facilities at the hospital;*
8. *Limited license physicians;*
9. *The security force;*
10. *An alleged incident of employee abuse of a patient.*

Acknowledgements. *Whereas some limited-license members of the medical staff leave much to be desired from the standpoint of their professional expertise, we do wish to acknowledge the dedication of the other employees to the welfare and interest of mentally retarded patients. We also gratefully acknowledge the fact that Senator Frank M. Ozinga's Legislative Commission to Visit and Examine State Institutions postponed its inspection of the Peoria State Hospital facilities pending the completion of our investigation. We trust that this report will be of assistance in connection with that Commission's forthcoming inspection. In that regard the Peoria State Hospital visitation reports of the Illinois Association for the Mentally Retarded should be helpful.*

In conclusion, we implore the legislature to do everything in its power to assure the people of Illinois that disasters such as those which occurred last summer at Peoria State will not recur there, nor anywhere else in the State mental health system. We also urge the General Assembly, through its appropriate committees and commissions, to redouble its efforts concerning the treatment of the mentally retarded. In the past 12 years Illinois has emerged from the "dark ages" to the point where our State is becoming a leader in the field. Much, however, remains to be done.

Institutions postponed its inspection of the Peoria State Hospital facilities pending the completion of our investigation. We trust that this report will be of assistance in connection with that Commission's forthcoming inspection. In that regard the Peoria State Hospital visitation reports of the Illinois Association for the Mentally Retarded should be helpful.

In conclusion, we implore the legislature to do everything in its power to assure the people of Illinois that disasters such as those which occurred last summer at Peoria State will not recur there, nor anywhere else in the State mental health system. We also urge the General Assembly, through its appropriate committees and commissions, to redouble its efforts concerning the treatment of the mentally retarded. In the past 12 years Illinois has emerged from the "dark ages" to the point where our State is becoming a leader in the field. Much, however, remains to be done.

Appendix VI

Governors of Illinois

Richard Yates	1901-1905
Charles Deneen	1905-1913
Edward Dunne	1913-1917
Frank Lowden	1917-1921
Lennington Small	1921-1929
Louis Emmerson	1929-1933
Henry Horner	1933-1940
John Stelle	1940-1941
Dwight Green	1941-1949
Adlai Stevenson	1949-1953
William Stratton	1953-1961
Otto Kerner	1961-1968
Samuel Shapiro	1968-1969
Richard Ogilve	1969-1973
Daniel Walker	1973-1977

Superintendents of Peoria State Hospital

F. C. Winslow & Henry Carriel	1901-1902
George A. Zeller	1902-1913
Ralph Hinton	1913-1917
Ralph Goodner	1917-1921
George A. Zeller	1921-1935
Dudley Dawson	1935
Walter Baer	1936-1939
Irving Turow*	1939-1942
George Wiltrakis*	
Phyllip Waters*	
Bernard Skorodin*	
James Ellingsworth	1942-1946
Richard Graff	1946-1949
Walter Baer	1949-1951
Henry Knowles	1951-1954
Daniel Manelli	1954-1957
Ernest Klein	1957-1963
Walter Garre	1963-1964
Henry Staras	1964-1973

* All served an undetermined length of time

Appendix VII
Significant Mental Health Legislation

Before 1847 - There were no state institutions for the mentally ill or mentally retarded. They were incarcerated in local community almshouses and jails.

1847-1869 - Institutions for the mentally disabled were established under separate Local Boards of Trustees appointed by and responsible only to the governor.

1869 - Creation of the Board of State Commissioners of Public Charities. This organization functioned for approximately 40 years. Its duties were primarily to visit and inspect institutions under Local Boards of Trustees.

1907 - A law was passed in which the state accepted full responsibility for the mentally ill and provided that all mentally ill persons should be transferred to state hospitals.

1910 - Creation of a Board of Administration to have full administrative powers over state institutions. All Local Boards of Trustees were abolished.

1917 - Creation of the Department of Public Welfare to replace the Board of Administration. This occurred during an extensive governmental reorganization which created the Civil Administrative Code in which the functions of state government were consolidated into 9 code departments. The Department of Public Welfare was responsible for the treatment and care of the mentally ill and mentally retarded but was also made responsible for the administration of the penal system, the licensing of child-placement agencies and the visitation of children placed in foster homes. At one time or another the Department has been responsible for the penal system, for services to children and families, and for public aid.

1941 - Penal institutions were transferred to the newly created Department of Public Safety. Soon afterwards, the Public Aid Commission was made responsible for public assistance programs.

1944 - Creation of the Mental Health Act which revised the laws in relation to commitment, admission, detention and care of the mentally ill. Seven regional offices were established.

1953 - The responsibility for delinquent youth was transferred to the Illinois Youth Commission.

1960 - The legislature approved a Public Welfare Building Bond Issue for 150 million dollars. Funds were thereby appropriated to renovate, rebuild and construct new buildings at the mental health facilities. Funds were also appropriated to establish seven zone centers.

1961 - The legislature established the Department of Mental Health to replace the Department of Public Welfare. At this time the Department was made solely responsible for the treatment and care of the mentally ill and mentally retarded.

1963 - Establishment of the Community Mental Health Act which established what are popularly known as 708 Boards. This legislation permits local communities to tax themselves in order to set up mental health boards to provide community mental health services.

1974 - (Effective 1976) creation of the Division of Alcoholism and "decriminalization of alcoholism."

Appendix VIII

Condensed Rules for the Guidance of Attendants and Nurses.*

No. 1.   A tour of duty is limited to eight hours a day, except in emergencies.

No. 2.   The inmates are not to be imprisoned or secluded.

No. 3.   Vigilance is the watchword of this institution.

No. 4.   Mechanical restraint will never, under any circumstances, be applied to any inmate.

No. 5.   Non-resistance should be the guiding rule in our attitude toward the inmates. It requires an antagonist to provoke a quarrel, hence, when inmates are unruly, they are to be soothed by gentle words and a gentle manner.

No. 6   "A Soft Answer Turneth Away Wrath."

No. 7.   Fire! Turn in the alarm, take down the hose and turn on the water while other attendants are removing the inmates. Be calm in the face of peril. Verify your list of inmates. Make no effort to save valuables so long as one life is in jeopardy.

No. 8.   Men visiting women's cottages for whatever purpose are to be chaperoned by the attendant in charge and the visit must be noted on the daily report.

No. 9.   No attendant is to leave her post until regularly relieved.

No. 10.   Meals are to be carefully inspected, the food impartially distributed, and all irregularities reported.

No. 11.   All clothing and effects must accompany each inmate when transferred, even temporarily.

No. 12.   The Head Attendant is supreme in the cottage and in her absence the Acting Head Attendant assumes her authority and carries out her orders.

No. 13.   Obedience must follow every order. No latitude is left the employe except where danger of the life of an inmate is involved.

No. 14.   The public demands courtesy of its servants. Never forget the misfortunes of your charges or the sorrow of their friends and relatives.

* These 14 rules were taken from the "Rules Governing the Conduct of the Illinois General Hospital for the Insane, Peoria, Illinois," which was compiled by George A. Zeller, M.D. Superintendent 1909. A copy was kept posted in each of the cottages.

NOTES:

Introduction.
1. "Marvelous Progress Made at Bartonville Insane Asylum." <u>Peoria Star.</u> February 10, 1907.
    Volume X-137. Page 24.
2. Ibid. Page 25.
3. Baker, Rick. <u>Mary, Me In Search of a Lost Life Time.</u> The Bakery, a Publishing Company,
    1989. Page 20.

Chapter I: The Birth of the Peoria State Hospital.
1. "Corner Stone Laid." <u>Peoria Daily Transcript.</u> June 6, 1896. Volume XLII. Page 1.
2. Ibid. Page 3.
3. Ibid. Page 2.
4. Kirkbride, Thomas. <u>On the Construction, Organization and General Arrangements of</u>
    <u>Hospitals for the Insane.</u> Arno Press-A New York Times Company, 1973. Page 293.
5. Ibid. Page 2.
6. "Memorial of Miss Dix." <u>Scope.</u> Reprinted Springfield, Springfield, Illinois. Volume No.2.
    January 28, 1972. Page 3.
7. Ibid. Page 3.
8. Ibid. Page 6.
9. Ibid. Page 5.
10. Gallahar, David. <u>Voice for the Mad the Life of Dorothea Dix.</u> The Free Press, 1995. Page 5.
11. "Corner Stone Laid." <u>Peoria Daily Transcript.</u> June 6, 1896. Volume XLII. Page 4.
12. Zeller, George A. M.D. <u>Befriending the Bereft.</u> Unpublished autobiography. Circa: 1930.
    Page 3.
13. Fifth Biennial Report of the Trustees, Superintendent and Treasures of the Illinois Asylum
    for the Incurable Insane at Peoria. June 30, 1904. Page 8.
14. Adams, Bill. "Clubs Building was City Cultural Center From Start. <u>Yester Days: Volume III.</u>
    Copyright <u>Peoria Journal Star.</u> May 31, 1993. Pages 130-131.
15. "Corner Stone Laid." <u>Peoria Daily Transcript.</u> June 6, 1896. Volume XLII. Page 1.
16. Ibid. Page 1.
17. Ibid. Page 1.
18. Ibid. Page 1.
19. Ibid. Page 1.
20. Ibid. Page 1.
21. Gallahar, David. <u>Voice for the Mad the Life of Dorothea Dix.</u> The Free Press 1995. Page 7.
22. Zeller, George A. M.D. <u>Befriending the Bereft.</u> Unpublished autobiography. Circa: 1930.
    Page 3.
23. Ibid. Page 4.
24. Ibid. Page 4.
25. Second Biennial Report of the Trustees and Treasurer of the Illinois Asylum for Incurable
    Insane at Peoria. July 1, 1898. Page 5
26. Zeller, George A. M.D. <u>Befriending the Bereft.</u> Unpublished autobiography. Circa: 1930.
    Page 3.
27. Ibid. Page 5.
28. Ibid. Page 5.

29. Second Biennial Report of the Trustees and Treasurer of the Illinois Asylum for Incurable Insane at Peoria. July 1, 1898. Page 5.

30. Zeller, George A. M.D. <u>Befriending the Bereft.</u> Unpublished autobiography. Circa: 1930. Page 5.

31. Zeller, George A. M.D. "Peoria State Hospital Peoria, Illinois (Formerly the General Hospital for the Insane; originally theIllinois Asylum for the Incurable Insane). Unpublished article.

32. Kirkbride, Thomas. <u>On the Construction, Organization, and General Arrangements of Hospitals for the Insane.</u> Arno Press- A New York Times Company, 1973. Page 303.

33. Ibid. Page 303.

34. Second Biennial Report of the Trustees and Treasurer of the Illinois Asylum for Incurable Insane at Peoria.July 1, 1898. Page 6.

35. Zeller, George A. M.D. <u>Befriending the Bereft.</u> Unpublished autobiography. Circa: 1930. Page 6.

36. Stanley, Theresa. "Peoria Women's Club: After 100 Years, Local Group Remains Dedicated to Educational Opportunity." <u>Peoria Observer.</u> October 9, 1995. Page 1.

Chapter II: The Walls Came Tumbling Down.

1. "Corner Stone Laid." <u>Peoria Daily Transcript.</u> June 6, 1986. Volume XLII. Page 1.

2. Ibid. Page 1.

3. Ibid. Page 1.

4. Ibid. Page 1.

5. Ibid. Page 1.

6. Ibid. Page 1.

7. Ibid. Page 1.

8. Ibid. Page 3.

9. Ibid. Page 1.

10. Second Biennial Report of the Trustees and Treasurer of the Illinois Asylum for Incurable Insane at Peoria.July 1, 1898. Page 15

11. Mehr, Joseph J. Ph.D. <u>An Illustrated History Illinois Public Mental Health Services 1847-2000.</u> A Santayana Publication 2002. Page 184.

12. "Governor Tanner and the Asylum." <u>Peoria Herald Transcript.</u> December 23, 1897. Page 4.

13. Ibid. Page 6.

14. Second Biennial Report of the Trustees and Treasurer of the Illinois Asylum for Incurable Insane at Peoria.July 1, 1898. Page 6.

15. Ibid. Page 10.

16. Ibid. Page 11.

17. Ibid. Page 13.

18. Ibid. Page 13.

19. Ibid. Page 19.

20. Ibid. Page 20.

21. "Denies the Rumors-Henry Alexander of Asylum Board Says Stories of His Resignation are False." <u>Peoria Herald Transcript.</u> Wednesday A.M. December 1, 1987. Page 6.

22. Ibid. Page 1.

23. Ibid. Page 4.

24. Ibid Page 1

25. Second Biennial Report of the Trustees and Treasurer of the Illinois Asylum for Incurable
    Insane at Peoria.July 1, 1898. Page 16.
26. Ibid. Page 16.
27. Ibid. Page 15.
28. Ibid. Page 16.
29. Ibid. Page 16.
30. Ibid. Page 16.
31. Ibid Page 16.
32. Ibid Page 16.

Chapter III: Day One Arrival of the First Patients.
1. "First Hundred Patients Here-Arrive at the Asylum Grounds at Noon Yesterday." Peoria Herald
    Transcript Tuesday, February 11, 1902. Page 10.
2. Ibid. Page 10.
3. Edward, Thomas, Peoria State Hospital Historic District Application for Listing in National
    Register of Historic Places. Prepared for the Reardon Company, July 24, 1980. Page 25.
4. Fourth Biennial Report of the Trustees, Superintendent and Treasurer of the Illinois Asylum
    for the Incurable Insane at Peoria. July 1, 1902. Page 12.
5. Ibid. Page 5.
6. Ibid. Page 11.

Chapter IV: Dr. Zeller's Appointment.
1. Zeller, George A. M.D. Befriending the Bereft. Unpublished autobiography. Circa: 1930.
    Page 22.
2. Ibid. Page 23.
3. Ibid. Page 23.
4. Ibid. Page 55.
5. Fourth Biennial Report of the Trustees, Superintendent and Treasurer of the Illinois Asylum
    for the Incurable Insane at Peoria. July 1, 1902. Page 10.
6. Zeller, George A. M.D. Befriending the Bereft. Unpublished autobiography. Circa: 1930.
    Page 34.
7. Fourth Biennial Report of the Trustees, Superintendent and Treasurer of the Illinois Asylum
    for the Incurable Insane at Peoria. July 1, 1902. Page 10.
8. Zeller, George A. M.D. Befriending the Bereft Unpublished autobiography. Circa: 1930.
     Page 55.

Chapter V: New Facility – Old Ideas.
1. Zeller, George A. M.D. Befriending the Bereft. Unpublished autobiography. Circa: 1930.
    Page 56.
2. Eighth Biennial Report of the Peoria State Hospital at Peoria – Formerly the Illinois General
    Hospital for The Insane – Originally the Illinois Asylum for the Incurable Insane. June 30,
    1910. Page 5.
3. Mehr, Joseph J. Ph.D. An Illustrated History Illinois Public Mental Health Services 1847-
    2000. A Santayana Publication 2002. Page 193.
4. Zeller, George A. M.D. Befriending the Bereft. Unpublished autobiography. Circa: 1930.
    Page 56.

5. Fifth Biennial Report of the Trustees, Superintendent and Treasurer of the Illinois Asylum for the Incurable Insane. June 30, 1904. Page 10.
6. Mehr, Joseph J. Ph.D. <u>An Illustrated History Illinois Public Mental Health Services 1847-2000.</u> A Santayana Publication 2002. Page 5.
7. "Memorial of Miss Dix." <u>Scope.</u> Volume No.8. Reprinted January 28, 1972.
8. "Marvelous Progress Made at Bartonville Insane Hospital." <u>Peoria Star.</u> Vol. X-137. February 10, 1907. Page 25.
9. Ibid. Page 24.
10. Zeller, George A. M.D. <u>Befriending the Bereft.</u> Unpublished autobiography. Circa: 1930. Pages 56-57.

Chapter VI: A Revolution in Mental Health Care.

1. Zeller, George A. M.D. <u>Befriending the Bereft.</u> Unpublished autobiography. Circa: 1930. Page 59.
2. Fifth Biennial Report of the Peoria State Hospital at Peoria Illinois – Formerly the Illinois General Hospital for the Insane – Originally the Illinois Asylum for the Incurable Insane. June 30, 1904. Page 11.
3. Sixth Biennial Report of the Commissioners, Superintendent and Treasurer of the Illinois Asylum for the Incurable Insane at Peoria. June 30, 1906. Page 14.
4. Ibid. Page 14.
5. Ibid. Page 14.
6. Fifth Biennial Report of the Peoria State Hospital at Peoria Illinois – Formerly the Illinois General Hospital for the Insane – Originally the Illinois Asylum for the Incurable Insane. June 30, 1904. Page 11.
7. Zeller, George A. M.D. <u>Befriending the Bereft</u> Unpublished autobiography. Circa 1930. Page 70.
8. Ninth Biennial Report of the Peoria State Hospital at Peoria, Illinois. July 1, 1910 to September 30, 1912. Page 8.
9. Zeller, George A. M.D. <u>Befriending the Bereft</u> Unpublished autobiography. Circa: 1930. Page 70.
10. Sixth Biennial Report of the Commissioners, Superintendent and Treasurer of the Illinois Asylum for the Incurable Insane at Peoria. June 30, 1906. Page 77.
11. "Nurse Graduate at Bartonville." <u>Peoria Journal.</u> Vol. XLIC No.13. Friday, June 18, 1909. Page 13.
12. Sixth Biennial Report of the Commissioners, Superintendent and Treasurer of the Illinois Asylum for the Incurable Insane. June 30, 1906. Page 14.
13. Ibid. Page 15.
14. Ibid. Page 18.
15. Zeller, George A. M.D. <u>Befriending the Bereft</u> Unpublished autobiography. Circa 1930. Page 60.
16. Ibid. Page 59.
17. Ibid. Page 59.
18. Ibid. Page 60.

Chapter VII: The Nursing School.

1. Ward, James S. M.D. Asylum Light – Stories From the Dr. <u>George A. Zeller Era and Beyond – Peoria State Hospital Galesburg Mental Health Center, and George A. Zeller Mental Health Center.</u> Mental Health Historic Preservation Society of Central Illinois. 2004. Page 82.

2. Seventh Biennial Report of the Illinois General Hospital for the Insane at Peoria. June 30, 1908. Page 13.

3. "Nurse Graduate at Bartonville." <u>Peoria Journal.</u> Vol. XLIC No.13. Friday, June 18, 1909. Page 13.

4. Seventh Biennial Report of the Illinois General Hospital for the Insane at Peoria. June 30,1908. Page 13.

5. "Nurse Graduate at Bartonville." <u>Peoria Journal.</u> Vol. XLIC No.13. Friday, June 18, 1909. Page 20.

6. Ninth Biennial Report of the Peoria State Hospital at Peoria Illinois. July 1, 1910 to September 30, 1912. Page 12.

7. Tenth Biennial Report of the Peoria State Hospital at Peoria Illinois. October 1, 1914. Page 10.

8. Zeller, George A. M.D. <u>Befriending the Bereft.</u> Unpublished autobiography. Circa: 1930. Page 78.

9. Ibid. Page 78.

10. Eleventh Biennial Report of the Peoria State Hospital at Peoria, Illinois. October 1, 1916. Page 14.

11. Ibid. Page 13.

12. State of Illinois Third Administrative Report of the Directors of Departments. July 1, 1919 to June 30, 1920. Page 430.

13. State of Illinois Seventh Administrative Report of the Directors of Departments. July 1, 1923 to June 30, 1924. Page 622.

14. Annual Reports of the Department of Welfare. July 1, 1930 to June 30, 1931. Page 199.

15. Annual Reports of the Department of Welfare. July 1, 1939 to June 30, 1940. Page 476.

16. Annual Reports of the Department of Welfare. July 1, 1936 to June 30, 1937. Page 334.

17. Ibid. Page 336.

18. Ibid. Page 335.

19. Ibid. Page 336.

20. Annual Reports of the Department of Welfare. July 1, 1937 to June 30, 1938. Page 364.

21. Annual Reports of the Department of Welfare. July 1, 1939 to June 30, 1940. Page 476.

22. Annual Reports of the Department of Welfare. July 1, 1939 to June 30, 1940. Page 38.

23. Ward, James S. M.D. Asylum Light – <u>Stories From the Dr. George A. Zeller Era and Beyond: Peoria State Hospital Galesburg Mental Health Center, and George A. Zeller Mental Health Center.</u> Mental Health Historic Preservation Society of Central Illinois. 2004. Page 83.

Chapter VIII: Women Attendants.

1. Fifth Biennial Report of the Peoria State Hospital at Peoria Illinois – Formerly the Illinois General Hospital for the Insane – Originally the Illinois Asylum for the Incurable Insane. June 30, 1904. Page 14.

2. Zeller, George A. M.D. <u>Befriending the Bereft.</u> Unpublished autobiography. Circa: 1930. Page 21.

3. Seventh Biennial Report of the Illinois General Hospital for the Insane at Peoria. June 30, 1908. Page 14.

4. Fifth Biennial Report of the Peoria State Hospital at Peoria Illinois – Formerly the Illinois General Hospital for the Insane – Originally the Illinois Asylum for the Incurable Insane. June 30, 1904. Page 11.

5. Sixth Biennial Report of the Commissioners, Superintendent and Treasurer of the Illinois Asylum for the Incurable Insane. June 30, 1906. Page 12.

6. Seventh Biennial Report of the Illinois General Hospital for the Insane at Peoria. June 30, 1908. Page 13.

Chapter IX: Monuments and Memories.

1. Fifth Biennial Report of the Peoria State Hospital at Peoria Illinois – Formerly the Illinois General Hospital for the Insane – Originally the Illinois Asylum for the Incurable Insane. June 30, 1904. Page 12.

2. Zeller, George A. M.D. A Series of Asylum Romances. Published by the Department of Welfare 1919. Page 95.

3. Zeller, George A. M.D. Befriending the Bereft. Unpublished autobiography. Circa: 1930. Page 33.

4. Zeller, George A. M.D. "Rules Governing the Conduct of the Illinois General Hospital for the Insane Peoria, Illinois. 1908." Page 19.

5. "Bowen Denies Laxity at Bartonville." Peoria Star. 1940. Page 10.

6. Ibid. Page 1.

7. Ibid. Page 3.

8. Baker, Rick. "Graves Without Bodies a Hospital Without Pity." Peoria Journal Star. Vol. 129 No. 208. June 30, 1985. Page D20.

9. Ibid. Page D20.

10. Ibid. Page D20.

11. McNett, William M. M.D. The Forgotten Residents of the Peoria State Hospital. Peoria Genealogical Society Inc. Peoria, Illinois 1995. Page 168.

12. Ibid. Page 167.

13. Ibid. Page 43.

14. Ibid. Page 43.

15. Ibid. Page 116.

Chapter X: Treatment and Therapy.

1. Altschule, Mark, M.D. Roots of Moder Psychiatry Essays in the History of Psychiatry. Gurne and Straton Inc. New York and London. 1957. Page 140.

2. Zeller, George A. M.D. Befriending the Bereft. Unpublished autobiography. Circa: 1930. Page 59.

3. Altschule, Mark, M.D. Roots of Moder Psychiatry Essays in the History of Psychiatry. Gurne and Straton Inc. New York and London. 1957. Page 147.

4. Ibid. Page 148.

5. "Yesterday Today Tomorrow." Illinois Department of Mental Health 1970. Annual Report. Page 3.

6. Fifth Biennial Report of the Peoria State Hospital at Peoria Illinois – Formerly the Illinois General Hospital for the Insane – Originally the Illinois Asylum for the Incurable Insane. June 30, 1904. Page 14.

7. Ibid. Page 14.

8. Ibid. Page 15.

9. Ibid. Page 15.

10. Sixth Biennial Report of the Commissioners, Superintendent and Treasurer of the Illinois Asylum for the Incurable Insane. June 30, 1906. Page 16.

11. Zeller, George A. M.D. Befriending the Bereft. Unpublished autobiography. Circa: 1930. Page 75.

12. Ward, James S. M.D. "Have We Come Full Circle." Unpublished article.

13. Sixth Biennial Report of the Commissioners, Superintendent and Treasurer of the Illinois Asylum for the Incurable Insane. June 30, 1906. Page 16.

14. Ibid. Page 16.

15. Seventh Biennial Report of the Illinois General Hospital for the Insane at Peoria. June 30, 1908. Page 10.

16. Ibid. Page 11.

17. Ward, James S. M.D. Asylum Light – Stories From the Dr. George A. Zeller Era and Beyond: Peoria State Hospital Galesburg Mental Health Center, and George A. Zeller Mental Health Center. Mental Health Historic Preservation Society of Central Illinois. 2004. Page 78.

18. Mehr, Joseph J. Ph.D. An Illustrated History Illinois Public Mental Health Services 1847-2000. A Santayana Publication 2002. Page 226.

19. Wright, Rebekah, M.D. Hydrotherapy in Hospital for Mental Disease. Tudor Press Inc. Boston Massachusetts. 1932. Page 19.

20. Kellog, J.H., M.D. A Manual of the Physiological and Therapeutic Effects of Hydriatic Procedures, and the Technique of Their Application in the Treatment of Disease. Moder Medicine Publication 1928. Page 21.

21. Ibid. Page 21.

22. Mehr, Joseph J. Ph.D. An Illustrated History Illinois Public Mental Health Services 1847-2000. A Santayana Publication 2002. Page 254.

23. Ibid. Page 256.

24. Sixth Biennial Report of the Commissioners, Superintendent and Treasurer of the Illinois Asylum for the Incurable Insane. June 30, 1906. Page 14.

25. Mehr, Joseph J. Ph.D. An Illustrated History Illinois Public Mental Health Services 1847-2000. A Santayana Publication 2002. Page 272.

26. Wright, Rebekah, M.D. Hydrotherapy in Hospital for Mental Disease. Tudor Press Inc. Boston Massachusetts. 1932. Page 19.

27. First Administrative Report of the Directors of Departments Under the Civil Administrative Code Together With the Adjutant General's Report. July 1, 1918 to June 30, 1919. Page 14.

28. Ibid. Page 320.

29. Annual Reports of the Department of Public Welfare. July 1, 1958 to June 30, 1959. Page 50.

30. Ibid. Page 50.

31. Wright, Rebekah, M.D. Hydrotherapy in Hospital for Mental Disease. Tudor Press Inc. Boston Massachusetts. 1932. Page 179.

32. Ibid. Page 212.

33. Ibid. Page 202.

34. Ibid. Page 202.

35. Mehr, Joseph J. Ph.D. <u>An Illustrated History Illinois Public Mental Health Services 1847-2000.</u> A Santayana Publication 2002. Page 378.

36. Ibid. Page 378.

37. "Asylum Light." Vol. 3 No.8. October 1938. Monthly newsletter produced at the Peoria State Hospital.

38. Annual Report of the Department of Public Welfare. June 30, 1938. Page 361.

39. Annual Report of the Department of Public Welfare. 1932 to 1933. Page 504.

40. Ward, James S. M.D. <u>Asylum Light – Stories From the Dr. George A. Zeller Era and Beyond : Peoria State Hospital, Galesburg Mental Health Center, and George A. Zeller Mental Health Center.</u> Mental Health Historic Preservation Society of Central Illinois. 2004. Page 78.

41. Mehr, Joseph J. Ph.D. <u>An Illustrated History Illinois Public Mental Health Services 1847-2000.</u> A Santayana Publication 2002. Page 380.

42. Ward, James S. M.D. <u>Asylum Light – Stories From the Dr. George A. Zeller Era and Beyond: Peoria State Hospital Galesburg Mental Health Center, and George A. Zeller Mental Health Center.</u> Mental Health Historic Preservation Society of Central Illinois. 2004. Page 79.

43. Annual Report of the Department of Public Welfare. July 1, 1949 to June 1950. Page 62.

44. Seventh Biennial Report of the Illinois General Hospital for the Insane at Peoria. June 30, 1908. Page 2.

45. Ibid. Page 5.

46. Third Administrative Report of the Directors of Departments Under the Civil Administrative Code Together With the Adjutant General's Report. July 1, 1919 to June 30, 1920. Page 325-326.

47. Ibid. Page 432.

48. Mehr, Joseph J. Ph.D. <u>An Illustrated History Illinois Public Mental Health Services 1847-2000.</u> A Santayana Publication 2002. Page 356.

Chapter XI: Unrelated Conditions and Treatments.

1. Zeller, George A. M.D. <u>Befriending the Bereft.</u> Unpublished autobiography. Circa: 1930. Page 65.

2. Ibid. Page 65.

3. Sixth Biennial Report of the Commissioners, Superintendent and Treasurer of the Illinois Asylum for the Incurable Insane. June 30, 1906. Page 17.

4. Ibid. Page 17.

5. Seventh Biennial Report of the Illinois General Hospital for the Insane at Peoria. June 30, 1908. Page 14.

6. Eighth Biennial Report of the Peoria State Hospital at Peoria, Illinois – Formerly the Illinois General Hospital for the Insane – Originally the Illinois Asylum for the Incurable Insane. June 30, 1910. Page 9.

7. Ninth Biennial Report of the Peoria State Hospital at Peoria Illinois. July 1, 1910 to September 30, 1912. Page 6.

8. Annual Reports of the Department of Public Welfare. June 30, 1940. Page 477.

9. Ibid. Page 488.

10. Zeller, George A. M.D. <u>Befriending the Bereft.</u> Unpublished autobiography. Circa: 1930. Page 64.

11. Ibid. Page 63.

12. Eighth Biennial Report of the Peoria State Hospital at Peoria, Illinois – Formerly the Illinois General Hospital for the Insane – Originally the Illinois Asylum for the Incurable Insane. June 30, 1910. Page 8.

13. Annual Reports of the Department of Public Welfare. June 30, 1938. Page 268.

14. The Welfare Bulletin. Illinois Department of Public Welfare. 1919. Page 4.

15. Annual Report of the Department of Public Welfare. 1908. Page 65.

16. Sixth Biennial Report of the Commissioners, Superintendent and Treasurer of the Illinois Asylum for the Incurable Insane. June 30, 1906. Page 17.

17. Fifth Biennial Report of the Peoria State Hospital at Peoria Illinois – Formerly the Illinois General Hospital for the Insane – Originally the Illinois Asylum for the Incurable Insane. June 30, 1904. Page 11.

18 Sixth Biennial Report of the Commissioners, Superintendent and Treasurer of the Illinois Asylum for the Incurable Insane. June 30, 1906. Page 18.

Chapter XII: The Young and Helpless of Peoria State Hospital.

1. Sixth Biennial Report of the Commissioners, Superintendent and Treasurer of the Illinois Asylum for the Incurable Insane. June 30, 1906. Pages 8-9.

2. Ibid. Page 9.

3. Annual Reports of the Department of Public Welfare. July 1, 1952 to June 30, 1953. Page 55.

4. Hoshler, Fred K. "The Abbott Children's Center." The Welfare Bulletin. Illinois Department of Welfare, November – December 1951. Page 1.

5. Ibid. Page 3.

6. Ibid. Page 4.

7. Annual Reports of the Department of Public Welfare. July 1, 1950 to June 30, 1951.

8. Annual Reports of the Department of Public Welfare. July 1, 1954 to June 30, 1955. Page 84.

9. Nelson, Robert, "Disturbed Children in State Hospital Special Worry, Care." Peoria Journal Star. Monday, April 8, 1957. Page B12.

10. Nelson, Robert, "Eight Young Patients at State Hospital Moving Into Wards of Their Own." Peoria Journal Star. Tuesday, April 15, 1958. Page B12.

11. Ibid. Page B12.

12. Annual Report of the Department of Public Welfare. July 1, 1957 to June 30, 1958. Page 113.

13. Annual Report of the Department of Public Welfare. July 1, 1959 to June 30, 1960. Page 118.

14. Annual Report of the Department of Public Welfare. July 1, 1961 to June 30, 1962. Page 75.

15. Annual Report of the Department of Public Welfare. July 1, 1963 to, June 30, 1964.

16. Bloch, Verne. "Eight Children Make Selves at Home as They Move Into Zeller Center Unit. Peoria Journal Star. September 19, 1967.

Chapter XIII: Peoria State Hospital: A Small City.

1. Illinois Department of Public Welfare Reports. July 1, 1921 to June 30, 1922. Pages 90-91.

2. Annual Reports of the Department of Public Welfare. July 1, 1950 to June 30, 1951. Page 62.

3. Annual Reports of the Department of Public Welfare. July 1, 1955 to June 30, 1956. Page 99.

4. The Welfare Bulletin. Illinois Department of Public Welfare. November to December, 1951. Page 4.

Chapter XIV: The End of an Era.

1. O'Connell, Bill. "State Hospital Here, 'Obsolete,' To Close." Peoria Journal Star. Vol. 118 No. 81. Tuesday, September 19, 1972. Page B1.

2. "No Letters, Visitors in 55 Years: Fete Hospital: Forgotten Man on 100th Birthday." Peoria Journal Star. Monday, June 16, 1958. Page B12.

3. Mehr, Joseph J. Ph.D. An Illustrated History Illinois Public Mental Health Services 1847-2000. A Santayana Publication 2002. Page 481.

4. Ibid. Page 482.

5. Ibid. Page 485.

6. Barry, Frank, "New Drug 'Dramatic Success' at Peoria State Hospital." Peoria Journal Star. Thursday, April 3, 1958. Page D-1.

7. Ward, James S. M.D. "History of Psychiatry in Central Illinois – During the 20th Century." Excerpted from an unpublished article.

8. Report of the Illinois Legislative Investigating Commission: Peoria State Hospital. February 1973. Page 53.

9. Ibid. Page 42.

10. Ibid. Page 4.

11. Ibid. Page 4.

12. Ibid. Page 1.

13. Ibid. Page 1.

14. "The Guards to Surrender to the Sheriff." Peoria Journal. Vol.XXXIII. No. 140. Thursday, October 23, 1903. Page 10.

15. Report of the Illinois Legislative Investigating Commission: Peoria State Hospital. February 1973. Page 40.

16. Ibid. Page 38.

Chapter XVI: Asylum Romances.

1. Baer, Walter and Pollak, Maxim. "The Friend of the Bereft" George Anthony Zeller, M.D. 1858-1938." Journal of the History of Medicine and Allied Sciences. Vol. VIII. No. 1. Page 69.

2. Sixth Biennial Report of the Commissioners, Superintendent and Treasurer of the Illinois Asylum for the Incurable Insane. June   30, 1906. Page 18.

3. Seventh Biennial Report of the Illinois General Hospital for the Insane at Peoria. June 30, 1908. Page 23.

4. "The Mystery of the Graveyard Elm." Peoria Journal Star. Sunday, June 30, 1974. Page C1.

5. "Fainting Bertha Skips the Tra-La-Lu." Peoria Journal. Vol. XLIII. No.12. Sunday, June 14, 1908. Page 20.

6. "Fainting Bertha, Will-O-Wisp." Peoria Journal. Vol. XLIII. No. 27. Monday, June 29, 1908. Page 9.

Bibliography

State of Illinois Biennial Reports:

Second Biennial Report of the Trustees and Treasurer of the Illinois Asylum for Incurable Insane at Peoria. July 1, 1898. Springfield, Illinois: Phillips Brothers, State Printers 1899.

Third Biennial Report of the Commissioners and Treasurer of the Illinois Asylum for Incurable Insane at Peoria. July 1, 1900. Springfield, Illinois: Phillips Brothers State Printers, 1901.

Fourth Biennial Report of the Trustees, Superintendent and Treasures of the Illinois Asylum for the Incurable Insane at Peoria. July 1, 1902.

Fifth Biennial Report of the Trustees, Superintendent and Treasurer of the Illinois Asylum for the Incurable Insane at Peoria. June 30, 1904. Springfield: Illinois State Journal Co., State Printers, 1905.

Sixth Biennial Report of the Commissioners, Superintendent and Treasurer of the Illinois Asylum for the Incurable Insane at Peoria. June 30, 1906. Springfield, Illinois. Phillips Brothers, State Printers, 1907.

Seventh Biennial Report of the Illinois General Hospital for the Insane at Peoria. June 30, 1908. Springfield, Illinois: Illinois State Journal Co., State Printers, 1909.

Eighth Biennial Report of the Peoria State Hospital at Peoria, Illinois. Formerly the Illinois General Hospital for the Insane. Originally the Illinois Asylum for the Incurable Insane. June 30, 1910. Springfield, Illinois: Illinois State Journal Co., State Printers, 1911.

Ninth Biennial Report of the Peoria State Hospital at Peoria, Illinois. July 1, 1910 to September 30, 1912.

Tenth Biennial Report of the Peoria State Hospital Peoria, Illinois. October 1, 1914. Printed by authority of the State of Illinois.

Eleventh Biennial Report of the Peoria State Hospital at Peoria, Illinois. October 1, 1916. Printed by authority of the State of Illinois.

Reports of the Illinois Department of Public Welfare, State of Illinois:

1919 First Administrative Report of the Directors of Departments Under the Civil Administrative Code Together With the Adjutant General's Report for the Year July 1, 1917 through June 30, 1918.

Second Administrative Report of the Directors of Departments Under the Civil Administrative Code Together With the Adjutant General's Report for the Year July 1, 1918 through June 30, 1919.

Third Administrative Report of the Directors of Departments Under the Civil Administrative Code Together With the Adjutant General's Report for the Year July 1, 1919 through June 30, 1920.

Fourth Administrative Report of the Directors of Departments Under the Civil Administrative Code Together With the Adjutant General's Report for the Year July 1, 1920 through June 30, 1921.

Fifth Administrative Report of the Directors of Departments Under the Civil Administrative Code Together With the Adjutant General's Report for the Year July 1, 1921 through June 30, 1922.

Sixth Administrative Report of the Directors of Departments Under the Civil Administrative Code Together With the Adjutant General's Report for the Year July 1, 1923 through June 30, 1924.

Seventh Administrative Report of the Directors of Departments Under the Civil Administrative Code Together With the Adjutant General's Report for the Year July 1, 1924.

Eighth Administrative Report of the Directors of Departments Under the Civil Administrative Code Together With the Adjutant General's Report for the Year July 1, 1925.

Ninth Administrative Report of the Directors of Departments Under the Civil Administrative Code Together With the Adjutant General's Report for the Year July 1, 1926.

Tenth Administrative Report of the Directors of Departments Under the Civil Administrative Code Together With the Adjutant General's Report for the Year July 1, 1927.

Eleventh Administrative Report of the Directors of Departments Under the Civil Administrative Code Together With the Adjutant General's Report for the Year July 1,1928.

Twelfth Administrative Report of the Directors of Departments Under the Civil Administrative Code Together With the Adjutant General's Report for the Year July 1,1929.

Annual Reports of the Department of Public Welfare:

Thirteenth Annual Report of the Department of Public Welfare July 1, 1929 through June 30, 1930. Printed by authority of the State of Illinois.

Fourteenth Annual Report of the Department of Public Welfare July 1, 1930 through June 30, 1931. Printed by authority of the State of Illinois.

Fifteenth Annual Report of the Department of Public Welfare July 1, 1931 through June 30, 1932. Printed by authority of the State of Illinois.

Sixteenth Annual Report of the Department of Public Welfare July 1, 1932 through June 30, 1933. Printed by authority of the State of Illinois.

Seventeenth Annual Report of the Department of Public Welfare July 1, 1933 through June 30, 1934. Printed by authority of the State of Illinois.

Eighteenth Annual Report of the Department of Public Welfare July 1, 1934 through June 30, 1935. Printed by authority of the State of Illinois.

Nineteenth Annual Report of the Department of Public Welfare July 1, 1935 through June 30, 1936. Printed by authority of the State of Illinois.

Twentieth Annual Report of the Department of Public Welfare July 1, 1936 through June 30, 1937. Printedby authority of the State of Illinois.

Twenty First Annual Report of the Department of Public Welfare July 1, 1937 through June 30, 1938. Printed by authority of the State of Illinois.

Twenty Second Annual Report of the Department of Public Welfare July 1, 1938 through June 30, 1939. Printed by authority of the State of Illinois.

Twenty Third Annual Report of the Department of Public Welfare July 1, 1939 through June 30, 1940. Printed by authority of the State of Illinois.

Twenty Fourth Annual Report of the Department of Public Welfare July 1, 1940 through June 30, 1941. Printed by authority of the State of Illinois.

Twenty Fifth Annual Report of the Department of Public Welfare July 1, 1941 through June 30, 1942. Printed by authority of the State of Illinois.

Twenty Sixth Annual Report of the Department of Public Welfare July 1, 1942 through June 30, 1947. Printed by authority of the State of Illinois. *(Combined records were issued for the years July 1, 1942 – June 30, 1947. This was done because of WWII.)*

Twenty Seventh Annual Report of the Department of Public Welfare July 1, 1947 through June 30, 1948. Printed by authority of the State of Illinois.

Twenty Eighth Annual Report of the Department of Public Welfare July 1, 1948 through June 30, 1949. Printed by authority of the State of Illinois.

Twenty Ninth Annual Report of the Department of Public Welfare July 1, 1949 through June 30, 1950. Printed by authority of the State of Illinois.

Thirtieth Annual Report of the Department of Public Welfare July 1, 1950 through June 30, 1951. Printed by authority of the State of Illinois.

Thirty First Annual Report of the Department of Public Welfare July 1, 1951 through June 30, 1952. Printed by authority of the State of Illinois.

Thirty Second Annual Report of the Department of Public Welfare July 1, 1953 through June 30, 1954. Printed by authority of the State of Illinois.

Thirty Third Annual Report of the Department of Public Welfare July 1, 1951 through June 30, 1955. Printed by authority of the State of Illinois.

Thirty Fourth Annual Report of the Department of Public Annual Report of the Department of Mental Health July 1, 1960 through June 30, 1961.

Thirty Fifth Annual Report of the Department of Public Welfare July 1, 1954 through June 30, 1957. Printed by authority of the State of Illinois.

Thirty Sixth Annual Report of the Department of Public Welfare July 1, 1955 through June 30, 1958. Printed by authority of the State of Illinois.

Thirty Seventh Annual Report of the Department of Public Welfare July 1, 1956 through June 30, 1959. Printed by authority of the State of Illinois.

Annual Reports of the Department of Mental Health:

Annual Report of the Department of Mental Health July 1, 1960 through June 30, 1961.

Annual Report of the Department of Mental Health July 1, 1962 through June 30, 1963.

Annual Report of the Department of Mental Health July 1, 1963 through June 30, 1964.

Other State Records:

"Asylum Light." Hospital Newsletter published by the patients and employees of the Peoria State Hospital. 1936 to 1940.

Journal of the History of Medicine and Allied Sciences. Vol. III. No.1. *Minutes of the meetings held by the Board of Trustees of the Asylum for the Incurable Insane located at Bartonville, Illinois. (March 18, 1897 through February 1, 1898.) "Rules Governing the Conduct of the Illinois General Hospital for the Insane Peoria, Illinois." Compiled by George A. Zeller, M.D., Superintendent. 1909.

"Scope." Volume 6, No. 4. January 28, 1972.

"Three Patients Deaths at Peoria State Hospital a Report to the Illinois General Assembly." By the Illinois Legislative Investigating Commission 300 West Washington Street, Chicago, Illinois 60606. February, 1973. Printed by the Authority of the State of Illinois.

"The Welfare Bulletin." Volume XXVI No. 5 Published monthly by the Illinois State Department of Public Welfare. May 1935.

"The Welfare Bulletin." Published monthly by the Illinois State Department of Welfare. June 30, 1938.

"The Welfare Bulletin." Published monthly by the Illinois State Department of Welfare. September – October 1951.

Newspapers:

The Daily Plaindealer. Tuesday, October 11, 1898.

Limestone Independent News. July 21, 2004

Penny Press. September, 28,1972.

Peoria Daily Transcript. 1895 to 1896.

Peoria Herald Transcript. June 6, 1896 to 1925.

Peoria Journal. June 14, 1908 to June 29 1938.

Peoria Times Observer. October 7, 1985 to August 29, 2001.

Peoria Journal Star. March 14, 1952 to June 30, 1985.

Peoria Star. February 10, 1907 to August 1940.

Books:

Adams, Bill. Yester Days: Volume III. Copyright by the Peoria Journal Star. May 31, 1993.

Altshule, Mark, M.D. Roots on Modern Psychiatry Essays in the History of Psychiatry. Gurne and Straton Inc. New York and London. 1957.

Baker, Rick. Mary, Me In Search of a Lost Life Time. The Bakery, a publishing Co. 1989. Copyright by Teresa M. Baker 1989.

Beam, Alex. Gracefully Insane the Rise and Fall of America's Premier Mental Hospital Public Affairs, New York, N.Y. 2001

Grob, Gerald N. The Mad Among Us a History of the Care of America's Mentally Ill. The Free
    Press. Copyright by: Gerald N. Grob 1994.

Johnson, Heidi. Angels in the Architecture - A Photographic Elegy to an American Asylum.
    Wayne State University Press, Detroit. Copyright by Heidi Johnson 2001.

Kellog, J.H., M.D. A Manual of the Physiological and Therapeutic Effects of Hydriatic
    Procedures, and the Technique of Their Application in the Treatment of Disease.
    Modern Medicine Publication 1928.

Kirkbride, Thomas, M.D. On the Construction, Organization and General Arrangements of
    Hospitals for the Insane. Arno Press – A New York Times Company, 1973.

Mehr, Joseph J., Ph.D. An Illustrate History Illinois Public Mental Health Services 1847 to 2000.
    A Santayana Publication. Copyright by Joseph Mehr 2002.

Packard, Elizabeth P.W. Modern Persecution on Insane Asylums Unveiled Volumes I and II.
    Arno Press, a New York Times Co.   1973.

Wright, Rebekah, M.D. Hydrotherapy in Hospitals for Mental Disease. Tudor Press Inc. Boston
    Massachusetts, 1932.

Ward, James Sheridan, M.D. Asylum Light Stories From the   George A. Zeller Era and
    Beyond :Peoria State Hospital – Galesburg Mental Health Center, and George A. Zeller
    Mental Health Center. Copyright 2004, by Mental Health Historic Preservation Society
    of Central Illinois.

Zeller George A. M.D., A Series of Asylum Romances. Published by the Department of Public
    Welfare. (Printed by the Authority of the State of Illinois.) 1919.

Unpublished Materials:

Belt, Leonard E. "Fifty Challenging Years." Speech given at the Peoria State Hospitals fiftieth
    anniversary. Circa: 1952.

Knowles, H.B., M.D. "Program for an open house at the Peoria State Hospital on May 3, 1953.

McCombs, Jack G. "Peoria State Hospital Annual Narrative Report: Intensive Treatment Day
    Hospital Center – Stone Cottage – July 1,1964 to June 30, 1965. Richardson, Walter E.
    "Restraint and Seclusion."

Richardson, Walter E. "Restraints and Seclusion"

Unknown Author. "The Care of the Insane in Illinois." Circa 1914.

Ward, James S., M.D. "Have We Come Full Circle."

Ward, James S., M.D. "The History of Mental Illness." Speech given at the dedication of the auditorium at the Zeller Zone Center.

Ward, James S., M.D. "History of Psychiatry in Central Illinois – During the 20th Century."

Zeller, George A., M.D. Befriending the Bereft. Circa:1930.

Zeller, George A., M.D. "Peoria State Hospital Peoria Illinois (Formerly the Illinois General Hospital for the Insane; Originally the Illinois Asylum for the Incurable Insane.) Circa: 1914.

Independent Studies:

Edwards, Tom. Peoria State Hospital Historic District – Application for Listing in National Register of Historic Places. July 25, 1980.

McNett, William M., M.D. The Forgotten Residents of the Peoria State Hospital. Peoria Genealogical Society Inc. Peoria, Illinois 1995.

Index

NOTE: No attempt has been made to record references to George A. Zeller, Peoria State Hospital, or the Memories.

ISBN 141203336-5

9 781412 033367